Assessing
the Achievement of
J. M. Synge

Recent Titles in
Contributions in Drama and Theatre Studies

Assessing the Achievement of J. M. Synge

Edited by
Alexander G. Gonzalez

Contributions in Drama and
Theatre Studies, Number 73

GREENWOOD PRESS
Westport, Connecticut • London

Library of Congress Cataloging-in-Publication Data

Assessing the achievement of J. M. Synge / edited by Alexander G.
Gonzalez.
    p. cm.—(Contributions in drama and theatre studies, ISSN
0163–3821 ; no. 73)
   Includes bibliographical references and index.
   ISBN 0–313–29714–2 (alk. paper)
   1. Synge, J. M. (John Millington), 1871–1909—Criticism and
interpretation. 2. Ireland—In literature. I. Gonzalez, Alexander
G. II. Series.
PR5534.A88   1996
822'.912—dc20   96–5430

British Library Cataloguing in Publication Data is available.

Library of Congress Catalog Card Number: 96–5430
ISBN: 0–313–29714–2
ISSN: 0163–3821

First published in 1996

Greenwood Press, 88 Post Road West, Westport, CT 06881
An imprint of Greenwood Publishing Group, Inc.

Printed in the United States of America

∞™

The paper used in this book complies with the
Permanent Paper Standard issued by the National
Information Standards Organization (Z39.48–1984).

10 9 8 7 6 5 4 3 2

For Abelardo and Margaret Martinez

Contents

Preface and Acknowledgments

J. M. Synge is an author whose plays we literary critics have long considered to be safely ensconced in the canon of Irish literature and the greater canon of modern drama. Essays on his plays and other works continue to appear, and productions of his greatest plays are staged occasionally, not only in Ireland and the United States, but also in many other countries, from France to Japan. But there are indicators, not all of which are subtle, that Synge's reputation may be slipping: year after year at the Modern Language Association (MLA) annual convention, Synge's name lags behind those of the other modern Irish greats in terms of frequency of sessions—none that I can actually recall over the last ten years—or even of papers dedicated to him or his work. Panels devoted exclusively to Synge have become rare indeed, even at Irish-studies conferences, and when one does appear, it almost always seems to have been born by accident: three scholars happened to have submitted essays on Synge. Perhaps most telling of all is the fact that at the 1995 American Conference for Irish Studies (ACIS) National Convention held in Belfast, not *one* of the three hundred papers presented was even *partially* on Synge. Furthermore, I was assured by ACIS president James MacKillop that none of the eighty rejected proposals was on Synge. The very idea of a major Irish-studies conference—attended by over five hundred scholars—having nothing to say about Synge is staggering.

Other forms of evidence are also becoming stark. In fact, the idea for this present collection of essays evolved not only from the poor response from scholars to a call for papers assessing Synge's work for a proposed MLA session a few years ago, but primarily from the recent radical increase in negative responses from students in the classroom—a place where Synge's work and reputation seemed perhaps safest of all—about even some of his greatest and historically most well-received plays. It is no longer a question of whether the problem may lie in merely one or two generally disgruntled students. A pattern is emerging.

It is difficult to rid myself of the memory of one particularly bright student laughing cynically at the outset of the class's discussion of *Riders to the Sea*, a play most critics consider to be of timeless tragic beauty and power. She has not been the only one, whereas once upon a time all students seemed to approach the play seriously and with compassion. This student's dissatisfaction had to do with an inability to suspend her disbelief: if six, and likely seven, male relatives have died at sea, how can Bartley, with this knowledge, follow the course of action that he does? How can readers accept the play's compression, that Bartley dies—conveniently, from this antagonistic point of view—on the same day that his brother, Michael, is confirmed dead? That coincidence and others lead to the cynicism. Even the manner of Bartley's death—that the gray pony knocks him into the sea before any sail is set—inspires laughter in some. Some of us may want to dismiss this attitude as attributable to the cynicism of contemporary society, and there may be something to this notion: I recently found a student laughing at Coleridge's great emotional and spiritual meditation in ''Frost at Midnight'' because his eyes' focus is on that puny bit of soot fluttering in the grate; each time Coleridge reminds us of that external correlative, the student was unable to suppress her laughter and openly explained that she found the image ''so funny.'' Her classmates did not come to Coleridge's rescue.

But this line of analysis is insufficient to explain the rejection of Synge's comedies. With most of our students being at perhaps the most intellectually rebellious stages of their lives, it is hard to fathom the rejection some feel toward such plays as *The Playboy of the Western World* and *The Tinker's Wedding*. Or is it precisely that rebelliousness itself that motivates their rejection of literature that we have complacently come to expect them to love almost automatically? Is Synge's drama a particularly weak spot to be exploited? Though Sean O'Casey is seeing similar attacks—in *The Shadow of a Gunman* especially—he seems to be more successful at retaining his appeal. Is the trend perhaps a continuation of society's general turn-of-the-century shift toward favoring literature and writers whose subject matter is urban?

At any rate, students seem unwilling to suspend their disbelief regarding the plots of the comedies. They increasingly refuse to accept, for example, that the two blind beggars in *The Well of the Saints* prefer to remain blind. Some of my Irish-American students—in a curious and complete revolution from the *Playboy*'s earliest receptions—still see Synge's most famous play as an attempt to belittle the Irish people and regard its plot—a patricide as an exalted act—as simply unbelievable.

I fully expect a good number of scholars and teachers of Irish literature to assume, therefore, the worst about my enthusiasm for the subject matter or my presentation of cultural context, but in the latter, I am very thorough. To use the *Playboy* as an example, I provide Synge's source, an actual newspaper account of a man who murdered his father and was then harbored by villagers until he could escape to America; I explain the not-unusual Irish attitude toward criminals, who are more esteemed than the police—for a variety of reasons familiar to those of us in Irish studies and in American inner cities; I also provide Lady Gregory's journals that tell us all about the tumult in both Dublin and New York when the play was first staged. Yet the intolerance continues. To be sure, that intolerance is, thankfully, not nearly absolute, but it is frequent enough and sometimes savage enough at least to prompt the question: How well is Synge's drama standing the test of time? Are tastes changing enough to warrant a reexamination of Synge's dramatic canon? Perhaps my perceptions have evolved because I teach at what some have called a "blue-collar school," where students tend to be more practical minded than elsewhere and have had little exposure to literature and the other arts. Perhaps the situation is also in part attributable to a more serious, even sometimes seemingly humorless, generation, which sees many occasions for laughter as politically incorrect. Whatever the reason or reasons, it cannot hurt to attempt to reestablish the relevance of Synge's plays to the lives of our students and the general reading public.

That is what the essays in this collection try primarily to do. Some are fresh types of formal reassessment. Others are fruitful comparisons of Synge's work to popular modern authors. Still others are completely original approaches to the plays. The result is new perspectives that ought to serve as helpful steps in preserving Synge's reputation. If there really is no problem—and the lull at the conferences and antipathy shown by students are mere temporary aberrations— then, at worst, we have a collection of fresh views on the plays, some by top academics in the field of Irish literature, others by enthusiastic and insightful scholars just beginning their careers. As we approach the centenary of the publication and production of Synge's plays, he deserves all the good things we can say about him, and if we can change a few minds to persuade them of his continued greatness, then so much the better.

"Tragic Self-Referral in *Riders to the Sea*" and " 'Cute Thinking Women': The Language of Synge's Female Vagrants" first appeared in somewhat different form in *Eire-Ireland*. Copyright © 1996 *Eire-Ireland*, A Journal of Irish Studies, published by the Irish American Cultural Institute of St. Paul, Minnesota. Reprinted by permission of the publisher.

I am grateful to James S. Rogers for granting the above-mentioned permission on behalf of the Irish American Cultural Institute. Special thanks also go to Patricia Hazard, secretary extraordinaire, and to Robert Rhodes for various forms of generosity at several stages of the development of this project.

Assessing
the Achievement of
J. M. Synge

1

Resentment, Relevance, and the Production History of *The Playboy of the Western World*

John P. Harrington

One memorable image of the work of John Millington Synge was provided by W. B. Yeats in a speech at the Abbey Theatre, in the midst of demonstrations against *The Playboy of the Western World* in Dublin in 1907. "When the curtain of *The Playboy* fell on Saturday night," Yeats said, "I am confident that I saw the rise in this country of a new thought, a new opinion, that we had long needed" (227). Despite Yeats's confidence, one interesting feature of Synge's literary status, which is now surely as canonical as that of any other modern Irish writer, is persistent grumbling; opinion is not divided, but even today some ostensible endorsements of Synge and Synge's work seem distinctly resentful. Opposition to Synge was evident from the start, of course, and especially so in reference to the most canonical of his works, *The Playboy of the Western World*. Most remember the rotund journal entry of that indefatigable Abbey Theatre witness, Joseph Holloway, whose comment on the play's opening night in Dublin in 1907 was: "I maintain that his play of *The Playboy* is not a truthful or just picture of the Irish peasants, but simply the outpouring of a morbid, unhealthy mind ever seeking on the dunghill of life for the nastiness that lies concealed there" (81). The same evening of the suppressed performance provoked Maud Gonne, a force both on- and off-stage in the early Abbey years, to a pronouncement seldom quoted (though Peter Costello believes these to be "terms that some still repeat"):

A play which pleases the men and women of Ireland who have sold their country for ease and wealth, who fraternise with their country's oppressors or have taken service with them, a play that will please the host of English functionaries and the English garrison, is a play that can never claim to be a national literature. (Costello 32)

Such sentiments are not just period malcontent, for they survive in the form of a peculiar vexation with Synge that is especially acute at home, in Ireland. Notable recent recurrences include Denis Donoghue's enigmatic condemnation, in the generally ecumenical context of *We Irish*, that Synge's "constitution was determined to be gloomy" (210), and Seamus Deane's unhappiness because "in Synge, the cause," largely nationalist, "is always lost" (53).

Synge is hardly alone among modern writers for pessimism, however, and gloominess scarcely inhibits production of *The Playboy*. Since the time of those relatively recent comments, the play has been memorably staged in Dublin at the Kilmainham Royal Hospital, which, by association, carries some of the historical freight of the jail and Shawn Keogh's outcry in the play that if locked up there, Christy Mahon would "burst from Kilmainham and he'd be sure and certain to destroy me" (*Plays* 117). In New York City, where the opening night uproar early in the century equaled or excelled that of Dublin, the Irish Repertory Theatre recently staged *The Playboy* to special applause by a loyal Irish-American following (precisely the demographic group most outraged in 1911), and to general celebration in the Irish-American press (the vehicle of condemnation in 1911). Is the stage success of the play, in the face of general gloom over critical Ireland, a fulfillment of Yeats's vision, or have productions and audiences sold out for ease, wealth, and self-gratification, as Maude Gonne believed?

Deane's objections are most useful because they pass beyond vague opprobrium to a quite specific charge:

In *The Playboy of the Western World* Pegeen Mike's desolate cry of loss brings to an end the prospect of a glorious future with Christy Mahon, one which Christy had invoked by articulating a vision of pastoral romance which properly belongs to the old Gaelic past. The failure of the community to bring the past Eden into a utopian future marks the boundary line of nationalist and romantic desire. The vagrant hero or heroine fades into legend or fantasy. (53)

Deane's point is that *The Playboy*, because of its outcome, fails to satisfy both nationalist and romantic expectations. Again, that hardly sets Synge apart among modern writers or even modern Irish playwrights. Synge and *The Playboy*, however, seem to offend more than others.

Some of the reasons why can be seen in what Synge did to an important source for the play (recorded in *The Aran Islands*). The famous passage paraphrases an anecdote about the Connaught man "who killed his father with the blow of a spade" and fled to the islands, where he was sheltered:

They hid him in a hole—which the old man has shown me—and kept him safe for weeks, though the police came and searched for him and he could hear their boots grinding on the stones over his head. In spite of a reward which was offered, the island was incorruptible, and after much trouble the man was shipped to America. (*Prose* 95)

This leads to Synge's discussion of the adversarial relationship between the islanders and the law, then British in jurisdiction, and to Synge's remarkably Arnoldian praise for native wisdom in respecting passion above all possible motives. This incident remains as premise in *The Playboy*, with its only slightly less remote "community" on the Mayo coast. The crime in the anecdote is parricide, as in the play, and the weapon in both is the dread loy. Synge's revision of the outcome, however, is striking. In the source story, the people are "incorruptible" in solidarity, in hiding the fugitive from the police, and in rising to the occasion of new and perplexing experience. In Deane's terms, the anecdote offers some prospect for the future, if not quite "glorious," and posits the success of the community in negotiating passage from a past to a future with some honor and verve. The story as recorded is the stuff of the nationalist and romantic side of the boundary line.

However, the success of the community was precisely what Synge wrote out of the tale in adaptation. He altered the source in actual experience, which is ordinary procedure, but he did so to introduce failure, not success. That reverses the pattern of composition in nationalist, romantic, and even nineteenth-century popular melodramatic literature. Thus *The Playboy* wholly justifies Maud Gonne's sense that the play cannot claim to be a "national literature." Her phrase evokes the quite defensible position that a national literature is a useful literature, an effective expression of the needs and desires of the people—of the collective folk—even if "the people" proves to be a most abstract and fictitious concept. This note was sounded much more loudly in 1931 by Daniel Corkery, who found the issue epitomized by Synge. "A national literature," Corkery wrote in *Synge and Anglo-Irish Literature*, "is written primarily for its own people: every new book in it—no matter what its theme—foreign or native—is referable to their life, and its literary traits to the traits already established in the literature. The nation's own critical opinion of it is the warrant of life or death for it" (2). In an earlier aside, Corkery referred to "nationalist Dublin" and "the 'rioting' it indulged in for semi-political and religious reasons when *The Playboy of the Western World* was first produced before it" (vii). Synge's play does not fail Corkery's test for national literature on form or style as traits required to be conventional. It once troubled many on Corkery's content test, but Synge's explanatory prefaces on anthropological fidelity and society's gradual acknowledgment of the fact of violent crime by its very own has satisfied most critics that murder, and even parricide, are at least referable to Irish life. Early in the century, the play failed the audience response test for national literature, for the voluble response was in disapproval. What can be added to Maud Gonne's sentiment is that the failure of *The Playboy* to be a national literature was quite intentional on the part of the author, and that thus far, this failure appears to be the warrant for the life, not the death, of the play.

It has often been noted that the text of *The Playboy* fulfills expectations for comic drama until well into the final act. A helpful comparison not commonly made is with Henrik Ibsen, apropos of George Bernard Shaw's comment that until late in the final act, *A Doll's House* could have been resolved with the denouement of conventional domestic drama. In the beginning of *The Playboy*, the cause is not lost, and an honorable prospect is a real possibility. In Synge's treatment of Christy's "small voice" (*Plays* 67) becoming a powerful voice out of all proportion with deeds, the "community" is an active factor. At the outset of the action, Philly Cullen prompts the tall tale with a series of escalating demands, culminating in, "Were you off east, young fellow, fighting bloody wars for Kruger and the freedom of the Boers?" (71). In the second act, the Widow Quin provokes an inflated tale: "Don't be letting on to be shy, a fine, gamey, treacherous lad the like of you. Was it in your house beyond you cracked his skull?" (101). On the brink of the exposure of the tale as a lie, Michael Flaherty, civic center of the community as owner of the pub that is its stage scene, fully certifies Christy by accepting him as son-in-law:

A daring fellow is the jewel of the world, and a man did split his father's middle with a single clout should have the bravery of ten, so may God and Mary and St. Patrick bless you and increase you from this mortal day. (157)

Old Mahon's reappearance immediately after these words belies the tale with fact, and the group denunciation—"You're a liar!" (161)—is delivered in the text by the "Crowd" rather than by a "community." Christy's analysis of the moment is delivered as he is captured by the crowd and returned to the status of solitary outsider:

Shut your yelling, for if you're after making a mighty man of me this day by the power of a lie, you're setting me now to think if it's a poor thing to be lonesome, it's worse maybe to go mixing with the fools of the earth. (165)

In a draft, Synge made contempt for the community more explicit: there Christy taunts, "You're the mighty moral strong men of a Mayo bog" (164). In the play's treatment of the Mayo characters, a prospect of change and achievement is within their capacity. They have language requisite for action; when they decry the action they have fostered, their failure is complete. The requisites for a nationalist audience are the dramatization of its victories or of the villainies of its enemies. Synge quite directly assaults these expectations by dramatizing the victory of a villain.

Of course, the crux of the issue (and the sudden departure from comic expectations) is the relationship between Christy and Pegeen Mike Flaherty. In the final act, a comic resolution is proposed:

PEGEEN [*with real tenderness*]. And what is it I have, Christy Mahon, to make me fitting entertainment for the like of you that has such poet's talking, and such bravery of heart?
CHRISTY [*in a low voice*]. Isn't there the light of seven heavens in your heart alone,

the way you'll be an angel's lamp to me from this out, and I abroad in the darkness spearing salmons in the Owen or the Carrowmore?

PEGEEN. If I was your wife, I'd be along with you those nights, Christy Mahon, the way you'd see I was a great hand at coaxing bailiffs, or coining funny nicknames for the stars of night. (149)

It is worth quoting these familiar lines one more time for the emphasis on speech, articulation, and identity, qualities poised as light against the dark even if associated with fiction or prevarication, as in "coaxing bailiffs" or "coining funny nicknames" (or altering stories from *The Aran Islands*). The comic endings of marriage for local bliss or of flight for married bliss are not delivered, and Pegeen Mike will not be "fitting entertainment" for the like of Christy or the audience. As Michael James is the civic center of the community, so Pegeen is the moral center, the decision maker from the opening lines of the play. Oddly, her decision in favor of the community over Christy Mahon is both its demise and his revival:

It's there your treachery is spurring me, till I'm hard set to think you're the one I'm after lacing in my heart-strings half-an-hour gone by. (*To Mahon.*) Take him on from this, for I think bad the world should see me raging for a Munster liar, and the fool of men. (161)

This moment is a quite calculated reversal of the anecdote from which Synge worked. Pegeen, finding herself presented with the opportunity to write a future, declines. Her father, near the curtain, phrases that capitulation in terms of submission to foreign jurisdiction by betrayal of the outlaw: "It is the will of God that all should guard their little cabins from the treachery of law" (173). Synge's taunt to his audience resembles Christy's to the mighty, moral Mayo men. This outcome—Michael capitulating to the threat of British law for protection of the "little cabins"—is delivered as bluntly as possible. It is small wonder that Gonne, Corkery, and others were disappointed.

Discussion of *The Playboy* throughout this century consistently returns to the production history and the Dublin origin. That is quite proper, though there is perhaps no other twentieth-century play that is so rigidly referred back to its opening nights. A useful supplement to that production history is the opening in New York City in 1911. The Dublin story is very well documented, and the New York City story is usually appended as a revival of the old dispute. But the scenes differ in important respects, most of which served to increase the distance between play and audience expectation. Any alleged libel of the Irish was a different matter in Dublin than in New York. In New York, the governing concern was not national autonomy but local hegemony; scandalous or patronizing suggestions about Irish backgrounds were set before a much more heterogeneous audience. There, self-examination of the Irish, even if by the Irish, amounted to external rather than internal review. Individual issues that were

forceful in the Dublin dispute, especially propriety of language and accounta-
bility of a national theater, were remote from the New York scene. It seems
astonishing now, but there were reasons to expect the play to please its audience,
and the reasons were different in Dublin and New York. In Dublin, approval
could reasonably be expected (wrongly, as it proved) for the play's appropriately
revivalist concentration on the Irish Ireland of the rural west. In New York, the
emigrant Irish-American audience could be thought predisposed to like the play
for other reasons. Yeats, in fact, made this point first, and in February 1907 in
the midst of the Dublin dispute. In a letter, Yeats proposed to John Quinn, the
art collector who would serve as sponsor in 1911, that Irish-Americans would
be flattered by *The Playboy* because

the play means that if Ireland goes on losing her strong men by emigration at the present
rate and submitting her will to every kind of political and religious domination, the young
men will grow so tame that the young girls will prefer any man of spirit, even though
he has killed his father. (Reid 49)

If we are to believe that Yeats wrote in all candor, he was remarkably wrong
in assuming that this Irish-American audience considered all political and religious organization to be domination or thought the spirit of strong men to be
the premium masculine quality.

   The first performance in New York City, which could not have been better
designed to outrage the Irish-American audience, was part of a five-month tour
by The Irish Players that would perform sixteen plays in thirty-one cities and
small towns from Boston to Chicago. During a mid-October extension of the
successful opening in Boston, the *Gaelic-American* printed a resolution of opposition by the United Irish-American Societies, which would organize protests
in New York. Citing *The Playboy* as "a gross libel on the Irish people" and
denouncing Yeats's advertisement of the play as "the mind of Ireland," the
resolution vowed "to induce those responsible for the presentation of *The Playboy* to withdraw it, and failing this we pledge to drive the vile thing from the
stage" (Gregory 222). However, by the time the tour opened in New York, on
November 20, 1911, the press was suggesting widespread boredom and only
selective, almost conspiratorial support. "Public interest in the enterprise has
already reached a low ebb," reported the *New York Sun*, adding, "To send
spectators to the Maxine Elliott Theatre with any such exalted expectation is to
prepare only disappointment for them and thus create a feeling against actors
so unjustly overpraised" ("Plays" 6). The public interest, however, was not the
target audience for The Irish Players. The chosen theater had been opened by
Maxine Elliott in 1908, and 1911, the year of *The Playboy*, was also the year
of her retirement from the stage. The building, with a capacity of 900, was
designed after the palace at Versailles, and the style was lush, including a marble
proscenium arch and seats framed in ivory (Van Hoogstraten 109–11). Elliott
had banned musicals from the theater, and the venue was distinctly "serious."

In this setting, the readers of the *Gaelic-American* could quite justly feel neglected. On opening night, attention was much more likely to focus on the five present or retired Supreme Court justices, or on John Dewey of Columbia University, who were all in the boxes. The second performance was attended by former president Theodore Roosevelt.

Though plainly not in control, the supporters of the *Gaelic-American* resolution were present in significant numbers on November 27, when, after an uneventful performance of Lady Gregory's *The Gaol Gate, The Playboy* opened at nine o'clock. Unlike Dublin, where the greatest dispute arose late in the play, in New York the disturbances began early in Act I, at the point when Shawn Keogh refuses to stay the night. "I would and welcome," he says to Michael Flaherty, "but I'm afeard of Father Reilly; and what at all would the Holy Father and the Cardinals of Rome be saying if they heard I did the like of that?" (63). Well before the entrance of Christy or mention of parricide, on this cue—this suggestion of church domination—the ordinary men of the audience began catcalls, which were countered by determined applause, to be, in turn, followed by a volley of vegetables, the weapon of preference by angry New York audiences. The actors continued, by some accounts even playing to the protesters. A force of fifty policemen outside entered and began forcible arrests and ejections. Then Fred O'Donovan, playing Christy, announced that the first act would be repeated, which it was. According to the *New York Times*, "This is the first time such a thing has happened in the history of the stage in this country" ("Riot in Theatre over an Irish Play" 1). Later, Lady Gregory had the wit to tell a reporter, "we have appeared before an audience that has demanded an encore of us" ("Riot in Theatre" 2). General disruptions continued until the final curtain dropped at eleven o'clock: the first act was presented twice, and then the remainder of *The Playboy*, all in two hours flat.

John Devoy, editor of the *Gaelic-American*, and so, publisher of the anti-*Playboy* resolution, remained in his seat throughout the performance, finally, no doubt, feeling chastened that the play had not been driven from the stage. That night, Lady Gregory reported her verdict to the *New York Sun*: "The whole intellect of America is with us," she said. "We found the most hearty approval of this play at Harvard, Yale, Vassar, Smith, and other colleges" ("Playboy Mobbed" 2). This was also the sentiment of the *Sun* review on the same page: "It became evident that under ordinary circumstances 'The Playboy of the Western World' would probably have met with a triumphant reception by the intelligent part of the audience that had gathered to welcome it. . . . The victory had been won by the drama before the curtain fell" ("'Playboy' as Drama" 2). Later, in *Our Irish Theatre*, Lady Gregory gave the police blotter report in pointed fashion: "Ten men were arrested. Two of them were bartenders; one a liquor dealer; two clerks; one a harness-maker; one an instructor; one a mason; one a carpenter; and one an electrician." There she repeated the verdict in terms that echoed the *Sun:* "our victory was complete in the end" (112). Her relish in this victory is evident: the play, which was favored by "the intellect of

America," triumphs over the "public" audience and gloats in the fashion of
Christy over the Mayo men.

In later accounts, the victory is often judged a purely aesthetic one. That
judgment deprives *The Playboy* of some of its power and distorts the record. In
its review, the *New York Times* did indeed credit the play with artistic power,
with having "the art of the poet. It is this quality, of course, which helps to
make Mr. Synge's play something more than a play in the ordinary sense, and
lifts it into the realm of fine art" ("Play" 3). This opinion, however, was
quickly corrected in an editorial. Conceding that "nobody doubts that the purpose of the Abbey Theatre and its players is wholly artistic," the editorial noted
that the "skill of the actors is somewhat deficient . . . in this queer, partly droll,
partly pathetic piece by the dead poet" (" 'Playboy' Row" 10). This reaction
is more representative of the general reception. The reviews generally praised
the text and qualified their praise of the performance. Hence, we should adjust
the image of *The Playboy* in 1911 as a stylistic breakthrough that changed
American drama, which is the image established in the (mostly retrospective)
accounts by notable witnesses from the theater world, such as Susan Glaspell,
Eugene O'Neill, and Robert Edmond Jones.

An observation closer to the sense of Lady Gregory's "victory" was supplied
by the *New York Post* in a later note: "It may be predicted with a fair degree
of confidence that when "The Playboy" is deprived of the free advertisement
bestowed upon it by Irish opprobrium, it will speedily disappear from the theater" ("Music and Drama" 6). Lady Gregory's claim to "victory" was a declaration cast directly into the face of opprobrium; opprobrium persists, and this
adds to the play's power. The relevance of *The Playboy* lies in its rather direct
assault on its audience, including the modern equivalent of the audience patron-
ized by Lady Gregory as clerks and bartenders. By exploiting an affluent theater
and soliciting "the whole intellect of America," the New York production illustrates the power of the play to offend. *The Playboy* is always in danger of
fulfilling Maud Gonne's criticism—in danger of merely pleasing. Contemporary
audiences risk that when they identify with Christy Mahon, with his ability to
seize the opportunity to leave and change. An alternative identification—one
made by the Irish-American audience in 1911—was with the people of Mayo,
with their inertia and maundering complicity with oppressive local codes and
equally oppressive hypocrisies. Seeing oneself in such light, of course, does not
please. However, it is the latter identification that evoked Yeats's premise of "a
new thought, a new opinion, that we had long needed." The play can serve the
purpose Yeats imagined only when, as in early productions, audiences identify
with the Mayo villagers and confront the text's excoriating exposure of those
failures as their own. In its assault on the audience, which was originally more
evident than it is now, *The Playboy of the Western World*, in text and in production history, demonstrates a capacity to agitate that prevents its speedy disappearance from the theater.

WORKS CITED

Corkery, Daniel. *Synge and Anglo-Irish Literature: A Study.* Dublin and Cork: Cork University Press; London: Longmans, Green, 1931. Reprint. New York: Russell and Russell, 1965.

Costello, Peter. *The Heart Grown Brutal: The Irish Revolution in Literature, from Parnell to the Death of Yeats, 1891–1939.* Dublin: Gill and Macmillan, 1977.

Deane, Seamus. *Celtic Revivals: Essays on Modern Irish Literature, 1880–1980.* Winston-Salem, N.C.: Wake Forest University Press, 1987.

Donoghue, Denis. *We Irish: Essays on Irish Literature and Society.* New York: Knopf, 1986.

Gregory, Lady Augusta. *Our Irish Theatre.* New York: Oxford University Press, 1972.

Holloway, Joseph. *Joseph Holloway's Abbey Theatre: A Selection from His Unpublished Journal "Impressions of a Dublin Playgoer",* ed. Robert Hogan and Michael J. O'Neill. Carbondale: Southern Illinois University Press, 1967.

"Music and Drama." *New York Post,* 2 Dec. 1911, 6.

"Play and the Acting, The." *New York Times,* 28 Nov. 1911, 3.

" 'Playboy' as Drama, The." *New York Sun,* 28 Nov. 1911, 2.

" 'Playboy' Mobbed." *New York Sun,* 28 Nov. 1911, 2.

" 'Playboy' Row, The." *New York Times,* 29 Nov. 1911, 10.

"Plays of the Irish Actors." *New York Sun,* 26 Nov. 1911, 6.

Reid, B. L. *The Man from New York: John Quinn and His Friends.* New York: Oxford University Press, 1968.

"Riot in Theatre; Irish Players Are Driven off Stage." *New York World,* 28 Nov. 1911, 2.

"Riot in Theatre over an Irish Play." *New York Times,* 28 Nov. 1911, 1, 3.

Synge, J. M. *Collected Works.* Vol. 2: *Prose,* ed. Alan Price. Gerrards Cross, U.K.: Colin Smythe, 1982. (Cited as *Prose.*)

———. *Collected Works.* Vol. 4: *Plays, Book II,* ed. Ann Saddlemyer. Gerrards Cross, U.K.: Colin Smythe, 1982. (Cited as *Plays.*)

Van Hoogstraten, Nicholas. *Lost Broadway Theatres.* Princeton, N.J.: Princeton University Press, 1991.

Yeats, William Butler. *Explorations.* New York: Macmillan, 1962.

2

The Playboy, Critics, and the Enduring Problem of the Audience

Ginger Strand

Both as text and as historical event, John Millington Synge's *The Playboy of the Western World* highlights the problem of the audience. Central to the critical history of the play is the question of why the Mayo villagers it depicts turn on the character Christy Mahon, the "playboy" they have lionized as a daring parricide until they actually see him commit what appears to be murder. Concurrently, theater history poses the presumably related question of why the Irish audience who first saw the play at the Abbey Theater in 1907 responded with violent and apparently organized attempts to have the play closed. Neither of these two questions has ever been answered simply "because it was right to do so." Both audiences—the Mayo villagers within the text and the Dublin audience who experienced it—have been continually approached by critics with antipathy. The inconsistency of the Mayo villagers, combined with the extremity of their brutality after they turn against Christy Mahon, seems to designate them the antagonists in Synge's play. Moreover, the censorious, "philistine" nature of the Irish audience's attempts to halt the presentation of the original *Playboy* seems to fit them only too well for the role of ignorant "howling mob" in which Yeats, for one, subsequently cast them.

The notoriety with which Synge's play was received has proven a mixed blessing. While the riots did guarantee, as Synge himself predicted in a letter to Molly Allgood, that the play would be "an event in the history of the Irish stage" (Greene and Stephens 257), they have received so much attention that the play *as an event* in theater history has all but upstaged the play as a work of literature. As Una Chaudhuri puts it, "the play remains strongly identified with its place of origin, with Ireland, and the question of its attitude to its characters is inevitably framed within a problematic of Synge's politico-national vision" (374).

If it is nearly impossible to separate Synge's play completely from the cultural politics that shaped it and the response it drew, it is useful to examine both—the play and the response—in the light of similar events outside what has become for many readers the very "literary" context of turn-of-the-century Irish nationalism. Recent American public debates about the representation of people struggling to define an identity have much in common with the "riots" that greeted *The Playboy* in 1907. While acknowledging vast differences of context and content in these debates, considering their similarities makes it significant to ask once again the question of why the villagers turn on Christy Mahon without the assumption of plain wrongheadedness that has marked intellectual approaches to the play. The 1992 riots following the acquittal of Los Angeles police officers in the beating of Rodney King, as well as that year's public dissent over the representation of gay subjects in a number of popular films—*The Silence of the Lambs*, *Basic Instinct*, and *JFK*—demonstrate the fact that audiences have something very real at stake in the representation of characters who claim to share some part of their identity, particularly when those representations enjoy authority (as in the case of the King verdict) or strong social sanction (as in the case of Hollywood films.)

Characterizing the original Irish audience as an ignorant "howling mob" seeking to shout down an opinion that differed from their own is in many ways misleading, particularly with respect to the pro-Irish writers who debated the issue in the years following 1907. Most writers sought not to suppress Synge but rather to discredit him. Even in the case of writers who did condone censoring the playwright, it must be acknowledged that the issues involved in Irish citizens' objections to *The Playboy* are complex, involving questions not only of nationalism, but also of identity and self-representation—issues that receive serious consideration today. Understanding these objections more fully can help us to understand contemporary audiences' objections to specific representations—be they the Christian fundamentalists' outcry against federal funding for "obscene art" or the gay audience's campaign against "homophobic films." It is clear from the persistence and violence of these objections that they are best addressed by an attempt to understand, rather than simply silence, the objections posed.

Synge understood well his relation to the issues of identity and representation. By the time he was writing *The Playboy*, the playwright was by no means unfamiliar with the kinds of public objections to his work that were to reach a peak in that play. As a metadrama, a play that self-consciously addresses questions of enactment and theatricality, *The Playboy* delves into the same issues of public representation that had caused public objections to *The Shadow of the Glen* and *The Well of the Saints*, both of which had also been declared to be misrepresentations of the Irish character (Greene and Stephens 154–92). Maud Gonne and Douglas Hyde had withdrawn their support of the Abbey Theatre over *The Shadow of the Glen*, and public protest had included a reactionary play called *In a Real Wicklow Glen*, which undertook to correct Synge's depiction of Irish peasants (Cairns and Richards 228). In *The Playboy*, Synge created a play dealing directly with issues of public presentation of the self and community representation—issues that had already influenced the reception of his previous work. Reading *The Playboy* partly as a metaphor for the process by which his representations had been received recasts Synge, not as the intuitive genius "incapable of a political idea" that Yeats appoints him (Yeats 353), but as a playwright self-consciously engaged with the contexts shaping his work and its reception. This suggests that we might turn to the play itself to understand the disturbances it provoked.

Why do the villagers turn against Christy Mahon? For most critics, this question has been intimately linked to the play's meaning. It may appear that the audience simply draws a line, albeit a much-contested line, between representations—in which an act can be cathartic—and reality, in which the same act is necessarily cruel. But in order to argue that the villagers simply police the distinction between reality and representation, one must assume that they, in fact, see Christy's story as a representation and never actually believe it to be true. This is clearly not so; the play's irony hinges upon the fact that the villagers are furious when they learn that Christy's father still lives. The contradiction in the villagers' behavior resides not only in the difference between their approval of the story and their disapproval of the deed, but in their anger when they find the story was not true, and their even greater anger when they later find that it has been made true. The villagers therefore seek to uphold not only the boundary between a representation and a reality, but the difference between two realities, one removed from them and one happening before their eyes. Critics tend to agree that this makes the villagers appear naive; they fail to recognize the fundamental sameness of what they try to differentiate.

In doing so, they also fail to see that Christy's attractions for them stem from the very action they deplore. As one critic notes of Pegeen: "It is the poet she had loved and not the murderer, and she fails to realize that the one is released by the other, that the murder of the father is, paradoxically, a life-giving act" (Gerstenberger 75). Pegeen's—and the audience's—ultimate rejection of Christy Mahon demonstrates their ignorance of the very relationship between violence and subjectivity that caused them to glorify Christy in the beginning. In rejecting the ugly act of brutality before their eyes, they contradict their own lionization of the parricide.

The contradiction in the villagers' behavior makes sense if it can be explained by a context of schematized self-division. The popular psychoanalytic reading of the play identifies Christy as the unconscious projection of the villagers' own repressed desires. Synge's biographers explain:

The villagers in that Mayo *shebeen* could applaud Christy for his desperate act of emancipation because it was an embodiment of their own subconscious desires. But when it became a reality—suddenly and violently—and they were asked to stand up and be counted, they had only the courage of their dreams. (Greene and Stephens 271)

The villagers thus construct the character of playboy for Christy as "a kind of neutral mirror upon which to project their own fears" (King 136). More importantly, the villagers also project their own desires onto Christy—especially Pegeen Mike, who is frustrated by her subjection to a patriarchal order, and for whom Christy "as a (purported) father-killer embodies the ideal that she would like to achieve metaphorically" (Finney 107). The villagers must thus be faulted in the end for failing to act on their own desires, for having, as Greene and Stephens put it, "only the courage of their dreams." In rejecting Christy, they ultimately reject their own desires.

The idea that the audience's anger represents a renunciation of recognizable aspects of self has also been extended to the crowds who disrupted performances of *The Playboy*. Yeats presents the dissent as the result of psychological repression: in "The Death of Synge" he writes that "Synge was the rushing up of the buried fire, an explosion of all that had been denied or refused, a furious impartiality, an indifferent turbulent sorrow" (Yeats 352). The audience's response to Synge's play, according to Yeats, is the rage of Caliban at seeing his face in the glass. In order to say so, one must read against the assertions of audience members, who insisted that the image presented was a false one. They objected not only to the fact that "dirty deeds" appeared before their eyes, but also to the claim that those deeds were specifically Irish.

Synge wrote *The Playboy* in Dublin at a time when the stage representation of Irish characters was a common subject for public discussion. Typical depictions of the Irish ranged from the "stage Irishman"—a demeaning caricature of the Irish as ignorant, comical louts—to the noble figure created to counterbalance him: what one critic calls "the unreal, impossibly virtuous, benign Irishman so popular with the Dublin audience" (Holder 541). Questionable as it is that audiences believed in the absolute truthfulness of the mythically good Irish character, critics have often suggested that they did and that their anger resulted from having this valued illusion shattered. T. R. Henn's explanation is typical:

The rancour of the mob centres on the fatal *shift*; in an access of outraged modesty, Victorian in character, but connected somehow with the idea that the very word was insulting to the womanhood of Ireland, whose chastity and purity had become a national myth, even as the saintliness of the island as a whole. It is probable that the audience, in their bewilderment at the more subtle ironies of the play, missed the full point of the phrase. (60)

Henn suggested that the audience was not only ignorant to "subtle ironies," but committed to two "myths": the myth of the purity of Irish womanhood and that of general Irish saintliness. Some contemporaries of Synge agreed with this reading. One Ellen Duncan, who wrote a letter to the *Irish Times*, conceded that Synge's debunking might be a welcome change, as "the banner of 'Erin and Virtue' has been worn a little threadbare of late" (Kain 177).

For the most part, however, contemporary protesters objected to the play neither as a simple manifestation of the "stage Irishman" nor as an unwelcome attack on the mythically perfect Irish peasant. What one finds in the copious writings on *The Playboy*—and in the catcalls and demonstrations that made up the "riots"—is an objection to Synge's depiction in the light of its claims to authority. The audience protested what they found to be an ugly depiction of Irish behavior. Crucially, this was an image not only presented by Synge but invested by him with the authority of a self-representation—an image created with the collaboration of the Irish themselves.

Synge took special pains to assign his play representative status. These efforts included an article appearing in the *Freeman's Journal* before the play opened. Titled "Mr. Synge's New Play," the widely quoted piece presented Synge as one who spoke for the peasants:

No one is better qualified than Mr. Synge to portray truthfully the Irish peasant living away in Western Ireland. He has lived with them for months at a stretch, in the Arran [*sic*] Islands and Mayo. He has noted their speech, their humors, their vices, and virtues. He is one of the best Irish speakers in the country, and is thus brought into closest contact with the people. "The Playboy" is founded on an incident that actually occurred. (Kain 173)

The preview makes manifest Synge's claim to realism. But one need not even turn to the newspaper for evidence of Synge's claims to authority. In the preface to *The Playboy*, Synge begins by invoking the Irish peasantry, acknowledging how much he owes to their folk imagination. He proceeds to outline in detail one particular debt:

When I was writing "The Shadow of the Glen," some years ago, I got more aid than any learning could have given me from a chink in the floor of the old Wicklow house where I was staying, that let me hear what was being said by the servant girls in the kitchen. (*Complete Plays* 3)

The implications are obvious. In a clear bid for "authenticity," Synge depicts his writing process as one of overhearing and transcribing dialogue as much as of creating it.

It seems likely that the playwright was being deliberately provocative. As noted, *The Shadow of the Glen* had been subject to the very same accusations of misrepresentation that *The Playboy* instigated, and Synge's portrait had been "corrected" by the upright morality depicted in *In a Real Wicklow Glen*. The almost comical image of Synge eavesdropping—through cracked floorboards—on the conversations of kitchen maids serves to reassert the playwright's claims to authority in an already ongoing discourse about the status of his representations, even as it represents him in the dubious position of "slumming" voyeur. By depicting him quite literally as a transcriber, it also deflates the assertion of greater accuracy made by the writers who had earlier sought to correct him.

Thus provoked, angry respondents to *The Playboy* set out to deny *its* professions of authenticity. Numerous accounts of the theater fracas relate the audience's comments on the impossibility of the events onstage. According to the *Daily Express* of January 30, 1907, during the melee in the theater, "the most frequent exclamation was 'That's not the West' " (Hogan and Kilroy 129). Often this assertion was backed up with its speaker's claim to authority; in testifying about the evening's scuffle, Inspector Flynn of the Northern Police Court stated: "I heard a number of young men ... say that the play did not represent Western Irish life as they understood it. Some of them said that they were from the West of Ireland themselves" (Hogan and Kilroy 136). A letter to the *Freeman's Journal* during the riots began with a common assertion of authenticity before attacking the play's depiction:

I am well acquainted with the conditions of life in the West, and not only does this play not truly represent these conditions, but it portrays the people of that part of Ireland as a coarse, besotted race, without one gleam of genuine honour or one sparkle of virtue. ... Could any Irish person accept this as a true picture of Irish life? (quoted in Kilroy 9–10)

The letter is signed, "a Western Girl."

Frank Hugh O'Donnell, author of *The Stage Irishman of the Pseudo-Celtic Drama* and one of the play's most persistent detractors, summed up the most common objection in a letter to Irish-American patron of the arts John Quinn:

Synge's Schopenhauerish pessimism and fatalism are simple bosh on the lips of Irish peasants with 15 centuries of Catholic Faith behind them. His use of the Religious exclamations of peasant devotion is continually revolting. It is all very clever and often powerful; but it is not Irish. It belongs to Syngeland. Only don't call it Ireland though it uses "Musha" and "wirrastrue." (quoted in Londraville and Londraville 78)

O'Donnell acknowledges Synge's talent here, allowing the play to be "clever and powerful," and denies the playwright only the claim to Irishness. In another letter, he declares that "the 'Irish Dramas' of Synge are forgeries" (quoted in Londraville and Londraville 81). Like the forger, O'Donnell declares, Synge transgressed, not by writing, but by writing under false pretenses—or in someone else's name.

O'Donnell's frustration extends to the entire group of what he labeled "Pseudo-Celtic" dramatists—Yeats, Lady Gregory, and Synge—highlighting the fact that *The Playboy*'s avowal of representative status was echoed by the Irish National Theatre. Audiences felt anger toward the Abbey, as well as toward Synge himself, not simply because the drama failed to represent the "real" Ireland, but because it failed while claiming that it was specifically designed to represent the Irish people and character. As an angry editorial in *The Irish Independent* fumed: "It was not for the purpose of lessening Ireland's self-respect and holding her people up to the ridicule of the world that the "National Theatre" was established" (quoted in Hogan and Kilroy 141). The reviewer for the *Irish Independent* agreed, declaring that Christy was "certainly not a type to be presented even in farce in an Irish theatre, and under the auspices of a movement that has for its very object the destruction of such stage-Irishman types as Christie Mahon" (quoted in Kilroy 12).

Detractors like O'Donnell sought not to abolish or silence Synge, as is commonly assumed, but rather to strip him of his claim to be truly representative. This becomes obvious in the angry response towards the Abbey. At some distance from the heat of the controversy, the *Irish News and Belfast Morning News* was able best to sum it up:

All this cant and rant about "Art" by Yeats and Synge is the veriest humbug—old, exploded, meaningless humbug, too. These men call their playhouse "The National Theatre." Let them shed the misnomer, remove the words "National" and "Irish" from their theatre, their programmes, their plays, and all their proceedings and belongings, and we, of Ireland and for Ireland, will have no further right to complain. (quoted in Kilroy 61)

The overriding concern in this passage is not for the play itself, but for the play's—and the Abbey's—claims to represent Ireland.

The problem of the failed representative is the problem not only of *The Playboy*, but *in The Playboy* as well. The villagers turn on Christy Mahon for exactly the same reason Irish audiences turned on Synge: in order to take from him the representative status that he claimed—and betrayed. On the most basic level, the problem of representation is what differentiates the parricide committed in what Christy lyrically describes as "a distant place . . . a windy corner of high, distant hills" from the parricide committed, as Pegeen says, "in your backyard." The villagers are quite literally implicated as an audience in the second place: "If we took pity on you," Michael tells Christy after the "second murder" of Old Mahon, "the Lord God would, maybe, bring us ruin from the law to-day." "Take him on from this," Pegeen agrees, "or the lot of us will be likely put on trial for his deed to-day" (77). Certainly the villagers would be seen by the law as accomplices had they witnessed the crime and not reported it. Their implication in the murder goes beyond countenancing it, however, for they have made Christy their representative.

In what appears to be the earliest outline for *The Playboy*, Synge sketched out a three-act play titled, "The Murderer (A Farce)." Act II, as it is briefly described, looks very much like the final version of Act II; Act I shows the scene in the potato garden, which Synge soon decided to leave out. Most interesting is Act III:

(he [Christy] is being elected county councillor) Old man comes in first, and shows his head to everybody. He is as proud of it as his son is, as he is going round the crowd.

His son comes out the elected member. He is put on a table to make a speech, he gets to the point where he is telling how he killed his father when the old man walks out— "You're a bloody liar, that's what you are." Son attacks father and is handcuffed, then with his former dejection. He says . . . (*Collected Works* 295)

Although the outline stops short, the final structure of Act III is complete here: in the midst of his enjoyment of his new position in the village, Christy is faced with his father, whom he attacks again. He is immediately handcuffed. Synge had not at this point worked out what would be Christy's final words, but the outline of Act III differs from the play mainly in that Christy is not only honored by the villagers, but made a "county councillor." In Synge's earliest version, the villagers do quite literally what they do figuratively in the finished play: they give Christy the power to represent them.

This consensual conferral of power provides the basis for the psychoanalytic reading of the play. In projecting their (conscious or unconscious) desires onto Christy, the villagers have chosen him to stand for some aspect of themselves. However, the psychoanalytic reading suggests that the villagers then reject that very aspect of themselves when it is made explicit. But to understand Christy as a figure who is made to represent the community is to posit a difference between the "first" murder and the "second," which is more than the difference between implicitness and explicitness. It is the difference between an individual act and a collective one.

Christy's rise to power is concurrent with his acquisition of the capacity for self-articulation (Spacks 321). Christy's transformation, however, could not have occurred without the help of the villagers; it is very much a collective endeavor. The audience can be read as coauthor of Christy's text. After all, they provide the paradigms and linguistic structures for his self re-creation. In the scenes in which Christy tells his tale, for instance, the hopeful guesses of the villagers lead the way through the slow construction of the narrative. As Chaudhuri has argued, "Christy's narrative cannot be said to be authored; rather, it is collectively produced, carved out of the shared imaginative experience of the Mayo people" (381). Christy borrows the villagers' speech in much the same way Synge claimed to borrow the overheard language of the Wicklow servant girls.

With Christy regarded as a product of the community, the community must try to maintain some control over his actions. Reading Christy in this way casts the villagers' turn against him in a new light: it becomes a crisis of representation, an assertion of control over a character they have created as their stand-in, but whom they no longer want to represent them. Christy, however, manages not only to escape the villagers' attempt at disciplining him, but also to maintain his capacity to represent them. In Old Mahon's final lines, he and Christy lay claim to the linguistic power to represent the community: "we'll have great times from this out telling stories of the villainy of Mayo, and the fools is here" (*Complete Plays* 80). Moreover, as he leaves in triumph, Christy points out that he does indeed remain the collective product of the townspeople: "Ten thousand blessings on all that's here, for *you've turned me* a likely gaffer in the end of all'' (80; emphasis mine).

The Mayo villagers are faced with the same problem that faced the Dublin audience: they find they have invested the powers of representation in a "likely gaffer" who will portray them as "villains" and "fools." Their displeasure was more complicated than a negative response to an ugly character. The role assigned to themselves offended them most. After playwright William Boyle withdrew from the Abbey in protest of *The Playboy*, Stephen Gwynn accused him, in the *Freeman's Journal*, of hypocrisy, pointing out that Shaun Gragon in Boyle's popular play, *The Building Fund*, was as despicable as Christy Mahon. D. J. O'Donoghue came to Boyle's defense in the same newspaper, declaring:

I cannot see the remotest analogy . . . Shaun Grogan is a hateful character, no doubt, mean and sordid, but Boyle does not make him a hero. Nobody in the play worships him, or applauds his courage—and he must have a considerable amount of it—and all his dodgery and meanness end in defeat. Where is the analogy between "The Building Fund" and "The Playboy"? (quoted in Kilroy 75)

Clearly, the problem as O'Donoghue saw it was not that the audience did not like villains, or even villainous Irishmen. But they resisted the implication that they themselves were villain-lovers.

If the *Playboy* audiences sought to silence Synge's play, it was in part because they felt silenced by it. The presence of the police—invoking an English justice system complicit in denying Ireland a voice—only confirmed the audience's conviction that they were being maligned without a chance to respond. But despite their objections on those grounds, police presence was increased throughout the run; with it increased the audience's refusal to be silent, and by the end, Yeats recalled, "we played it under police protection, seventy police in the theatre the last night and five hundred, some newspaper said, keeping order in the streets outside" (569). Every possible articulation of resistance was foreseen and countered: Berrow noted that on Thursday night after the opening, with police present, the Abbey floor was padded with felt to prevent the sound of the audience stomping its feet to signify displeasure (85).

The Abbey management's attempt to silence the audience resonated with particular potency in the context of Irish nationalism's struggle for a voice. In defending its very strong editorial position against Synge's freedom of speech, the *Freeman's Journal* attempted to connect the playwright's representation with attempts to silence the Irish, ominously alluding to English suppression:

Grossness of language is, of course, an offense to be condemned. But the calumny of the Irish people, of which the whole play is an embodiment, deserves still more scathing condemnation. Let us remember this calumny runs on old and familiar lines. It has ever been the custom of traducers of the Irish people to charge them with sympathy with all forms of crime. Over and over again this same lie has been made the justification for Coercion. (quoted in Kilroy 19)

The writer sees the audience as under attack here: the Irish are implicated by Synge's play not as parricides, but as criminal sympathizers. Moreover, such an accusation becomes a means of coercion. The Abbey's attempt to "libel" the Irish with a nonrepresentative play parallels English attempts to silence the Irish in much more tangible ways.

The angry response to *The Playboy* for the most part took the form of literary or journalistic language. The newspapers were full of satiric verse as well as prose commentary following the play's opening, including a parody of Yeats's *Cathleen Ni Houlihan*. At least one entire volume of material was published, titled *The Abbey Row, NOT Edited by W. B. Yeats*. As one satiric versifier described the fracas in the theater:

> Part of the audience we may
> Term quite enthusiastic,
> While others keen to stop the play
> Adopted measures drastic,
> With many a hiss and stamp and yell,
> Essayed to stop the action,
> Which didn't in the slightest quell
> Cheers of the other faction.
> And as these vocal gladiators—
> All of them—were stayers,
> The stage became spectators
> And the audience the players. (quoted in Berrow 81)

Interestingly, the author of this piece described the situation as one in which spectators and players exchange places. The traditionally silenced audience become "vocal gladiators," while those on the stage fall silent. Ironic as the image is, it depicts the real desires of the audience quite clearly: to be the ones heard, rather than the ones represented.

These literary rebuttals to Synge took shape as attempts to "debunk" him, satirizing his claims to authenticity explicitly. A song written on the occasion, and performed by Cathel M'Garvey in County Monaghan, begins:

> Come all ye bogus Irishmen, and hear my Synge-y song;
> In Abbey street my form you'll meet, 'mid peelers hundreds strong,
> 'Tis I'm the "Man for Galway," boys so raise a joyful shout;
> I'm the rattling lad that killed his dad—I'm the dirty stuttering lout. (quoted in
>   Berrow 83)

Of the four lines here, obviously only the last one actually parodies the play itself. The first directs attention to the "bogus" nature of the representation; the second mentions the police presence; the third recreates the kind of authenticity claim Synge made for the play. Again, Synge's claims to represent Irish truth were most at stake. Other satiric verses suggest that these claims were rejected specifically because of Synge's status as an Anglo-Irish writer:

> You come, sir, with your English ways
>   Your morals of the Cockney cabby
> Corrupting with unseemly phrase
>   The Abbey babby.
> Unless we watch your wanton text,
>   And waken shame with boos and knockings,
> You'll want that poor Miss Allgood next
>   To mention st-ck-ngs. (quoted in Berrow 84)

Even here, however, where Synge's "English ways" are definitely suspect, the apparent self-righteousness of the audience—parodied in the refusal to spell out "stockings"—was as subject to ridicule as Synge himself.

The anger and frustration attending misrepresentations granted authority are as familiar now as they were in Synge's day. A similarly angry response resulted from what were perceived as misrepresentations of the gay community in the series of recent films mentioned earlier. During Carolco Pictures' filming of the big-budget thriller *Basic Instinct*, for instance, dozens of protesters were arrested for disrupting shooting. The *Washington Post* took a transcendant attitude with respect to the fray, calling the demonstrations "a basic street brawl" (4 June 1991, B1). The filmmakers' official statement was very much like that of Yeats in 1907: "Censorship by street action will not be tolerated" (B2).

The street actions in which demonstrators engaged were similar in intent to the actions of *Playboy* audiences: they attempted to disrupt the "performance" by drowning it out. Protesters chanted, blew whistles, and induced cars passing by to honk their horns during the filming. As with *The Playboy*, *Basic Instinct*'s actors were not stopped, but they were severely antagonized. Activists justified their actions by arguing that the images of lesbian and gay people generated by the film were not only inaccurate, but socially harmful. Peter Nardi, a professor of sociology and copresident of the Los Angeles chapter of the Gay and Lesbian Alliance against Defamation, elaborates in the *Washington Post* on *Basic Instinct*'s physically dangerous message:

Accumulated with other films, it adds up that there's something evil about *those* people. That's enough to cause [viewers] to act in a negative way, be it passing a law that forbids a gay person from being a Boy Scout all the way up to bashing. If there's someone crazy enough to believe these images of what it means to be gay or lesbian, there may be a lesbian killed, or a heterosexual who "looks" like a lesbian. (4 June 1991, B2)

Nardi perceives a relationship between representation and reality that the *Playboy* audience was often labeled naive for seeing. In both cases, the representation alone is not the culprit, but the real social power that attends it—for the Irish audience, the representative status attributed to the Irish National Theatre; for gay audiences, the awesome cultural potency of Hollywood's constructs.

Interestingly, *Basic Instinct*'s writer, Joe Eszterhas, seems to have understood exactly that point from the activists' demonstrations. Explaining in the *Washington Post* his decision to make some changes in the original screenplay, Eszterhas referred to the specific power of assertions in the Hollywood machine:

The whole notion that you can write something that will hurt someone is a horrifying thought. I have learned to weigh very carefully the societal impact of an action or line in a screenplay when it's delivered by a star with the international stature of Michael Douglas. (4 June 1991, B2)

While *Basic Instinct* made even less claim to representativeness than *The Playboy*, Eszterhas's cautious statement acknowledges the power of representations to intervene in constructions of real identity.

Reading the screenwriter's statement in the light of the similar debates about Synge eighty-five years ago certainly challenges assumptions made by all factions in the "political correctness" debates. The *Washington Post* reported that the Gay and Lesbian Alliance against Defamation was undertaking "sensitivity training" at several major film studios. As useful—and overdue—as the notion of filmmakers becoming sensitive to gay and lesbian issues seems, would proponents of sensitivity training argue that Synge, Yeats, and Lady Gregory would have benefited from similar training at the Irish National Theatre? Our sense of the sanctity of Synge's—or any artist's—creative process probably makes such a suggestion sound ludicrous, and yet the arguments made by Nardi, and by Eszterhas himself, are compelling.

Relating the *Playboy* "riots" to the uproar over *Basic Instinct* thus obliges critics to take a new look at both. Both cases present the puzzling spectacle of an audience that ought to be sensitive to the dangers of censorship yet demands the suppression of a text. Before crying foul, however, it is necessary to question to what extent each audience felt itself to be silenced by the text it sought to suppress. For each, it turns out, the text itself was not problematic; it became so only when it claimed an authority that was resisted by those it alleged to represent.

To acknowledge that the attempt to repress a text is often a defensive strategy by a constituency that feels itself being silenced is not to justify censorship, but to begin to understand its motives in cases like those of *Basic Instinct* and Synge's *Playboy*. It may also shed light on more mainstream debates. Republicans, for instance, have repeatedly argued that federal funding for what they label "obscene art" misrepresents the desires and tastes of the populations implicitly represented by that funding. Social conservatives, like the *Playboy* audience, claim that they are made unwilling collaborators by the National Endowment's support for certain projects. The National Endowment for the Arts

(NEA) would have been best defended not by denying this constituency's claim to be in some way represented by federal arts funding, but rather by separating the NEA's representative status from the texts or images created by individual artists. The National Endowment for the Arts, like the federal government, can survive only if it is understood to represent a society's commitment to freedom of expression. Individual works of art are not endorsed by this commitment, but rather their right to exist.

It is crucial to distinguish between attempts to suppress texts and attempts to deny them representative status. Demands for suppression are unpleasant in the mouths of any audience. At the same time, an audience's resistance to misrepresentation must be recognized as a valid concern and addressed as such. Unfortunately, artists and their supporters cried "censorship" in the face of a much more complex issue, not addressing the fact that many of their own arguments about the importance of representations had been co-opted and turned against them. The refusal of those on the left to take seriously conservative claims of misrepresentation has allowed opponents of the NEA to begin dismantling federal funding for the arts.

"All art is collaboration," Synge asserted in his preface to *The Playboy of the Western World* (*Complete Plays* 10). It is perhaps a sign of the enduring power of audiences that the role reversal that occurred at performances of the play, when "the stage became spectators/ And the audience the players" (quoted in Berrow 81), was first incited not by the audience's attempt to steal the stage, but by the author's own original effort to usurp the position of the audience— his portrayal of himself as transcribing eavesdropper. Even in what may appear a disingenuous attempt to force the audience to validate his depiction of them, the playwright acknowledges that the immense powers of articulation he deploys are really in the hands of the audience. In that respect, Synge's audience did nothing more than agree with him.

WORKS CITED

Berrow, Hilary. "Eight Nights at the Abbey." In *J. M. Synge: Centenary Papers 1971*, ed. Maurice Harmon. Dublin: Dolmen Press, 1972, 75–87.

Cairns, David, and Shaun Richards. "Reading a Riot: The 'Reading Formation' of Synge's Abbey Audience." *Literature and History* 13(2) (Autumn 1987): 219–37.

Chaudhuri, Una. "The Dramaturgy of the Other: Diegetic Patterns in Synge's *The Playboy of the Western World.*" *Modern Drama* 32(3) (Sept. 1989): 374–86.

Finney, Gail. *Women in Modern Drama: Freud, Feminism, and European Theater at the Turn of the Century*. Ithaca, N.Y.: Cornell University Press, 1989.

Gerstenberger, Donna. *John Millington Synge*. New York: Twayne, 1964. Rev. ed. Boston: G. K. Hall, 1990.

Greene, David H., and Edward M. Stephens. *J. M. Synge, 1871–1909*. New York: Macmillan, 1959. Rev. ed. New York: Columbia University Press, 1989.

Henn, T. R. *"The Playboy of the Western World."* In *The Plays and Poems of J. M. Synge*, ed. T. R. Henn. London: Methuen, 1963, 56–67.

Hogan, Robert, and James Kilroy. *The Abbey Theatre: The Years of Synge 1905–1909.* Modern Irish Drama: A Documentary History III. Dublin: Dolmen Press, 1978.

Holder, Heidi J. "Between Fiction and Reality: Synge's *Playboy* and Its Audience." *Journal of Modern Literature* 14(4) (Spring 1988): 527–42.

Kain, Richard M. "The *Playboy* Riots." In *A Centenary Tribute to John Millington Synge, 1871–1909*, ed. S. B. Bushrui. New York: Barnes and Noble, 1972, 173–88.

Kilroy, James. *The Playboy Riots*. Dublin: Dolmen Press, 1971.

King, Mary C. *The Drama of J. M. Synge.* Syracuse, N.Y.: Syracuse University Press, 1985.

Londraville, Janis, and Richard Londraville. "The Stage Irishman and Pseudo-Celtic Drama: Selections from the Correspondence between Frank Hugh O'Donnell and John Quinn." *Yeats: An Annual of Critical and Textual Studies* 9 (1991): 66–86.

Spacks, Patricia Meyer. "The Making of the Playboy." *Modern Drama* 4(2) (Dec. 1961): 314–23.

Synge, John Millington. *Collected Works*, Vol. 4, ed. Ann Saddlemyer. London: Oxford University Press, 1968.

———. *The Complete Plays.* 1935. Reprint. New York: Random House, 1960.

Yeats, William Butler. "The Death of Synge." In *The Autobiography of William Butler Yeats.* New York: Macmillan, 1965.

3

A Young Man's Ghost: J. M. Synge, *The Playboy of the Western World*, and W. B. Yeats's *A Vision*

Ellen Powers Stengel

In October 1917, W. B. Yeats's young bride, Georgie, began to perform "automatic writing" under the alleged possession of "supernatural" beings. The mortal secretary, perhaps ascertaining how best to secure the affections of an occultist husband, transcribed by planchette "an elaborate classification of men [*sic*] according to their more or less complete expression of one type or the other" (*Vision* 9). Manifest among these paradigms is an analysis of Yeats's friend and colleague John Millington Synge, dead since 1909 but now metaphorically resurrected to chair the Yeatses' remarkable new school of philosophy. Gratefully, the Yeatsean system reciprocates, providing new insights into Synge's body of work, especially *The Playboy of the Western World* (1907). Indeed, Yeats's *Vision* offers an unprecedented guide to the "romping" career of the eponymous Christy Mahon.

The ground shared by *Playboy* and *Vision* is germinated by Yeats's propagative zeal: Yeats asserted that he and his wife were chosen to receive "the Vision" due to his erstwhile-published perceptions concerning "the perfection that is from a man's combat with himself and that which is from a combat with circumstance" (13). Whatever the reason for their supernatural selection, the Yeatses continued their relationship with the "ghostly" communicators, thereupon tracing the antithesis between man's true being and "the opposite of his true being" (13). Moreover, at the time when Yeats was verbalizing the Vision, he was also, hardly coincidentally, highlighting the meaning of his alliance with Synge: in his acceptance speech at the Nobel Prize ceremony of 1925, Yeats insisted that the true parents of the realistic Irish drama were Lady Gregory—and Synge. In the closing words of his speech (also the closing words of his *Autobiography*), Yeats reiterated his aesthetic debt to his friend: "When I received from the hands of your king the great honor your Academy has conferred upon me, I felt that a young man's ghost should have stood upon one side of me'' (387).

Not for the first time did Yeats so insist on Synge's inspiration. In fact, as Ann Saddlemyer, editor of the correspondence of the three Abbey Theatre founding codirectors, has reminded us, ''Synge . . . and the theatre they [the Abbey directors] tried to create . . . rested in Yeats's private mythology'' (17). Far from ''resting,'' though, Yeats's memories drove him to tout Synge's reputation. Indeed, Robin Skelton has pointed out that ''at times, Yeats seems almost obsessed with the need to establish Synge's greatness; his claims on his behalf are those made for a prophet'' (169). Thus we find Yeats penning, in 1911, his version of *In Memoriam*, or *J. M. Synge and the Ireland of His Time* (Saddlemyer 11). We also observe, with Skelton, ''the shift in Yeats' style that occurred in the years 1908–10,'' an evolution Skelton attributes directly to Synge's influence (Skelton 172).[1] Then, at the moment of Yeats's greatest worldwide prestige, came that effort at communication as urgently delivered as the messages of Georgie Yeats's supernatural beings. There is even a subtle hint that Synge, as a kind of aesthetic Holy Ghost, inspired Yeats along with the other communicators of *A Vision*.

True, Yeats never explicitly included ''the young man's ghost'' among his communicators. Instead, the Vision's spokesman is Michael Robartes, a middle-aged, well-traveled Irish sage. Robartes, who appears in both Yeats's prose and poetry, is a vital oracle, or popularizer, of the Vision. Employing as a concrete symbol the purported ''egg of Leda,'' he serves up the meaning of life, death, and marriage:

[R]eality is a congeries of beings and a single being; nor is this antinomy an appearance imposed upon us by the form of thought but life itself which turns, now here, now there, a whirling and a bitterness. . . . Death cannot solve the antinomy. . . . The marriage bed is the symbol of the solved antinomy. (*Vision* 52)

But that this middle-aged symbolic presence is not antithetical to ''the young man's ghost'' is demonstrated later in Yeats's exposition of the Vision when he names Synge as the definitive ''receptive'' genius: that is, one who most excels at ''laying bare—to hand and eye, as distinguished from thought and emotion— general humanity'' (164). Thus, the image of Robartes, cupping in his hands the egg of Leda, replicates Synge's gift to the world (perhaps not incidentally, Synge was an avid amateur ornithologist—a nest and egg collector, according to biographers Greene and Stephens).

The association between Synge and Robartes holds true even as the subject matter of Yeats's Vision becomes more and more convoluted: ultimately, Leda's egg is hatched in Yeats's writings as a ''double cone or vortex.'' One of these cones is time or subjectivity—''the antithetical tincture''; the other cone is space or objectivity—''the primary tincture.'' Whirling and ''gyring'' into and out of each other perpetually, the cones weave paths of motion (see Figure 1 in Appendix). As each cone is in "continual conflict with its opposite," the life of every person whirls back and forth between objectivity (which "brings us back to the mass where we begin") and subjectivity (which "tends to separate man from man"). When Yeats later classified Synge as a "primary" man, he was saying that his friend's muse had inspired an "objective" type of drama (*Vision* 71–72, 163–68).

The visualization of the cones that first whirred through Synge's drama should include a description of the points that make up the cones in space and time and that, therefore, link the operation of the principles of life to its gyrings. These points, dubbed the "Four Faculties," are the means for classifying each being: (1) Will is the way of being, the "is" of existence as opposed to the "ought." It is the mechanic that allows for the operation of choice in everyone's life. It partakes of the "antithetical tincture," or subjective cone. (2) Mask is the ideal of being, the "ought" of existence and antithetical to Will. Thus, these two Faculties "can be represented by two opposing cones so drawn that the Will of the one is the Mask of the other" (73, 87). (3) Creative Mind is a primary Faculty, defined as the knower, or thought, of the thinker, and formed by the memory of universals (like Plato's essences or Carl Jung's archetypes). (4) Body of Fate, the fourth Faculty, is also primary, but it is antithetical to Creative Mind. It is that which is known, or the object of the thought of the thinker (73, 87).

Next, the Yeatsean system superimposes the conflict of the opposing cones onto the Great Wheel of Being, a symbol derived from the natural phenomenon of the twenty-eight phases of the moon. The plotting begins by classifying Phase 1, the dark of the moon, under the heading of "complete objectivity." Then the phases fall around the two cones (see Figure 2 in Appendix): Phases 22 through 8 are points on the primary cone; Phase 22 is described as "the breaking up of [subjective] strength" (*Vision* 87) and Phase 8 as "the gathering of strength." Phase 8 and Phase 22 are also points on the antithetical cone that has Phase 15, or "complete subjectivity," as its apex.

Yeats relates the Great Wheel to the Four Faculties when he tells us, "Man seeks his opposite or the opposite of his condition, attains his object so far as it is attainable at Phase 15 and returns to Phase 1 again" (*Vision* 81). Thus Will and Mask whirl against each other from Phase 1, move counterclockwise around the Great Wheel, and begin moving again through the cones when they return to Phase 1. Meanwhile, Creative Mind and Body of Fate are whirling against each other clockwise around the Wheel and through the cones. The result of the changing positions of two conflicting sets (each of two conflicting Faculties) is that a type of person is associated with each phase of the Great Wheel. Every phase imparts a unique "tincture" and set of Faculties to the people belonging to it. A general description of the phases notes that the motive of "primary man" is (objective) service, while that of the "antithetical man" is (subjective) self-expression. The conflicts between Will and Mask and between Creative

Mind and Body of Fate will either impede or further the goal of service or expression, depending upon the phase (80–84).

When, Yeats informs us, the supernatural communicator of *A Vision* had completed his picture of the Great Wheel (formed by the two conflicting cones and the whirling Four Faculties), he presented a detailed description of each of the twenty-eight "phases of man," complete with historical and fictional examples of each type. Interestingly, Phase 23 is exemplified by John M. Synge himself—he who is naturally receptive to images of reality (Synge's Will). Synge's internal conflict is caused by the frustration of his search for subjective wisdom by self-pity (True Mask versus False Mask). His creative powers arise from his ability to empathize with humanity as an organic whole. This ability, however, is undermined when selfish considerations eclipse the vision of humanity (Creative Mind). In spite of these struggles, Synge manages, in Yeats's estimation, to produce successful and ingenious art (Body of Fate; *Vision* 163–67). Having donned his True Mask (ideal being) of "Wisdom," Synge, as "Phase 23 man," sets out upon his mission of imitating reality in the "audacious, joyous, ironical" manner that Yeats so admired (167).

Synge's preferred medium—"traditional" comedy—was ideal for such an "objective" technician. The form allowed him to exercise his predilection for "startling events," for the "shock of new material," for bursting out into original rhythms (*Autobiography* 168, 358). Sweeping away the decorum of tragedy left space in three acts for wild gyrings between subjectivity and objectivity, between various ways of being (Wills) and ideals of being (Masks). But Synge's characters are not free-floating signifiers. Neither are they beings constituted only as "an effect of transient or liminal spaces that lie between places," as asserted recently by Una Chaudhuri (382, 381, 384). Rather, they are forced through the same sort of recurrent changes that Yeats was later to symbolize in the Great Wheel of Being. In fact, a viewing (reviewing), especially of Synge's *The Playboy of the Western World*, shows that Vision-like terms such as the "Four Faculties," the "Great Wheel," and the "Phases of the Moon" may voice Yeats's divinations of Synge's drama.

The symbiosis between Syngean dramatic construction and the terms of Yeatsean visionary mythology (intensified by the complexity of the play's structure and the intricate pattern of characters-in-action) typifies a multidimensional search of Wills for True Masks. In particular, the evolution of the protagonist, Christy Mahon, is a spectacularly involved progression from downtrodden peasant boy to wanderer, novelty, poet, gamester, hero, fraud, murderer, and, finally, "Playboy." In fact, the proliferating growth in the plot of *The Playboy* even obscures the play's roots in an observation made years before by Synge in his travel journal, which was later published as *The Aran Islands*:

The impulse to protect the criminal is universal in the west [of Ireland]. It seems partly due to the association between justice and the hated English jurisdiction, but more directly to the primitive feeling of these people, who are never criminals yet always capable of crime, that a man will do no wrong unless he is under the influence of a passion which is as irresponsible as a storm on the sea. If a man has killed his father, . . . they ask, "Would any one kill his father if he was able to help it?" (*Aran Islands* 95)

Grown from such a relatively simple seed, this complex play has, of course, invited many interpretations. But the Yeatsean strategy can particularly help us follow the text as it spins around the Great Wheel of Being. We can start by drawing a circle: by definition, a circle must be plotted with at least three points in order to distinguish the first point, or point of origin, from the third point, or endpoint. Similarly, the three-act structure of *The Playboy* completes an arc as Christy-in-action moves through several of the numbered phases on the Great Wheel of Being.

As the comedy progresses, the Will of the playboy changes position on one or the other of the cones of subjectivity (the "antithetical cone") and of objectivity (the "primary cone"); these cones form a sphere whose circumference may be traced on Yeats's Great Wheel if we bear in mind that the apex of subjectivity in Yeats's system is identified with Phase 15 on the Wheel and the apex of objectivity, with Phase 1. We can turn the Wheel around 180 degrees so that the first phase encountered is the subjectivity that "tends to separate man from man" and the later phase is the objectivity that "brings us back to the mass where we begin" (*Vision* 168) (see Figure 3 in Appendix). Around the circle of the play's three acts, Christy analogously circumnavigates the entire diameter from subjectivity to objectivity and around to subjectivity again.

Christy's initially subjective phase is highlighted as he arrives at Michael James Flaherty's *shebeen* (public house) on the wild coast of Mayo. We have already come to know the inhabitants of the *shebeen*—the jovial "publican," Michael James; his young daughter, Pegeen; her pusillanimous fiancé, Shawn Keogh; and their friends, the choleric Philly Cullen and the "amorous" Jimmy Farrell. They already seem to comprise a cohesive society over and against Christy, the intruder identified by Shawn as "the queer dying fellow . . . looking over the ditch" (*Plays* 13). Christy's phase is antithetical not only to the *shebeen* circle; the supposed murder of his father makes him antithetical to the laws of government and of morality. He is also antithetical to his own later image as a self-confident playboy, a term that has been translated from the Irish *buachaill barra* as "an athlete or champion" (Bourgeois 193n). Moreover, he has been ostracized by his family and even by his native village—witness the claim of his father, Old Mahon, that his son has been nicknamed "the looney of Mahon's" (*Plays* 49). Now, however, Christy commences to move from the subjective role of loner to the more integrated, objective roles of requited lover, eloquent poet, and all-around social success. By the end of Act I, he has won, not only the trust of all the men (save Shawn), but also the hearts of both the young Pegeen and the older Widow Quin (see Figure 4 in Appendix).

Throughout the play, character interactions tend to veer suddenly from combinations of similar Wills to radical conflicts between the antitheses of Will and

Mask: at his entrance, Christy can be described by Chaudhuri as an alien, an Other "based on difference and distance" from every other personality and situation in the world of the play (376, 384). Ironically, at this low point in his relationship with convention, Christy most closely approximates the ineffectuality of Shawn Keogh, being bound by the dictates of the church—in the person of the village priest, Father Reilly—and state—in the persons of the village "peelers." It is not surprising, then, that Christy's initial appearance elicits Pegeen's latent brutality—after all, she has just barely managed to keep herself from striking Shawn during the preceding speculation about the "fellow above in the furzy ditch" (15). Now she first patronizes, next callously mocks, then physically threatens the cringing Christy: "Would you have me knock the head of you with the butt of the broom?" (15, 17). However, Christy suddenly is spotlighted for all his audience, and especially for Pegeen, in radical antithesis to Shawn:

CHRISTY [*twisting round on her with a sharp cry of horror*]: Don't strike me. I killed my poor father, Tuesday was a week, for doing the like of that.

PEGEEN [*with blank amazement*]: Is it killed your father? (17)

Probably for the first time in her life, Pegeen finds herself unsure of how to deal with a man or a situation. From now on, in Pegeen's eyes, Christy is distinct from Shawn, from her father, and from the other villagers. Even her condemnation of him at play's end is couched in terms of Christy's "playing off the hero" (73).

From this abrupt beginning to its abrupt end, Christy and Pegeen's love affair features both the opposition and the intercourse of two quite dissimilar Wills. Their first encounter is only possible due to Pegeen's voluntary condescension to Christy and the almost involuntary halting of the arc of her broom. Christy's sudden confession so fascinates her that she manages to ignore her antithetical relationship to him and begins the double process of drawing near to him and attracting him to herself. The mechanics of this "gyring" are established with the hiring of Christy as Flaherty's pot-boy, the exit of the three middle-aged men, and the eviction of the now-superfluous Shawn.

The foreplay in Pegeen and Christy's verbal, lyrical intercourse now ensues: Pegeen flatters him first by praising his looks, then by continuing with the far more subtle flattery of assuming that he has heard it all before and has pronounced similar sweet nothings in the ears of all the women of Ireland. Christy's confidence builds until he can actually announce that he and Pegeen are "alike, so" (23). Pegeen concurs but unintentionally distances herself from Christy by idealizing him. This worshipful admiration encourages Christy to exercise his natural talents as a bard by the eloquent denunciation of his father. Pegeen gracefully acknowledges this: "I never cursed my father the like of that, though I'm twenty and more years of age" (25). This acknowledgment is followed by the literal and figurative stretching out of a hospitable hand to Christy and by his pleased acceptance of both:

PEGEEN: . . . Well, you'll have peace in this place, Christy Mahon, and none to trouble you, and it's near time a fine lad like you should have your good share of the earth.

CHRISTY: It's time surely, and I a seemly fellow with great strength in me and bravery of. . . . (26)

A sudden knock at the door signals the entrance of the formidable husband killer, the Widow Quin, who stimulates Pegeen's rhetoric and Christy's confidence to new heights. The Widow Quin even makes the first equation of Christy's deed—and her own—to the material of legend and poetry: "you'll find we're great company, young fellow, when it's the like of you and me you'd hear the penny poets singing in an August fair" (27). No wonder Christy falls asleep that night saying to himself,

Well, it's a clean bed and soft with it, and it's great luck and company I've won me in the end of time—two fine women fighting for the likes of me—till I'm thinking this night wasn't I a foolish fellow not to kill my father in the years gone by. (30)

Already in this first act, an intricate dance of Wills and Masks has been choreographed. Pegeen and the Widow have revealed to Christy the possibilities of his personality. He begins to conceive of himself as a shrine to which offerings should be made, so that although he is already in love with Pegeen, he assigns to her the role of a Vestal Virgin who must maintain the fires of his poetry. Strangely, he seems to have cast the distinctly nonvirginal Widow Quin in a similar role. The requirement for this position of Vestal Virgin at Christy Mahon's altar is to establish—a priori to classification as a worshiper—a similarity to his nature: Pegeen and Christy are "alike, so"; the Widow Quin and Christy are both legends in their own time. Pegeen, with her broom; the Widow Quin, with her rusty pick; and Christy, with his loy, have merged into one and the same grotesque image. Thus, the gyring between Wills and Masks, at this point, includes a temporary fusion of Wills to Masks—of ways of being to ideals of being.

The procession of Christy-worshipers lengthens in Act II. Christy adds himself narcissistically to the number as he makes a fascinated self-examination in a looking-glass: "Didn't I know rightly I was handsome, though it was the divil's own mirror we had beyond, would twist a squint across an angel's brow" (31). In fact, his newly discovered self-confidence quickly dissolves even his initial paranoia at the entrance of the "stranger girls." In contrast, the night before he had prolongedly quailed at the Widow's solitary entrance. Now, however, his language grows along with his ego, as it is watered and sunned in female adoration: the tale of the murder of the father gains in color with every retelling, so that the father has become, through the mouth of Christy, an archetypal symbol of tyrannical power—"naked as an ash tree in the moon of May"; "shying clods against the visage of the stars"; yelling, "God have mercy on your soul" as he hoists a scythe (25, 37). The reaction of the girls to this virtuoso verbalization is to equate Christy's bravery to that of the Widow Quin, and therefore to proclaim a joint toast "to the wonders of the western world" (37). Christy and the Widow Quin drink a toast of porter with their arms linked, thus symbolizing their shared public image and their potential sexual relationship. Thus, Will intersects Will in brief physical conjunction.

The sudden entrance of Pegeen with her milk can splashes frigid white onto the colorful, porter-rich scene. True to character, Pegeen efficiently clears the stage of her rivals and commences to bring Christy down to earth with ominous reports of a newspaper story that "filled half a page of the hanging of a man" (41). This sadistic streak of Pegeen's is perversely functional for bringing Christy back into conjunction with herself. Her pronouncements are thus—and, again, ironically—moral in that they purge Christy of his superfluous pride and prepare him for the creation of a more heartfelt poetry during the lovers' consequent lyrical intermezzo. Christy's lovely words first puzzle, then enchant Pegeen:

CHRISTY [*with rapture*]: And I'll have your words from this day filling my ears, and that look is come upon you meeting my two eyes, and I watching you loafing around in the warm sun, or rinsing your ankles when the night is come.

PEGEEN [*kindly but a little embarrassed*]: . . . if you vexed me a while since with your leaguing with the girls, I wouldn't give a thraneen for a lad hadn't a mighty spirit in him and a gamey heart. (43)

Enter upon this speech Shawn Keogh (just such a lad as Pegeen "wouldn't give a thraneen for") and the Widow Quin. As did Pegeen in the preceding scene, Shawn bears a physical object that will serve as an instrument of peripeteia: he carries a *cleeve* (satchel) that contains such interesting objects as a one-way "ticket to the Western States" and a magnificent suit of clothes. With the Widow Quin now managing to force her rival's exit, the pattern of relationships has been suddenly altered; Christy-the-Will faces alternative Masks, offered by Wills that have insinuated themselves into the position of Pegeen-the-Will. Both the Widow and Shawn try to bribe Christy into ceding the contest for Pegeen to Shawn, the first-comer to the field. Christy has no intention of acceding to their Wills but every intention of wearing Shawn's clothes, of embracing the conventional life and the marriage with Pegeen that Shawn has been planning for himself. As Christy tries on the clothes, the terms of the contest are further defined: the Widow Quin throws out her lure—passionate sex. Indeed, her lusty language momentarily counterpoints the romantic words of Pegeen and Christy's lyrical intermezzo—but Christy, resplendent in Shawn's False Mask, is swaggering again. He is thus unable to accept the Widow's terms.

The resurrection of Old Mahon will soon facilitate belief in a creed offered to Christy-the-Will by the Widow Quin: Old Mahon immediately complicates the dance of Wills and Masks in that he is more a ludicrous, swaggering counterpart of Christy than the terrifying ogre depicted earlier. Besides suggesting a Will similar to Christy's, Mahon also fleshes out the portrait of Christy's earlier Will (or way of being) with his tales of Christy's foolishness, inadequacy with drink, ineffectuality with women, and unattractiveness. Amusedly, the Widow Quin notes family resemblances, proclaiming Christy a "hideous, fearful villain and the spit of you" (50), even as she looks from the cocksure father to his now far-from-cocksure son, who has been reduced to cowering behind the door. She manages to send Old Mahon on a wild-goose chase and to berate Christy gently for misleading Pegeen and the village with his False "walking Playboy of the Western World" Mask (50). However, Christy pulls himself together, even as he clings to that Mask, by inflicting adamant curses (instead of a loy) on his father's head.

Desperately, he hearkens to the Widow's offer of a companionship that will mitigate their mutual loneliness:

CHRISTY [*interested*]: You're like me so.

WIDOW QUIN: I am your like and it's for that I'm taking a fancy to you, and I with my little houseen above where there'd be myself to tend you, and none to ask were you a murderer or what at all. (52)

Christy's consideration of this way of being is shattered by the calls of the young girls to the games. As he goes off to "lick the world" (53), he recalls that Pegeen and his Playboy image go together. Nothing must disrupt that congenial Mask, or ideal of being. Thus, he acquiesces to the new terms of bribery offered by the Widow Quin only so that she will protect his affair with Pegeen by removing the irritating presence of his father from the scene. Obviously, Christy is losing his grip on his True Mask.

In spite of Christy's refusal to take into account his father's indestructibility, the dance of Wills and Masks is drawing to a finale in which Christy's Will will be linked with that of his father rather than with the Widow Quin's or Pegeen's. The beginning of Act III rehearses its end: Philly and Jimmy, upon their return from Kate Cassidy's wake, begin to interrogate Old Mahon and to elicit his story, even as they interrogated Christy and elicited *his* story in the first scene. Old Mahon himself reveals another quality shared with his son—a distinct pride in his power to tell a whopping good tale:

I'm after walking hundreds and long scores of miles, winning clean beds and the fill of my belly four times in the day, and I doing nothing but telling stories of that naked truth. . . . Give me a little supeen and I'll tell you now. (56)

The Widow Quin's subsequent efforts to paint over Old Mahon's accusations against his son with the color of madness are wasted. Even if the suspicious Philly were not impossible to fool, Christy would not escape his father's sharp eyes: he has won all the games at the fair on the strand and is being hoisted on the shoulders of the crowd and proclaimed "the champion Playboy of the Western World." Old Mahon cannot believe that his son, "the fool of men," could be so proclaimed—until Christy becomes all too visible over the heads of the crowd (58). As has been observed since the days when the Chorus of Thebans mourned over Oedipus, a hero on a mountaintop is easily toppled.

Christy's downfall is forestalled when Widow Quin leads Old Mahon into questioning his own sanity and Pegeen manages to banish all the villagers from the *shebeen*. Thereupon follows the final—and most sensual—of the lyrical intermezzos between Pegeen and Christy, wherein Christy proposes marriage and is accepted. A final vision of Christy and herself joined Will-to-Will is sculpted by Pegeen: "Well, the heart's a wonder; and, I'm thinking, there won't be our like in Mayo, for gallant lovers from this hour, to-day" (66). However, as his situation rapidly deteriorates, Christy soon realizes that he has been cast out from the Mayoite community. He can, though, perceive no particularly attractive alternative to the life he has lately been enjoying. To return home with his father, "to go back into [his] torment" (73), would be regressive. The second attempted murder of his father, therefore, is as much a violent search for a new Mask as an attempt to regain his Playboy laurels. After the apparent murder, Christy's hope (obviously irrational) is that now "Pegeen'll be giving [him] praises the same as in the hours gone by" (75). That Christy can so overlook the fact that rigor mortis is setting into Pegeen's feelings for him indicates that he is still confusing Pegeen's Will with his own Playboy Mask. And he also fools himself when he pretends not to cling to the Mask that is being torn from his grasp. It takes the undeniable physical reality of *Pegeen* tying the noose around him, attempting to cripple him with the burning sod, and having become a far more lethal castrator than even the Widow Quin to make him drop the Mask.

A Death Mask seems to be the only—and ghoulish—choice left to Christy's Will. But Old Mahon manages to resurrect himself once more, probably wanting to be reassured that Christy still wants to kill him. Promptly his wish is granted as Christy cries, "Are you coming to be killed a third time, or what ails you now?" (79). In fact, Old Mahon is absurdly like a figure from a hyperbolic Freudian dream in which a father is delighted to learn that his son would like to castrate him because that desire certifies his offspring as a bona fide heterosexual. At any rate, Christy's honest rage delivers him from the Death Mask. Now he can attempt to don a new Mask, which he tentatively identifies as that of "a likely gaffer in the end of all" (80). Since, indeed, this ideal of being leaves Christy a loner, alienated from all the play's other characters save his father, it seemingly justifies a time-honored critical approach to the play: to analyze the discourse of "two distinct groups" of characters, the Mayoites and the Mahons (Chaudhuri 374, 376).

However, the traditional heuristic does not take into account what Chaudhuri calls the discourse of the "signifying space" (377). As cogent for analysis, though, as Chaudhuri's concept of "spatial transformation" are the Yeatsean terms derived from conning this very text. They can help the story of Christy's growth and of his love affair with Pegeen emerge as an arc upon the antithetical side of the Great Wheel of Being (see Figure 5): that is, Christy's Will or way of being at curtain's rising partakes of the qualities of Phase 7 on the Great Wheel:

Will—Assertion of Individuality.

Mask . . . True—Altruism. *False*—Efficiency.

Creative Mind . . . True—Heroic sentiment. *False*—Dogmatic sentimentality.

Body of Fate . . . —Adventure that excites the individuality. (*Vision* 114–15)

The main cause of the Playboy's internal conflict, though, arises from his progression to Phase 8, which is defined by conflict, "the West," and "the gathering of strength":

Will—War between Individuality and Race.

Mask . . . True—Courage. *False*—Fear.

Creative Mind . . . True—Versatility. *False*—Impotence.

Body of Fate . . . —The beginning of strength. (116–17)

However, Christy does not progress to this Phase—that of a Playboy of the Western World—until he defends himself courageously against his persecutions at the hands of Pegeen and the other Mayoites. Then and only then can he discard his False Mask and find a Mask that will imbue him with "true" personal courage. This is the special courage of Phase 8, "the courage unbroken through defeat":

It is the very nature of a struggle, where the soul must lose all form received from the objectively accepted conscience of the world [perhaps the dictates of Father Reilly]. . . . The being clings like a drowning man to every straw . . . amidst the collapse of all these public thoughts and habits. . . . Till he has begun groping for strength within his own being, his thought and emotion bring him to judgment but they cannot help. (117–19)

In the moments of crisis in Act III, Christy jumps through several phases in a development analogous to the rapid expenditure of several of his catlike father's lives. At the play's end, Christy approximates the man of Phase 12, whose Will is of "the Forerunner" and whose Masks are "Self-exaggeration" and "Self-abandonment":

He defines himself mainly through an image of the mind begun or beginning. . . . [T]he sanity of the being is no longer from its relation to facts, but from its approximation to its own unity. . . . [T]hat which it would be [is] the lonely, imperturbable, proud Mask. (126–28)

A new play, or perhaps just an epilogue, in which Christy acts out his intentions to "go romancing through a romping lifetime" may be projected from Pegeen's mourning memory of "the only Playboy of the Western World" and Yeats's praise of the Will of "the Hero" (Synge, *Plays* 80; Yeats, *Vision* 127).

In several ways, then, Yeats's revelations spring from Synge's complex *Playboy*: first, *A Vision* traces back to the *Playboy* its gyrings between subjectivity and objectivity. Thus marked off is the apposition between the three-act form and the comic material, especially the pattern of Christy and Pegeen's romance, which in turn is complementary to the gyrings of the characters between various ideals of being, or Masks. Second, the symbols of Will and Mask can focus attention on the multiple movements danced by Synge's dramatis personae. Finally, the correspondence of the characters to antithetical or primary phases on the Great Wheel of Being indicates the geometrically increasing possibilities of intersecting realities: parallel developments make the play aesthetically beautiful and add to the comic effect; antithetical relationships become, by play's end, ironic associations due to their continual joint presence in the eyes of the audience. That is why the confrontations between, for instance, Christy and his father are as rich in connotation as they are in laughter. In Synge's dramatic world, he who laughs last laughs best, for a mocker can suddenly become a keener: as the curtain falls, we lament with Pegeen, "Oh my grief, I've lost him surely. I've lost the only Playboy of the Western World" (80).

Perhaps, then, it is fitting to award at least the penultimate word to Yeats, who was, like Christy, a master of self-transformation: in "The Municipal Gallery Revisited," he points to the portrait of John Synge and perhaps (in an otherwise paradoxical allusion) links his hero's power of " '[f]orgetting human words' " to the linguistic legerdemain of the Vision's preternatural poets. Most poignantly, though, he begs the viewer to discount the Yeatsean oeuvre and "[s]ay my glory was I had such friends" (Yeats, *Poems* 318). Certainly Yeats continually reiterated his debt to Synge, that unlikely Muse. Does Synge owe a similar debt to Yeats? If we can acknowledge that Synge, together with his Playboy, helped energize Georgie Yeats's visionary planchette and thereby bequeathed "metaphors" to a review of his own drama as well as to the creation of his friend's poetry, we can answer in the affirmative.

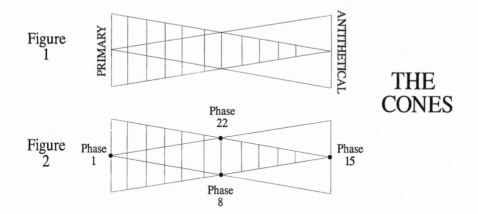

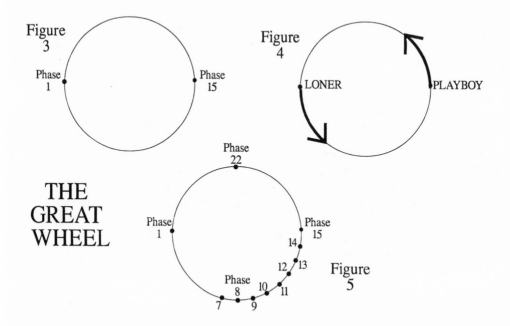

NOTE

1. In 1972, a collection entitled *A Centenary Tribute to John Millington Synge* (ed. S. B. Bushrui) included ''Yeats's Conception of Synge'' by Robert O'Driscoll. The essay declares that ''Yeats's concept of the mask and his theory of tragic ecstasy developed about the figure of Synge'' (Kopper 16). In the same year I developed independently a more complex linkage between Yeats's concepts and Synge's work (Powers).

WORKS CITED

Bourgeois, Maurice. *John Millington Synge and the Irish Theatre*. London: Constable, 1913.

Chaudhuri, Una. ''The Dramaturgy of the Other: Diegetic Patterns in Synge's *The Playboy of the Western World*.'' *Modern Drama* 32(3) (1989): 374–86.

Greene, David H., and Edward M. Stephens. *J. M. Synge, 1871–1909*. New York: Macmillan, 1959. Reprint. New York: Collier, 1961.

Kopper, Edward A., Jr. *Synge: A Review of the Criticism*. Modern Irish Literature Monographs Series 1. Lyndora, Pa.: Kopper, 1990.

Powers, Ellen Ann. ''A Search for the Yeatsean Masks in the Comedies of John Millington Synge.'' Honors thesis, Smith College, 1973.

Saddlemyer, Ann, ed. *Theatre Business: The Correspondence of the First Abbey Theatre Directors: William Butler Yeats, Lady Gregory and J. M. Synge*. University Park: Pennsylvania State University Press, 1982.

Skelton, Robin. *The Writings of J. M. Synge*. Indianapolis, Ind.: Bobbs-Merrill, 1971.

Synge, John M. *The Aran Islands*. In *Prose*, ed. Alan Price. Vol. 2 of *J. M. Synge: Collected Works*. 4 vols. London: Oxford University Press, 1966, 45–184.

———. *The Complete Plays of John M. Synge*. New York: Vintage, 1960. (Cited as *Plays*.)

Yeats, W. B. *The Autobiography of William Butler Yeats*. New York: Collier, 1971.

———. *The Collected Poems of William Butler Yeats*. New York: Macmillan, 1972.

———. *A Vision*. New York: Collier, 1972.

4

Tragic Self-Referral in *Riders to the Sea*

Daniel Davy

One of the most basic critical issues of *Riders to the Sea*—the nature of the tragic experience expressed in the play—continues to be a matter of dispute. For many critics, the play's brevity, monochromatic emotional tone and the quality of purely passive suffering it exhibits render it far too insubstantial to be labelled "tragedy" at all, particularly when weighed against its mighty predecessors, which define the genre.[1] Others are equally emphatic in affirming the "tragic" stature of *Riders to the Sea*, but even among the play's proponents there is considerable dispute about the precise nature of this experience and the dramaturgical method that the play employs to evoke an authentic tragic response.[2] Perhaps chief among the various issues in contention is the allegedly "static" quality of the play, its failure to provide a fully articulated "action" in an Aristotelian sense, and, as a kind of Aristotelian corollary to this reputed structural defect, the perceived haplessness of Maurya as protagonist—her status, not as "subject," but as helpless and passive "object" before the intentions of the cruel and implacable sea. Additional controversy arises from the interplay of "natural" and "supernatural" perspectives in the work, from the play's curious, and perhaps unique, ability to participate in the radically divergent *epistemes* of both "classical" and "modern" worlds.[3] There is, in my view, a single, vital element in the play that is capable of harmonizing these various clashing perspectives, and that has been, to a large degree, overlooked by previous criticism: Maurya's "vision" at the spring well of her still-living, but doomed, son Bartley, followed by the ghostly Michael astride the grey horse of death. An analysis of this vision as it relates to other elements of character, structure, and theme in the play will perhaps reveal a previously unsuspected complexity in the apparently simple organization of the play's materials.

One of the most striking features of this incident is the fact that it in no way appears anomalous, despite its appearance in a play that is otherwise expressed within a wholly naturalistic idiom. As Nicholas Grene has noted: "The supernatural in Synge is oddly matter-of-fact and unmysterious. . . . In *Riders* he presented Maurya's vision as though there could be no doubt that she actually saw what she said she saw. No one in the play questions its reality" (Grene 53–54). Nor do we doubt its veracity, a point emphasized by Simon Williams:

Though the style of representation may be naturalistic, the perspective adopted towards the supernatural does not invite us to analyse it. . . . The supernatural is neither explored nor explained, it just gains in credibility to the point where we unquestioningly accept the reality of Maurya's vision of Bartley being followed by Michael on the grey pony. Equally unquestioningly, we accept the fact of Bartley's death as a result of this pursuit. (83)

How does the play succeed in this apparently seamless integration of what would appear to be an anomalous element? I believe we can obtain a clue to answer this question by momentarily shifting our attention from the play to Synge's prose narrative *The Aran Islands*, a work that is, of course, very closely associated with *Riders to the Sea*.

In one respect, the apparent straightforward simplicity and detached quality of Synge's narrative of island life seems as deceptive as the dramatic work the playwright later fashioned from his experience on the islands. Consider the following account of the funeral rites of one of the inhabitants:

When the coffin was in the grave . . . the keen broke out again more passionately than before. This grief of the keen is no personal complaint for the death of one woman over eighty years, but seems to contain the whole passionate rage that lurks somewhere in every native of the island. In this cry of pain the inner consciousness of the people seems to lay itself bare for an instant, and to reveal the mood of beings who feel their isolation in the face of a universe that wars on them with winds and seas. (*Aran Islands* 75)

Synge's own perspective here—his sensitive response to the feelings of the islanders notwithstanding—is very much that of the "reporter" giving an objective account of this event. From such a perspective, the notion of the "inner consciousness" of the people revealing and expressing acute "isolation" in the face of an obviously hostile environment is perfectly reasonable and normal. However, such a "normative" and objective perspective on the relationship of the islanders' psyche to their environment is, in fact, very atypical of *The Aran Islands*. Consider, for example, the following passages:

In Inishmaan one is forced to believe in a *sympathy between man and nature*. . . .

Many women here are too sturdy and contented to have more than the decorative interest of wild deer, but I have found a couple *that have been turned in on themselves* by some circumstance of their lives *and seem to sum up in the expression of their blue grey eyes the whole external symphony of the sky and seas.* . . .

The charm I have found among these people is not easy to describe. *Their minds have been coloured by endless suggestions from the sea and sky, and seem to form a unity in which all kinds of emotion match one another like the leaves or petals of a flower....*

I cannot say it too often, the supreme interest of the island lies in *the strange concord that exists between the people and the impersonal limited but powerful impulses of the nature that is round them.* (*Aran Islands* 75, 143, 102, 75; my emphases)

There is, quite obviously, a dramatic difference in the perspective adopted in these passages, and in the relationship they establish, compared to the first passage quoted. What is notable here is not only the expression of an integral connection between the subjectivity of the islanders and the outer environment, but also the fact that Synge's *own* perspective is so clearly subjective here, markedly differing from the "reporter's" point of view cited earlier. Another observer might not perceive any "strange concord" here at all, but only the pain of "isolation" induced by a harsh and alien environment. But Synge is not simply an observer or a reporter, he is a poet and a dramatist, and it is that perspective—that unique *consciousness*—that is persistently in evidence, in various subtle ways, throughout his narrative of Aran and its inhabitants.

There are, therefore, two separate points to be emphasized here: first, Synge's own capacity for an altered perspective, or consciousness, and second, on the basis of this altered perception and in the context of Aran, the repeated emphasis on the "unity, concord," and so forth of subject and object: the integral connection perceived by Synge between the psyches of the islanders and the external environment.[4] It should also be noted, as a corollary to this second point, that Synge repeatedly emphasized in his writings the influence of a specific locale over time on the minds and spirits of its inhabitants.[5]

Of course, these passages are extrinsic to the text of *Riders to the Sea*, but they nevertheless seem clearly suggestive of one possible avenue of investigation. With these points in mind, let us return to the play and its pivotal event, Maurya's "vision" at the spring well. What exactly is the nature of this manifestation? The emphasis of virtually all the various critical responses to this question is on the vision as an "object" in the landscape, on the *seen*, but there are none on the *seer*.[6] Nonetheless, if we accept "vision," why not "visionary?" I would argue that Maurya's "vision" cannot be legitimately construed as suddenly "appearing" as a manifestation of reality as objective as any other in the heretofore natural terrain of the island, but rather should be seen in its true context as the specific "object" of a *subject*, of Maurya's perception and consciousness. It is, of course, also true that the apparition of the dead Michael astride the grey horse is of supernatural origin, and it is also, certainly, an expression of the deadly power of the sea. There are, therefore, three separate components here: supernatural presence, the natural sea, and, as the agency organizing the three components into the unitary image of the vision, Maurya considered as consciousness. In determining the relationship between these three components as they function in the drama, we will, in my view, be able to come to a clearer understanding of the nature of the tragic experience in the play.

Let us begin with Maurya's subjective relationship to the natural sea, and remind ourselves as we do of Synge's belief in the influence of a specific environment on the psyche over time. If we are to take this point seriously, we can only regard the sea's influence on Maurya as overwhelming. We are given to understand that Maurya has spent an entire lifetime wholly surrounded by the sea, and indeed "isolated" from any other mode of life. But the sea's pervasive presence exerts far more than simply a passive influence. Maurya is forever *intent* upon the sea, as the sea holds within its power all that she values, and virtually the entire content of her life. Its power over the life and death of her sons and other menfolk is made abundantly clear in the play; of secondary importance, but still very significant, are the bounty and living it yields and the specter of poverty and dependence it casts up along with the bodies of its two most recent victims.[7] We can picture Maurya forever confronting the sea, forever staring out over its expanse; what can the "influence" *be* in such an activity, persisting over decades, with the attendant attrition of one death slowly and inevitably following another? The very concept of "attrition," in the context of Synge's dramatization of the culminating hours of this scenario, seems to me to take on a double meaning. Many critics have spoken of Maurya as "worn out" by the play's end, a conventional but apt image signifying a lifetime of care and fatigue. However, it would also seem accurate to refer to Maurya— specifically as the perceiving and responding *subject* here—not as "worn out," but as worn *down* or worn *away*, in the manner of rocks on the seashore, by the unceasing movement and action of the sea. There is a sense in this play of the sea invading the very mind of Maurya; the sea *washes through consciousness* as it were, incessantly wearing away the "natural" or "normative" substance of the psyche and leaving behind the prepared potentiality for an altered or, we may well say, "visionary" state of consciousness. For what is the sea in this play? Certainly it is, and remains at all times throughout the play, a "natural" sea, indeed the most basic and dominant element of the natural world. At the same time we would probably be justified in asserting (many have done so) that the sea, by virtue of the "vision" as its metaphysical extension, both symbolizes and, in a sense, becomes a supernatural presence in the play. Third and, I think, very important, the sea is a vehicle and a catalyst, a *way of knowing*; it is the bridge that connects the supernatural with Maurya's interior self in the moment of vision and makes them, temporarily, one.

The deadly sea and the vision of death that emerges from it structure an imaginative continuum: the "natural" sea extends into the metaphysical, and we sense this transcendental strength in the natural movement of the waves. In like manner, Maurya's "natural" consciousness extends into the supernatural; the natural sons are destroyed by the natural sea, but it is the metaphysical power beyond, but at the same time within, the natural that is "seen" in the moment of vision by Maurya; she is transfigured from within as the exterior world is transfigured from without by the specter of the dead Michael astride the grey horse.

The sense of unity established here at the very core of the play—created by this integral relationship between the subjective and the objective, *mind* and *reality*, the human and the inhuman—is, in my view, responsible for the overall dramatic power of the play. This relationship is also powerfully suggested throughout by the play's overall ambience. The emotional "tone" of mourning humanity is externalized as the bleak topography of the island and its environs: the grey overcast of the outer environment suggests the greyness within the twilight of the heart; the salt of the sea unites with the salt tears of grief and endless mourning for lost sons and husbands. The island and the sea become, in a sense, an extension of the physical bodies of Maurya and the others in the community; they certainly seem to be as aware of—as *connected*—to the movements and moods of the sea as they are to the rhythms within their own bodies. This relationship is immediately established by many of the lines in the play's opening speeches, which are spoken variously by all three of the women (Nora, Cathleen, and Maurya):

There's a great roaring in the west, and it's worse it'll be getting when the tide's turned to the wind. . . . maybe when the tide turns she'll be going down to see would he be floating from the east. . . . He won't go this day with the wind rising from the south and west. . . . The tide's turning at the green head, and the hooker's tacking from the east. (*Riders* 96, 97)

And the relationship is again illustrated near the very end of the play in Maurya's concluding lamentation:

I'll have no call now to be up crying and praying when the wind breaks from the south, and you can hear the surf is in the east, and the surf is in the west. . . . I won't care what way the sea is when the other women will be keening. (*Riders* 105)

This deep and intimate concern with the mood of the sea is found throughout *Riders to the Sea*; as Ann Saddlemyer has noted, the word "sea" appears on every page of the play (*Modern Comedy* 15).

In addition to the play's powerfully suggestive general ambience, there are a number of specific elements in the text that strongly suggest a similar identification and relationship. Shortly before her departure for the spring well, a stage direction reads, "Maurya sways herself on her stool" (*Riders* 99), an action that is repeated by the battery of "old women" who enter the cottage in a mourning processional immediately preceding the entry of Bartley's body, which is borne by the men: "The women are keening softly and swaying themselves with a slow movement" (105). This action clearly replicates the action of the sea, and it identifies Maurya, as well as the primitive chorus of old women—who are themselves replicas of Maurya—with the sea's primal rhythms.

Immediately following this entrance, Maurya inquires after the identity of the body: "Is it Patch, or Michael, or what is it at all?" The quality of this inquiry, indicated in a stage direction—"half in a dream, to Cathleen"—is strongly suggestive both of the subjective element in the play and, also, of fluctuating subjective perspectives. Maurya is told by Cathleen that it could not be Michael, as he has been found in the "far north," whereupon Maurya replies: "There does be a power of young men floating round in the sea" (104). The imagery of this line suggests that the accumulating dead bodies of the sea's victims ("a power") do not decompose and revert to nature but rather remain forever "young men," an image that transforms the objective sea into a subjective phantasmagoria of staring eyes and dead faces moving forever in the waves.

In addition to these points, which connect Maurya directly to the sea, there are also elements in the text that connect Maurya to the transcendental power behind—and within—the sea. Donna Gerstenberger has observed that the weaving function of the "spinning wheel" indicated in the opening stage directions suggests the Greek *moira*, or "fates" (47); the image of the wheel also suggests the cyclic pattern of the action of the play, and specifically designates "fate" from yet another angle as the "wheel of karma" in Eastern philosophy and religion. Additionally, as Clifford Leech has pointed out, there is a strong connection between *moira* and the name *Maurya*, an allusion that Synge almost certainly intended (230).

Such a perspective on *Riders to the Sea*, which I term "self-referral," in that the play's structure of objective referents functions simultaneously to express an interior dynamic of subjectivity, can perhaps give us new insight into many of the contradictory critical perspectives. On the level of consciousness that gives rise to Maurya's vision, "opposites" become one: "futility" and "reverence" are fused within the mind, which beholds death in a living form in the visionary image of the dead son, and both "natural" and "supernatural" perspectives blend in the fluctuating values of consciousness within the mind of the protagonist and in the simultaneously oscillating status of the all-pervasive sea. This juxtaposition of "opposites" in conjunction rather than in their natural bipolar relationship, a fundamental characteristic of the altered state of consciousness experienced by Maurya in the play's central event, is found throughout the drama and its seemingly "natural" landscape, establishing from yet another angle the dynamic of self-referral in the play.

It is significant that the vision itself, which is given substantive existence by metaphysical power, nevertheless takes a *human* form; the supernatural and the natural are thus conjoined in a single image. Similar conjunctions of opposing values—life and death, as well as past and present—also occur in Maurya's account of this experience, which begins, "I've seen the fearfullest thing any person has seen since the day Bride Dara seen the dead man with the child in his arms" (*Riders* 102). Here birth is found clasped in the embrace of death, in an image "seen" by the new bride, who is soon to be a new mother and, soon enough, an "old mother" as well. The play's major conjunction of past and present occurs, however, as Maurya's account of the visionary experience nears its conclusion. While she utters her own replication of "Bride Dara's" experience, her mind is in the present as she recalls the past; with the ritualistic entry of another dead son borne by the living, this relationship is reversed, as the "dreamlike" Maurya recounts a past simultaneously occurring in the present:

MAURYA: I was sitting here with Bartley, and he a baby lying on my two knees, and
    I seen two women, and three women, and four women coming in, and they crossing
    themselves and not saying a word. I look out then, and there were men coming after
    them, and they holding a thing in the half of a red sail, and water dripping out of
    it—it was a dry day, Nora—and leaving a track to the door.
    [*She pauses again with her hand stretched out towards the door. It opens softly
    and old women begin to come in, crossing themselves on the threshold, and kneeling
    down in front of the stage with red petticoats over their heads.*]
    [*Half in a dream to Cathleen.*] Is it Patch, or Michael, or what is it at all? (104)

Similar conjunctions of opposing values are found in the theatrical imagery of the play, as indicated in Synge's stage directions. Synge's use of the color red is striking in this regard. The deeply saturated color of the "red petticoats" ostentatiously displayed by the chorus of mourning women who precede the entry of Bartley's body into the cottage contrasts markedly with the pallor of the lifeless body itself, which is, in turn, covered by a red sail, but is also covered and "saturated" by the gray salt water of the sea that has taken it.[8] This theatrical juxtaposition of the color red—so suggestive of the vibrancy of life— with the grey of death and the sea also refers back to the earlier, clearly symbolic juxtaposition of the red and grey ponies ridden by the living and dead brothers, respectively, in the visionary moment.

The presence of both "nets" and "new boards" indicated in the opening stage directions is also highly suggestive in this context. T. R. Henn has pointed out that the "new boards"—which are on hand, we quickly discover, as coffin boards held in readiness for the next death—would have been imported from the mainland, as the infertile soil of the islands will not support the growth of substantial trees (280). Here, in a single image, lie numerous juxtapositions of opposing values in conjunction: the island's "sea" environment is joined with the land, the vegetable life of mainland forests is used to form the casements of death, and the aspect of island infertility itself suggests the island locale as a locus of both death and life.[9]

The "nets" are obviously on hand as the principal tool in the livelihood of the islanders, but, as Errol Durbach has pointed out, they "clearly perform a counter-function, as well, to their primary connotation. Draped along the walls and rafters of the cottage, they evoke an insidious atmosphere of entrapment" (367). The nets, which are so suggestive of the presence of the sea, thus function simultaneously to symbolize life, generated by humanity in opposition to the sea, and death, generated by the sea's opposition to humanity.

Finally, the sea itself assumes a metaphysical presence correspondent with the conditions of visionary consciousness. The insistent suggestions of its presence are virtually overwhelming throughout the play and yet, in purely theatrical terms, it is not seen and is, strictly speaking, absent. It is thus both there and not there—a state of being entirely in harmony with its enigmatic life.

Such a perspective on *Riders to the Sea* would seem to clarify a number of the disputed critical issues noted in this chapter. In thus "seeing" the vision of death on the basis of her hitherto dormant potential for an altered state of consciousness, Maurya consciously and actively participates in the essential "event" of the play (if not "action"), and in so doing moves beyond her status of passive "object"—and locus of dramatic "stasis"—which so many have criticized as the principal defect in the work. Life (and the love that proceeds from it) and death, as engendered by mortality, are both elevated to the same plane of conscious activity. From the perspective of the play as a structure of self-referral relationships, we see revealed a subtle level of unity underlying the overtly antagonistic relationship between Maurya and the sea, a unity that co-exists with the oppositional duality of the two adversaries, which leads to the play's catastrophe. From such a perspective, the omnipresence of the sea in the play functions as an integral component and extension of the play's human presence, and the sea's omnipotent power operates throughout as a kind of buried peripety, an inverse index and perpetual comment on fatal human limitation. Second, our "unquestioning acceptance" of the supernatural is derived, in my view, from its fundamental relationship to the subjective element in the play and the various ways in which this element, extending "outward" in the perception of an "objective" apparition in the moment of vision, alters, in turn, the operation of the entire outer landscape of the play. This landscape can be seen as expressing objective reality, on the one hand, while, on the other, simultaneously suggesting a corresponding "inner" plane of experience.

As so much of the controversy surrounding *Riders to the Sea* has turned on the notion of "action" as discussed in Aristotle's *Poetics*, I would like to conclude with a consideration of this concept and its related cluster of key ideas— *hamartia, peripety, anagnorisis, catharsis*, and so forth—as they seem to me ultimately quite relevant to Synge's play. An examination of the *Poetics* quickly reveals that Aristotle's focus on the "structuring of the incidents" as the key element in tragic drama was not intended to assert the priority of "action" as an end in itself, but to reveal the disjunctive relationship, in the context of a tragic action, between "moral character," on the one hand, and metaphysical presence—and implicit intention—on the other.[10] The Aristotelian paradigm of "action" reveals the relationship of metaphysical presence to character indirectly—its very art lies in the subtlety of its indirection—through a structure that is linear, temporal, and objective. It is this aspect of objective linearity, expressed or "structured" along a temporal continuum, that requires the apparatus of hamartia, peripety, anagnorisis, and so forth (peripety as a consequence of hamartia can only be expressed through a structure grounded in time relationships). On the basis of such a model, Synge's play could certainly be considered "flawed"; the only element that can unequivocally be said to be present is anagnorisis.[11] However, it is just this "recognition," by virtue of its role as the central and dominant element in the play and in the context of a structure of self-referral relationships, that lends itself to the proposition that the *entire play* can be regarded as an anagnorisis. From such a perspective, those very qualities which have been attributed to the play as liabilities—stasis and the relative absence of action and temporal conflict—operate as structural assets. Whereas a play such as *Oedipus Rex* is organized "objectively" along a linear plane extending through time, *Riders to the Sea* is structured "subjectively": the action of the play is organized centripetally around the central event of the visionary experience, in a structure that more directly expresses, via its very "stasis," the timelessness of subjective experience.[12] In the Aristotelian paradigm, metaphysical presence is intimately associated with character by virtue of the *metabasis*, a sequence of actions that has been set in motion by subjective intention but that leads to metaphysical purpose. In *Riders to the Sea*, metaphysical presence dwells within the visionary "object," which is formed from the psyche of the protagonist subject, and extends "outward"—and "inward"—throughout the entire structure of the play.

The "self-referral" tragic scheme outlined here is clearly very different from the classic Aristotelian model, and yet the ultimate distillation of the two models is quite similar. Both result in the eerie sense of *participation* in an experience that is simultaneously natural and transcendental, and that ruthlessly reduces the protagonist to the status of object even as it expands his awareness and status as participating subject. For Aristotle, the culmination of this process was catharsis: the purgation of "pity and fear," and the restoration of order and equilibrium at the end of the play. I would like to end my own analysis here as well, with a few observations on catharsis as it seems to me to function in Synge's play.

Within the self-referral structure of *Riders to the Sea*, the subjective "action" of dread, agitation, and mourning is folded within an inner stillness of self. The play both begins and, in a sense, ends with sleep: at the outset, the daughters speak in muted tones as they examine the bundle of clothes so as not to disturb Maurya, who is resting in the next room, and Maurya's final lament concludes with, "It's a great rest I'll have now, and it's time, surely. It's a great rest I'll have now, and great sleeping in the long nights after Samhain" (*Riders* 105). The end is thus located in the beginning; at the end of the play, and of her life's journey, Maurya can rest in what is perhaps a uniquely "modern" catharsis: with respect to the power of the sea—and of life—there is, as Samuel Beckett's protagonist will put it fifty years later, "nothing to be done"—but nothing now need be done.

Following the visionary experience, Maurya's reaction to Bartley's death—which is also near the end of the play—is quite different from her anticipation of Michael's, as witness Nora's words, "She's quite now and easy; but the day Michael was drowned you could hear her crying out from this to the spring well'' (106). But the germ of the catharsis, it seems to me, can be located at a prior point in the action. It is not simply *after* the heat of conflict has passed— at the ''end'' of a linear process—that ''great rest'' and ''quiet'' descend, but in the very center of the tragic experience itself. As within Macbeth, during the interminable and terrible moments of inner stillness following Macduff's words, ''Let the Angel, whom thou still hast serv'd,/ Tell thee, Macduff was from his mother's womb/ Untimely ripp'd'' (Shakespeare) (Act V, Scene 8, 14–16), so it is as well within Maurya during the moments of vision.[13] Within these moments, Bartley and Michael, the living and the dead, merge together as one, as do the eternal sea and its mortal adversary. From the perspective of the natural world, Maurya here suffers total defeat, but it is a defeat achieved through total certitude: *Maurya knows*. From such a unity comes the purgation of duality and also the purgation of pity and fear arising from the ground of duality—the separation of subject and object that gives rise to all conflict. Maurya becomes, here and in the ''end,'' in the great rest of the long nights after Samhain, no longer the object of mortality, but the subject.

NOTES

1. The play has been variously described as possessing only the ''atmosphere of tragedy''; as a ''dramatic fragment,'' a ''tragic poem,'' or simply a ''lament.'' See Darrell Figgis (42), Raymond Williams (133), James Joyce cited in Richard Ellmann (129), and Robert Heilman (39), respectively.

2. Among those who grant the play status as tragedy are Thomas F. Van Laan, Errol Durbach, David R. Clark, and Leslie D. Foster.

3. ''Classical'' in the sense of an integral connection between the fate of humanity and the operation of metaphysical forces; ''modern'' in the sense of an equally fundamental *disjunction* between humanity and the ''world'': here, of course, ''world'' means the bleakly naturalistic landscape of ''an Island off the West of Ireland'' and the omnipotent, but indifferent, sea that surrounds it. What is of interest here is that the play's apparently simple organization of these divergent frames of reference is nevertheless capable of giving rise to directly contradictory interpretive perspectives on a number of very basic points. Both Figgis (42) and John Gassner found the play ''static,'' although what Figgis found flawed is termed a ''masterpiece'' by Gassner, despite the fact that ''nothing by way of plot and conflict occurs'' (Gassner 219). For Leslie D. Foster, however, the play ''may best be . . . understood by formulating the plot in the conventional terms of plot structure: exposition[;] . . . complication; turning point; *denouement*; . . . and catastrophe'' (106–7). Observations on other, equally fundamental, aspects of the play diverge along similar lines. Raymond Williams, for example, found that the play ''deals with man only in the simple exercise of his routine existence. The tragedy is natural, in the most common sense of that term'' (60). However, for Simon Williams, ''*Riders to the Sea* is the only one of Synge's plays in which the supernatural has a dominant and entirely determining presence'' (83). On the other hand, Thomas Van Laan spoke of ''the futility of human life'' as the ''play's statement'' (360). Otto Reinert referred to a ''reverence for life and the sea . . . [as] the sustaining emotion of *Riders to the Sea*'' (590). Even the identity of the play's protagonist is a matter of dispute. Al-

though the majority of commentators automatically have assigned this role to Maurya, a number of critics, pursuing the logic of Maurya as "passive, helpless, overwhelmed," variously find that "fate," "nature," or the "sea" operate as the true protagonist of the play. Van Laan (363) and Una Ellis-Fermor (169) are among those who discuss the play in these terms.

4. One of the few Synge critics to explicitly recognize this capacity for an altered perspective as a facet of his work is Ann Saddlemyer, who has collected numerous instances of what she terms "heightened consciousness" in Synge's work. Saddlemyer summarized:

All these . . . [instances] bear the same intense perception of the sudden shock of recognition, of heightened awareness to sensations, of the transfiguration in place and time, that we see scattered throughout his published works. But in these private confessions . . . *that which is transfigured is not the observed object, but the observer himself.* (102, my emphasis)

5. This is true, for Synge, not only of the islands and the islanders, but for the Irish mainland as well. The following account occurs in Synge's other "travel" book, *In Wicklow, West Kerry and Connemara*:

Among the cottages that are scattered through the hills of Country Wicklow I have met with many people who show in a singular way the influence of a particular locality. These people live for the most part beside old roads and pathways where hardly one man passes in the day, and look out all the year on unbroken barriers of heath. At every season heavy rains fall for often a week at a time; . . . the winds come down through the narrow glens with the congested whirl and roar of a torrent, breaking at times for sudden moments of silence that keep up the tension of the mind. (209)

6. By "seer" here I mean in the sense of "one who sees"; it is, however, certainly worth noting in this context that in ancient Gaelic the word for "poet"—*fili*—originally meant "seer" in the sense of divination, or one possessing supernatural "sight." See Myles Dillon (17).

7. Considerable evidence in the play supports this stark fact of life. Maurya attempts to prevent Bartley from going to the mainland by arguing, "It's hard set we'll be surely the day you're drowned with the rest. What way will I live and the girls with me, and I an old woman looking for the grave?" Following the visionary experience, Nora speaks of Maurya becoming "destitute with no son living," and Maurya's final lament concludes with, "It's a great rest I'll have now . . . if it's only a bit of wet flour we do have to eat, and maybe a fish that would be stinking." (*Riders* 98, 103, 105)

8. The "red petticoats" of the play are taken directly from Synge's experiences as recounted in *The Aran Islands*. Synge commented, on more than one occasion in this volume, on the striking red color of this article of clothing, so in contrast with the relative colorlessness of most of the bleak island environment. The "red sail" was mentioned by Maurya in the dialogue cited here as covering Patch's body in the much earlier drowning, and is not indicated specifically in the play's stage directions to cover Bartley's body; it is, however, obviously an appropriate choice for a director to make in stage presentation.

9. The conjunction of sea and land is also replicated via the location of Bartley's death: as a "rider" (land) to the "sea" he perishes not "out" at sea, but in the "surf," which is the border and junction point of the two opposing elements.

10.

The greatest of these elements is the structuring of the incidents. For tragedy is an imitation not of men but of a life, an action, and they have moral quality in accordance with their characters but are happy or unhappy in accordance with their actions; hence they are not active in order to imitate their characters, but they include the characters along with the actions for the sake of the latter. Thus the structure of events, the plot, is the goal of tragedy, and the goal is the greatest thing of all. (Aristotle 27)

11. There seems to me no substantive hamartia in the play (apart from the fact of mortality itself); nor is there, in the absence of any real linear progression of events, peripety. Maurya's fortunes, which were already melancholy and declining, cannot really be said to "reverse" as a result of what occurs, although there is a "reversal" of another kind in the abrupt shift of the play's energies from natural to supernatural as the visionary experience is revealed. "Pity and fear" do seem to me to be present in the play, but these are really the consequence of a successful structure rather than structural elements themselves. I will touch on the element of catharsis in the conclusion of this chapter.

12. It is perhaps worth pointing out here that the tragic paradigm articulated in the *Poetics*, although frequently taken to refer to "Greek tragedy" in a general sense, really refers very specifically to the type of dramatic structure first created by Sophocles, wherein the idiosyncrasies of an individual "character" assume a new significance. The earlier tragedy of Aeschylus was relatively "plotless,"—and "characterless" as we understand it—and it was, in contradistinction to the later, linear model of Sophocles, organized "analytically," or as a series of multiple perspectives on a single significant event. Indeed, Aeschylus' most famous work, *Agamemnon*, could also be said to be organized centripetally around the solitary "action" of the killing of Agamemnon, although the logic of this structure is, in other respects, of course, very different from *Riders to the Sea*. However, it is also worth pointing out here that the spontaneous reaction of W. B. Yeats (who was primarily responsible for first staging the play in the Abbey Theater) on first reading the play aloud was: "Aeschylus!"—or so it was reported (Gogarty 308).

13. By this comparison I do not mean that the psychological and spiritual implications arising *out of* these experiences are the same, but that the quality of *inner silence* is identical.

WORKS CITED

Aristotle. *Poetics*, trans. Gerald F. Else. Ann Arbor: University of Michigan Press, 1967.

Clark, David R. "Synge's 'Perpetual Last Day': Remarks on *Riders to the Sea*." In *A Centenary Tribute to John Millington Synge, 1871–1909: Sunshine and the Moon's Delight*, ed. S. B. Bushrui. New York: Barnes and Noble, 1972, 41–51.

Dillon, Myles. *The Archaism of the Irish Tradition*. Oxford: Oxford University Press, 1947.

Durbach, Errol. "Synge's Tragic Vision of the Old Mother and the Sea." *Modern Drama* 14(4) (Feb. 1972): 363–72.

Ellis-Fermor, Una. *The Irish Dramatic Movement*. London: Methuen, 1939.

Ellman, Richard. *James Joyce*. New York: Oxford University Press, 1959.

Figgis, Darrell. *Studies and Appreciations*. 1912. Reprint. Norwood, Pa.: Norwood Editions, 1977.

Foster, Leslie D. "Maurya: Tragic Error and Limited Transcendence in *Riders to the Sea*." *Eire-Ireland* 16(3) (1981): 98–117.

Gassner, John. *The Theatre in Our Times*. New York: Crown, 1954.

Gerstenberger, Donna. *John Millington Synge*. New York: Twayne, 1964.

Gogarty, Oliver St. John. *As I Was Going Down Sackville Street: A Phantasy in Fact*. New York: Reynal and Hitchcock, 1937.

Grene, Nicholas. *Synge: A Critical Study of the Plays*. Totowa, N.J.: Rowman and Littlefield, 1975.

Heilman, Robert. *Tragedy and Melodrama: Versions of Experience*. Seattle: University of Washington Press, 1968.

Henn, T. R. "General Introduction" and "Notes." In *J. M. Synge: The Complete Plays*, ed. T. R. Henn. London and New York: Methuen, 1963. Reprint. 1981, 1–21, 274–311.

Leech, Clifford. "Synge and the Drama of His Time." *Modern Drama* 16 (Dec. 1973): 223–37.

Reinert, Otto. *Classic through Modern Drama*. Boston: Little, Brown, 1970.

Saddlemyer, Ann. *J. M. Synge and Modern Comedy*. Dublin: Dolmen Press, 1967.

———. "Synge and the Doors of Perception." In *Place, Personality and the Irish Writer*, ed. Andrew Carpenter. Gerrards Cross, U.K.: Colin Smythe, 1977, 97–120.

Shakespeare, William. *Macbeth*, ed. Kenneth Muir. In *The Arden Shakespeare*. London and New York: Methuen, 1984.

Synge, John Millington. *The Aran Islands*. In *J. M. Synge: Collected Works*, vol. 2, ed. Alan Price. London: Oxford University Press, 1966, 75–143.

———. *In Wicklow, West Kerry and Connemara*. In *J. M. Synge: Collected Works*, vol. 3, ed. Alan Price. London: Oxford University Press, 1966, 187–338.

———. *Riders to the Sea*. In *J. M. Synge: The Complete Plays*, ed. T. R. Henn. London and New York: Methuen, 1981, 96–106.

Van Laan, Thomas F. "Form as Agent in Synge's *Riders to the Sea*." *Drama Survey* 3 (1964): 352–66.

Williams, Raymond. *Drama from Ibsen to Brecht*. London: Chatto and Windus, 1961. Reprint. New York: Oxford University Press, 1969.

Williams, Simon. "John Millington Synge: Transforming Myths of Ireland." In *Facets of European Modernism*, ed. Janet Garton. Norwich, U.K.: University of East Anglia Press, 1985, 79–92.

5

Death and the Colleen: *The Shadow of the Glen*

Mary Fitzgerald-Hoyt

Initially, *The Shadow of the Glen*, J. M. Synge's one-act play about an unhappy marriage in a remote area of County Wicklow, appears far removed from the concerns of the contemporary world. More dated are the virulent attacks the play received from Irish nationalists after its premiere in 1903. Outraged at the play's depiction of Nora Burke, an unhappily married wife who longs for sexual and emotional fulfillment, some Irish theatergoers viewed the play as an unflattering attack on the virtuousness of Irish women. Maud Gonne walked out on the first performance of the play, "in protest against Synge's portrayal of Irish womanhood" (Gerstenberger 33).

Today such an attempt to perpetuate the misguided stereotype of the Irish woman as blissfully ignorant of sexuality invites laughter or scorn. The anger the play elicited has become a historical curiosity, the same sort of hypersensitivity in an emergent nation that plagued Nathaniel Hawthorne when he depicted Colonial America as a society riddled with moral ambiguity. As Edward A. Kopper, Jr., has observed:

It is no wonder that *The Shadow* was disquieting for Synge's audiences. It depicts an Irish rustic set completely opposed to the image that nationalistic Ireland was promoting: a cold and brutal husband; a cowardly and mean-spirited would-be lover; a tramp, who, while exhibiting some kindness toward Nora at the end, is filled with blather and blarney; and a thoroughly discontented woman. (35)

And as David Cairns and Shaun Richards have argued, the Irish nationalists' reaction ironically placed them, albeit unknowingly, in alliance with the forces of colonialism (43). They point out that supporters of English colonialism, including Matthew Arnold, associated the Irish with the allegedly "feminine" qualities of emotionalism, dreaminess, and otherworldliness. In political terms, such an association was used to justify England's dominance of Ireland on the grounds that such people were surely incapable of self-determination. Cairns and Richards have argued that those Irish nationalists who condemned Nora Burke, who attempts to control her own fate—as the nationalists themselves wished to do—unwittingly adopted English justifications for a colonial presence in Ireland.

The Shadow of the Glen is no mere historical curiosity, however. The play remains a haunting, compelling piece of drama whose concerns reach beyond the confines of a lonely glen in County Wicklow. In the character of Nora Burke, Synge explores such timeless themes as the plight of the lonely individual in a forbidding landscape and the misery of an emotionally and sexually unfulfilling marriage. But of particular note to a contemporary audience is the fact that in so doing, Synge delivered a stunning blow to stereotypes of Irish women. Nora is no colleen, nor is she an old woman longing for the liberation of her four green fields. Imaginative but not unworldly, Nora longs for an escape from the lowering landscape and loveless marriage that confine her.

Living in a world where economic need determines marital choice, Nora marries Dan Burke, an elderly man who offers her financial security; but she eventually realizes that her husband "was always cold, every day since I knew him—and every night" (*Shadow of the Glen* 102). As she reveals to Michael Dara, a young man who evidently attracts her, the price of marriage to such a man was too high:

I do be thinking in the long nights it was a big fool I was that time, Michael Dara, for what good is a bit of a farm with cows on it, and sheep on the back hills, when you do be sitting looking out from a door the like of that door, and seeing nothing but the mists rolling down the bog, and the mists again, and they rolling up the bog, and hearing nothing but the wind crying out in the bits of broken trees were left from the great storm, and the streams roaring with the rain. (112)

Nora knows all too well the power of this landscape, for she has witnessed the bitter fates of Patch Darcy and Peggy Cavanagh, who were both driven mad in this desolate setting. Patch, a skilled herdsman whose companionship once helped assuage Nora's loneliness, died "queer in the head"; Peggy, now a wreck of her former self, is a living warning to Nora of what she herself might become.

Synge's inspiration for the play was a story told him by Pat Dirane, an Aran Islands *seanachie*, about a man who feigned death in order to catch his wife in adultery. Dirane's tale is spare, teasingly so, for we learn little about the participants, although Dirane claimed to have witnessed the events—the husband even furnished him with a stick to help in the attack on the guilty lovers (though Dirane never discloses whether he participated)—he never completes the story. The ending is compellingly ambiguous:

Then the dead man got up, and he took one stick, and he gave the other to myself. We went in and saw them lying together with her head on his arm.

The dead man hit him a blow with the stick so that the blood out of him leapt up and hit the gallery [presumably, the loft in the cottage]. (*Collected Works* 72)

Does the husband kill his rival? Does he also attack his wife? The story never answers these questions. Of the nameless wife, we know only of her hospitality to the wandering Dirane, her use of him to watch by the body while she summons her lover, and the chilling detail that the sticks the husband uses to attack the lover are the very same "fine sticks he had to keep down his wife" (72). That Dirane seems to find nothing untoward in the husband's possession of such sticks is likewise disturbing. One can well imagine how Synge, an artist who was extremely interested in the characters of women, might have wondered about the silences in this story.

From his travels in Wicklow and the Aran Islands, Synge had heard disturbing stories of madness and death in a lonely landscape. As Eugene Benson has noted (70), in the essays that Synge wrote about life in Wicklow, he underlined the fearful effects of rough landscape and harsh weather on an isolated populace:

This peculiar climate, acting on a population that is already lonely and dwindling, has caused or increased a tendency to nervous depression among the people, and every degree of sadness, from that of the man who is merely mournful to that of the man who has spent half of his life in the madhouse, is common among these hills. (*Collected Works* 209)

Synge draws on this knowledge of the effects of landscape on the psyche throughout *The Shadow of the Glen*, particularly in the character of Nora. Her speech reveals her to be a passionate, sensual woman all too aware of her marital and geographical entrapment and preyed upon by brooding thoughts of old age and death. She has a fleeting hope for change in the person of Michael Dara, whose youth and ardent speech contrast with the complaints of her elderly, passionless husband. But while Dan lies feigning death and Michael speaks wheedlingly of the pleasures of marriage to a young man, Nora reveals depths of character that both men lack. Michael lacks Nora's insight: eagerly counting Nora's cache of money, he reveals himself to be materialistic and unimaginative. Nora sees no great salvation in his plans for their marriage, for she has faced the inevitability of aging and death, including the likelihood that Michael will age as unappealingly as Dan has:

And why would I marry you, Mike Dara? You'll be getting old and I'll be getting old, and in a little while I'm telling you, you'll be sitting up in your bed—the way himself was sitting—with a shake in your face, and your teeth falling, and the white hair sticking out round you like an old bush where sheep do be leaping a gap. (*Shadow of the Glen* 114)

Nora has felt profoundly the isolation of the glen, but her longing for sympathetic companionship and "talk" has been largely unassuaged. When Dan "comes back to life," his harshness reveals how ill-suited a husband he is for this sensitive woman. Dan orders Nora from their house, and when the Tramp remonstrates that Nora will find it difficult to survive life in the open countryside, her husband cruelly taunts her with predictions that she will end up like the dreaded Peggy Cavanagh:

It's lonesome roads she'll be going and hiding herself away till the end will come, and they find her stretched like a dead sheep with the frost on her, or the big spiders, maybe, and they putting their webs on her, in the butt of a ditch. (116)

Dan's "resurrection" likewise confirms that Michael Dara is no solution to her loneliness. Having already revealed himself to be more interested in Nora's money than in Nora herself, Michael is now exposed in all his weakness and cowardice. Michael fails to reassure Nora when Dan offers his frightful picture of her future, and offers only the timid suggestion that "there's a fine Union below in Rathdrum" (115). The Tramp, who has overheard Michael's earlier proposal of marriage, suggests that the couple go away together, for at least the young man could offer Nora "the half of a dry bed, and good food in your mouth" (116); his suggestion is answered with Michael's silence. Nor does her former suitor intervene when the Tramp suggests that Nora join him in his wandering life: Michael watches her depart, breaking his silence only when he blesses Dan for sharing whiskey with him.

Even the Tramp, who sympathizes with Nora and moves her with his "fine bit of talk," is a poor match for her, for despite his romantic (and Romantic) description of the itinerant life, she soberly recognizes the harsh realities lurking behind his fine words, and "undercuts the Wordsworthian cast of this view of Nature" (Benson 78). To this poetic description of birds' songs and the beauties of the wild, she counters with the health-impairing hardships of life in the open countryside. Driven away by her husband, she decides that life with the Tramp is the best of her limited choices, even as she recognizes that what he "and nature offer is *distraction* from the processes of aging, not a halt to them" (Kopper 35). As Ann Saddlemyer has noted:

It is she who first recognizes in the comically shabby Tramp a kindred spirit, one whose imaginative sympathy and perceptiveness can help her find refuge in the very eye of the storm, the intensity of nature itself. But she also recognizes the quality of that refuge, when she interrupts with a fine ironic sense the Tramp's rhapsodies over grand evenings and wild nights. (62–63)

What makes *The Shadow of the Glen* such a memorable play is Synge's continual reversal of the predictable. As Weldon Thornton has noted:

Part of Synge's purpose . . . was to produce this aesthetic shock of eliciting the traditional stereotype of the lovers' triangle . . . and then shattering the stereotype by allowing the true natures and affinities of the characters to emerge at the end. (100)

Synge begins with an old story—the marital problems of a couple that is disparate in age—but he departs from the usual variations on that theme: Dan does not assume the role of the comic cuckold as, for instance, in Chaucer's tale of the Miller. And although Nora is expelled from her home—even though there is no evidence that she has been literally unfaithful—she does not assume the role of the punished ''bad'' wife: as we have seen, her future, however daunting, offers her more hope than does marriage to Dan.

Furthermore, Synge maintains what seems to be a deliberate ambiguity regarding Nora's sexual experience. Though her complaints of Dan's coldness and her evident interest in the company of other men, especially the late Patch Darcy, would suggest that Nora is sexually aware, Synge's reticence about her actual relationship with both Patch and Michael would seem to suggest that it is not Nora's sexuality that is of primary importance. Though commentators on the play have disagreed about Nora's sexual experience—with Edward A. Kopper, Jr., asserting that, despite the comments of literary critics and the accusations of Dan, there is no evidence that Nora has been literally unfaithful, and with David Cairns and Shaun Richards asserting that ''The clear implication is that she has found satisfaction in the now dead Patch Darcy and intends to do so with the young Michael Dara'' (51–52)—ultimately, we do not need to know. This is because Synge demonstrates that what Nora truly desires is not sex, but rather *transcendence*. Nora needs to believe that life is more than loneliness and decay; she engages in a desperate struggle to avoid the mean-spiritedness, materialism, and madness that have become the lot of those around her. Sexual warmth might assuage her loneliness, but she does deceive herself that life with any man will render her immune to mortality.

Synge likewise reverses expectations by rendering Nora, not a stereotype or a transparent symbol, but a real woman. At a time when women in Irish literature had too long been done the disservice of being transformed into symbols of Ireland itself, whether the mournful woman with the harp, Dark Rosaleen awaiting rescue, or the old woman longing for the restoration of her stolen land, Synge, in one act, undermines such reductive images. Though Nora may reflect the plight of Irish women and men caught in a society ruled by economic exigency, she is an individual, not the symbol of a country. Nor is Nora relegated to the ranks of the sexually unaware colleen, whose purity and innocence became the fodder for much bad art.

Most important of all, though Nora is victimized, she is not a victim. Her gender and her economic status severely curtail her choices, as is revealed in her unfortunate marriage. Particularly chilling for a contemporary reader is the implication that she is viewed as near-chattel toward the end of the play. As her truculent husband orders her from the house, rendering her destitute, the Tramp suggests of Michael, "Maybe himself would take her" (116). When Michael remains silent at this suggestion, the Tramp persuades Nora to accompany him. However, Nora will not let herself be passed around like one of the mountain ewes in Michael's poorly controlled herd: she *chooses* to go with the Tramp, despite, as we have seen, her refusal to be seduced by his image of an idyllic life in the wild. Nora, whose moving speeches have revealed her to have the soul of a poet, accepts the company of a man gifted with a "fine bit of talk," and courageously faces an uncertain future. As C. L. Innes has asserted, "Nora is the first of many Synge heroines who actually participate in the making of their destinies, rebelling against patriarchal control and, to the outrage of Irish audiences, expressing their sexuality as they do so" (52).

In our own time, when Irish women have joined women throughout the world in attempting to overturn reductive stereotypes, Nora is a "creation . . . more truly liberating than that preferred and presented by those for whom holy Ireland could only be adequately represented by those who had the morality of the Virgin" (Cairns and Richards 51). She conceals neither her sexual desire nor her despair; she refuses to be controlled by men who have suffered less profoundly and thought less deeply than she. Stoic, courageous, and individual, she is Synge's prophetic death knell to that creature so curiously tenacious of life, the Irish colleen.

WORKS CITED

Benson, Eugene. *J. M. Synge*. New York: Grove Press, 1983.

Cairns, David, and Shaun Richards. " 'WOMAN' in the Discourse of Celticism: A Reading of *The Shadow of the Glen*." *Canadian Journal of Irish Studies* 13(1) (June 1987): 43–60.

Gerstenberger, Donna. *John Millington Synge*. New York: Twayne, 1964.

Innes, C. L. *Woman and Nation in Irish Literature and Society, 1880–1935*. Athens: University of Georgia Press, 1993.

Kopper, Edward A., Jr. *"The Shadow of the Glen*." In *A J. M. Synge Literary Companion*, ed. Edward A. Kopper, Jr. Westport, Conn.: Greenwood Press, 1988, 25–37.

Saddlemyer, Ann. "Synge and the Nature of Woman." In *Woman in Irish Legend, Life and Literature*, ed. S. F. Gallagher. Gerrards Cross, U.K.: Colin Smythe; Totowa, N.J.: Barnes and Noble, 1983, 58–73.

Synge, J. M. *J. M. Synge: Collected Works*. Gen. ed., Robin Skelton. 4 vols. London: Oxford University Press, 1962–1968. Vol. 2, *Prose*, ed. Alan Price. 1966. Reprint. Washington, D.C.: Catholic University of America Press, 1982.

———. *The Shadow of the Glen*. In *The Complete Plays*. New York: Vintage, 1935, 101–118.

Thornton, Weldon. *J. M. Synge and the Western Mind*. New York: Barnes and Noble; Gerrards Cross, U.K.: Colin Smythe, 1979.

6

The Wooing of Étaín: Celtic Myth and *The Shadow of the Glen*

Cóilín D. Owens

Even before its first production—at the Molesworth Hall on October 8–10, 1903—*The Shadow of the Glen* was the subject of debate as to its Irishness. Maire T. Quinn and Dudley Digges had resigned from the Irish National Theatre Society in protest, and the *Irish Independent* attacked it in its October 8 editions. John Butler Yeats defended it in the *United Irishman* (October 10) on the grounds that a satire on the arranged, loveless marriage was fair game for satirical attack (Murphy quotes John Butler Yeats's "Ireland out of the Dock," 256–58). Then, Maud Gonne's theatrical exit that evening seemed a calculated reaction to the prominence given Lord Lieutenant Wyndham, who sat in a red seat in the front row (Cardozo 236–37). The subsequent controversy, which resumed with the second Irish production in December 1904, veered from one issue to another: whether Nora Burke was a plausible Irishwoman, whether the story was a version of the story of "The Widow of Ephesus" (Griffith), and whether the play derived from Henrik Ibsen and Dion Boucicault (Maud Gonne). It was defended on social grounds (John Butler Yeats), on grounds of artistic freedom (William B. Yeats), and eventually on its origin in Pat Dirane's story (Synge himself). Not all contemporary accounts were so inclined to follow party lines: for instance, Joseph Holloway, who had been attending rehearsals in August and early September, considered it a "curious play," Daniel sympathetic, Nora "frivolous," and the windup "strange." Of the opening night, he reported audience reaction as divided. Edward A. Kopper nicely summarizes all this familiar controversy ("*Shadow of the Glen*" 25–30).

An unfortunate effect of these original arguments has been to focus subsequent critical attention on the verisimilitude of the play: how many Irish marriages were like the Burkes'? What proportion of Irish wives committed adultery? How many Irishwomen would run off with a tinker? But questions such as these imply that Synge was writing a socially realistic problem play. Now, Synge was not insensitive to social injustice, as we see in his reports in "In Connemara" (1905–1906). There he wrote of poverty, ignorance, unemployment, emigration, excessive drinking, fights, degradation, oppressive landlords, and inadequate Congested Boards plans to counter these evils (Synge 2: 283–343). Nowhere, however, does he make any observations on the loveless marriage. Moreover, none of his creative works is concerned with solutions to social problems. *Riders to the Sea* is not an attack on the boat service to the Aran Islands.

The flashpoint in all this controversy was Arthur Griffith's charge that the play was a version of "The Widow of Ephesus," from Petronius's satire, *Trimalchio's Feast*. This Synge denied, but it was not until January 1905 that he produced the text of Pat Dirane's story (Synge 2:70–72). Now, if readers are willing to accept Synge's word that his play "differs essentially from any version of the story of the Widow of Ephesus with which he was acquainted" (*United Irishman*, 11 Feb. 1905, 1)—and I am willing to accept it with them— why have they been so uncritically accepting of his claim that the Pat Dirane story—also "essentially different"—is his source? In fact, the Dirane story provides little more than a pretext for Synge's play, with its sympathetic treatment of the character of Nora Burke, soulful language, evocation of place, complexity of the action, and resolution. On closer examination, Dirane's story seems less a source than a device to defend its native origins against Griffith, Maud Gonne, and the Irish-Irelanders. The Dirane story has, indeed, been found in many variations throughout Ireland, as Éilís Ní Dhuibhne-Almqvist shows. If this is indeed a source, then it has undergone a profound metamorphosis in *The Shadow of the Glen*.

The most abrupt element in Synge's transformation of Dirane's source is Nora's departure with the Tramp and the reconciliation of the erstwhile rivals, Dan and Michael Dara. William Yeats found in this conclusion a "perfection of ironic humour"; Eric Bentley considers Synge even more cynical than Petronius, while he re-creates traditional genres in the form of a comedy with an unhappy ending (see Benson 81); Declan Kiberd has argued that it looks back to the license associated with wake customs (168–75); and Weldon Thornton has argued that all Synge's plays, *The Shadow* included, were written against stereotypes (156).

Following Thornton, then, this chapter argues that *The Shadow of the Glen* resists the realistic stereotype into which it has been placed by most readers, even its defenders. Synge was writing a folk play in which the hard realities of everyday life are more likely to be interrupted by ghosts and fairies, representatives of the preternatural order, than by the preachments of social revolutionaries or rationalistic critics. *The Shadow* cannot be reduced to an exercise in fine language with focus on the real world (*pace* Maxwell 31). Just as in *Riders to the Sea*, Maurya's vision is no less real than any other aspect; each element— the pig with the black feet, the nets, Bartley's death—partakes of two worlds.

The ambiguities of *The Shadow of the Glen* similarly disconcert sound judgment and common sense.

Any reader of Synge's journals must be struck by the fact that for all the acuteness of their social observations, they are the expressions of an outsider from the lives of his subjects, indeed, of a profoundly solitary man. Separated by class, sect, and language from the people on whom he based his plays, he was by temperament even inclined to withdraw from the company of his peers; and although a patriot, he sought to protect himself from argument, action, and political party, which he deemed the enemies of the creative faculty. Requesting the removal of his name from the list of members of *Irland Libre*, he told Maud Gonne (6 Apr. 1897):

You already know how widely my theory of regeneration for Ireland differs from your and most of the other members of the *Jeune Irland*. . . . I wish to work in my own way for the cause of Ireland and I will never be able to do so if I get mixed up with a revolutionary and semi-military movement. (Saddlemyer, *Collected Letters* 47).

Synge guarded his private vision from intellection, abstraction, and dogma: "All theorizing is bad for the artist because it makes him live in the intelligence instead of the half sub-conscious faculties by which all real creation is performed." This vision emanates from the creative consciousness and precedes and shapes observation: "What is highest in poetry is always reached where the dreamer is leaning out to reality" (Synge 2:347). Thus, Synge sought to avoid what he privately considered as the subjective miasma of Yeats's *The Shadowy Waters*. As he confided in Stephen McKenna:

I do not believe in the possibility of "purely fantastic, unmodern, ideal, spring-dayish, cuchulanoid National Theatre," because no drama—that is to hold the public—can grow out of anything but the fundamental realities of life which are neither modern nor unmodern, and, as I see them, are rarely fantastic or spring-dayish" (Saddlemyer, *Collected Letters* 74).

For all its vision, it must be rooted in the clay: "No personal originality is enough to make a rich work unique, unless it has also the characteristic of a particular [time] and locality and the life that is in it" (Synge 2:350). That meant having the courage to face unpleasant social facts: "I think squeamishness is a disease and that Ireland will gain if Irish writers deal manfully, directly, and decently with the entire reality of life" (Saddlemyer, *Collected Letters* 76). Such considerations inform this reading of *The Shadow of the Glen*. Interpretations that selectively foreground the theme of the desire for escape from a loveless marriage apprehend but one aspect of Synge's purpose and fail to account for the power of the play as an expression of "the entire reality of life." That entire reality embraces both the struggle for subsistence on the back hills and the finer realities of a vision enabled by fairy lore and Celtic myth.

The Shadow of the Glen dramatizes the sexual yearnings of Nora Burke, a Wicklow farmer's wife. As she expresses these frustrations to a sympathetic tramp, they enlarge into a *cri d'esprit* against all mundane constraints, as symbolized by the mists moving up and down the remote glen. Synge's sympathies are with Nora and his identification, with the Tramp (the two developing characters in the play); his enmity is with the static counterparts, Daniel Burke and Michael Dara. The Tramp's emotional sympathy and colorful talk arouse Nora's hitherto dormant imaginative reserves, so that the surroundings of mountain mist and road become reinvested with their primal magic. Thus, the play dramatizes Synge's central preoccupations: a morose reflection on the conflict between actuality and human aspiration, mortality, and the consolation of an intimacy with the natural world.

The Shadow of the Glen dramatizes life-and-death issues in many ways, literally and metaphorically, and on different levels of seriousness and comedy. Daniel Burke appears dead but rises twice; his ploy is to test the validity of one of life's conventions (his wife's fidelity) from the vantage point of death, and he succeeds in exposing that convention as an illusion; the audience begins with the conventional view of death, proceeds, after Dan's first resurrection (through a sharing of his vantage point, but not his point of view), to a seriocomic view of life, and ends, after his second resurrection, with a romantic sharing of the Tramp's vantage point and point of view on both life and death. As its sympathies shift, the audience proceeds from an ironic view of Nora's infidelity to an ironic view of Dan's righteousness. The first revelation is that the conventional phenomena of death are deceptive, and the final revelation, that the conventional phenomena of life are equally so; we begin by believing Dan to be dead in body, and we end believing him to be dead in soul.

The language and imagery of the play reflect these ambiguities and shifts in the plot in a variety of ways. These devices make relative the states of being alive or dead by reference to animality, madness, and age. To the Tramp, Dan's death is dubious, for despite appearances, he has a "queer look" and is not properly laid out or waked; to Nora, however, his death was a dramatic event:

Then he went into his bed and he was saying it was destroyed he was, the time the shadow was going up through the glen, and when the sun set on the bog beyond he made a great lep, and let a great cry out of him, and stiffened himself out the like of a dead sheep" (Synge 3:35).

Nevertheless, the ironies in her remarks, "He's after dying on me, God forgive him" (33), and "Lay your hand on him now, and tell me if it's cold he is surely," and his observations on Dan's queerness, and coldness in both life and death (35) suggest the instability of appearances, for on her return with Michael Dara, her first enquiry is, "There was no sign from himself?" (45). The characters share a superstitious fear of the dead, though Dan assures the Tramp that "a man that's dead can do no hurt" (41). Clearly, the dead are not nonexistent, as Nora's remark indicates: "Isn't a dead man itself more company than to be sitting above?" (41). When Dan announces his presence with the comical tests, "How would I be dead, and I as dry as a baked bone?" and "It's near dead I was wanting to sneeze" (43), he further modifies the term.

Nora's reflections on age, time, and mortality raise the stakes above this verbal play, when she speaks of the death of her heart (49–51). Thus, her response to Dan's second resurrection, "Is it dead he is or living?" (53), while echoing the Tramp's reaction to the first rising, is now tragicomic. Forced to face the implications of her impossible love for the dead Patch Darcy, she taunts Dan's limitations, his literal-mindedness about life and death. Her rejection of Michael Dara is an easy afterthought, for, his temporary youth aside, he is Dan's counterpart. The image of these living dead sharing the water of life is a perfectly ironic coda to this interrogation of life's appearances. In these respects, the Ibsen play closest in spirit and technique to *The Shadow* is not *A Doll House* (1879), but *When We Dead Awaken* (1899).

Patch Darcy and the Tramp are another pair of living-dead counterparts. Of the "power of men" Nora is "after knowing," Patch was her favorite, by contrast with Michael Dara, who is highly estimated for his ability to "walk through five hundred sheep and miss one of them, and he not reckoning them at all" (47). Darcy, however, "went queer in his head" and died on the mountainside within the past year. The first mention of his name startles, then moves, Nora; and when the Tramp confides that he was "the last one heard his living voice in the whole world" (39), the associations between the anonymous Tramp and this mountain wanderer cumulate to motivate Nora's departure with the Tramp in the end. Having followed Darcy's nighttime footsteps to her door, the Tramp makes the significant remark, "There aren't two living souls would see the little light you have shining from the glass" (37). And just as we learn that Darcy's end was foreshadowed by "queer talk," insanity, and his nights on the mountainside, so, too, are we invited to share Dan's view of the Tramp's future: his talk is "blather," and his improvident life is passed on the roads, mountains, and glens. Although the Tramp appears to have a conventionally superstitious fear of the dead, to Nora he seems to offer a release from such fear. If at first she appears hesitant to greet death—"Is it walking on your feet, stranger?" (33)—by the end, she explicitly embraces it: "I'm thinking it's myself will be wheezing that time with lying down under the Heavens when the night is cold, but you've a nice bit of talk, stranger, and it's with yourself I'll go" (57). Their conversation is full of humorous remarks linking Patch, the Tramp, and death; for example, "He was a great man surely, stranger, and isn't it a grand thing when you hear a living man saying a good word of a dead man, and he a man dying?" (47). The Tramp may offer Nora freedom from convention and hypocrisy, but he also offers death. Could this mysterious stranger be the ghost of Nora's dead lover? At the very least, Nora's rapt response to him is due psychologically to the transference of her feelings of one to the other. She seems to recognize the affinity, at first dimly but with sufficient clarity in the end, so that she follows her Patch into the mists on the mountainside to romance, and possibly to madness and death.

Nora's decision to accept the Tramp's offer is the crux of the play. Even taking into account the ways in which he evokes inarticulate memories of her dead lover, this decision seems insufficiently motivated. We need to consider that Nora's yearnings are more than sexual and more than can be assuaged by physical security: they suggest a world-weariness, a longing for deliverance to another sphere for which she has an appetite. In fact, the swiftness of her final decision, if one can call it that, implies that she is going somewhere vaguely recollected rather than crossing into terra incognita. The climactic scene of the play turns less on one of her decisions than on her acceptance of a preordained condition. If the Tramp is psychologically an unconscious reminder of Darcy, then, from the perspective of folklore, may he not be considered a species of ghostly revenant, a visitant from the world of *sídhe*, or, mythologically, Darcy somehow after a metempsychosis? Before dismissing these possibilities as no more than wild speculations, it may be worthwhile to try to recover some premises overlooked by Synge's critics.

In his estimable book, *J. M. Synge and the Western Mind*, Weldon Thornton argues persuasively that throughout this period of his life, Synge was in a state of "permanent religious crisis." Citing his religious reading—Nutt, Besant, Blavatsky, Mead, Locke, Spinoza, Nietzsche, Thomas á Kempis, and so forth (27–28)—he quoted E. R. Dodds to the effect that one thing that Synge and Stephen McKenna shared was "an unresting curiosity about the secrets of religious experience" (30). In the Aran Islands he discovered an archaism with which modern society had lost touch—a strange blend of orthodoxy and unorthodoxy, of Christianity and paganism—which involved a sympathy toward a wide range of "supernatural" phenomena that would have struck any typical modern person as inconsistent and anomalous (63). The islanders believed in Christ and the angels, but also in the *sídhe*, which they considered to be real and dangerous creatures. Synge was attracted to the ease with which they moved between pagan and orthodox ideas, and their ability to move without apparent remorse or guilt between supposedly contradictory, or at least mutually exclusive, worldviews. This contrasted with the dogmatism of his Church of Ireland upbringing (65). Thornton concludes that:

His experience on the islands served not to make him into a primitive, but to permit him, standing between the two cultures as he did, to see how large a role "perspective" plays and how arbitrary and incomplete any single view of reality is. It was this awareness more than the primitive attitudes *per se* that enabled his plays and that determined many of their themes and devices. (45)

His observations of the Aran Islanders were complemented by what he was reading at the time he began *The Shadow of the Glen*.

As shown by his reviews, and the evidence of Kiberd and others, between

1898 and the spring of 1902, Synge was reading widely in Celtic mythology, Irish literary history, and folklore, and attending Professor Henry d'Arbois de Jubainville's lectures on Celtic literature at the Sorbonne (Greene and Stephens 77; Synge 2, pt. 4). The content of these lectures can be inferred from the professor's *Le Cycle Mythologique Irlandais*, Richard Irving Best's translation of which Synge later reviewed (Synge 2:364–66). There was also Alfred Nutt's two-volume study of the Celtic otherworld accompanying Kuno Meyer's translation of *The Voyage of Bran*, on which Synge took extensive notes (Kiberd 167). His March 1902 essay, "La Veille Literature Irlandaise," cites this work and de Jubainville (Synge 2:352–55). One of his observations reflects his intellectual interest in comparative religion and the conflicts within his personal faith:

Rien . . . dans la littérature n'est aussi primitif que cette foi commune aux Grecs et Irlandais, foi en un autre monde où les morts continuent une vie semblable à l'existence terrestre sans espoir d'être récompensés pour leurs vertus ni appréhension d'être punis pour leur méfaits. (Synge 2:354)[1]

It was at about this time (April), before returning home from Paris, that Synge began his verse plays. Moreover, between July 21 and September 6, while residing at his mother's rented house in Tomrilands, Annamoe, County Wicklow, he revised and completed both *Riders* and *Shadow*. Later that year (October–November), on his way to the Aran Islands (Inishere) for the last time, he left both manuscripts with Lady Gregory at Coole Park.

In his perusal of various Celtic tales, Nutt has the two principal aims of uncovering their representation of the otherworld and eliciting evidence of the doctrine of metempsychosis. In the course of this rambling disquisition—with excursions into Greek, Roman, and oriental analogues—he examines a number of Irish texts. One of the tales that he summarizes, *Tocmarc Étaíne*, or "The Wooing of Étaín" (1:175–77), must have caught Synge's attention. Nutt's source for this lovely story was Professor Heinrich Zimmer's edition of *Lebhar na hUidhre* (The Book of the Dun Cow), an eleventh-century fusion of older, discordant versions from possibly as early as the seventh century. A superior text was subsequently discovered in the *The Yellow Book of Lecan* and became available in a scholarly edition in 1938 (Best and Bergin). A good modern translation can be found in Gantz.

In the course of his book, Nutt gives two summaries of "The Wooing of Étaín," each designed to illustrate one of the themes of his book. The first, which should startle any reader of Synge's play, runs:

Étaín, originally the wife of Mider, one of the Tuatha Dé [Danann], is reborn as a mortal and weds Eochaid Airem, high king of Ireland. Mider still loves her, and when she refuses to follow him he games for her with her husband and wins. But Étaín is still unwilling to leave Eochaid, and to decide her he sings the following song:

"Woman of the white skin, wilt thou come with me to the wonderland where reigns sweet-blended song; there primrose blossoms on the hair; snowfair the bodies from top to toe.

"There neither turmoil nor silence; white the teeth there, black the eyebrows; a delight of the eye the throng of our hosts; on every cheek the hue of the foxglove.

"Though fair the sight of Erin's plains, hardly will they seem so after you have once known the Great Plain.

"Heady to you the ale of Erin, but headier the ale of the Great Land. A wonder of a land the land of which I speak, no youth there grows to old age.

"Streams gentle and sweet flow through that land, the choicest mead and wine. Handsome [?] people without blemish; conception without sin, without crime.

"We behold and are not beheld. The darkness produced by Adam's fall hides us from being numbered.

"When thou comest, woman, to my strong folk, a crown shall deck thy brow—fresh swine's flesh and beer, new milk as a drink shall be given thee by me, O white-skinned woman." (1:175–76)

This speech of Mider's, Nutt observes, although affected by Christian reinterpretation, is a typically Celtic characterization of the ideal of the Happy Otherworld (1:176).

Later in his discussion, Nutt distinguishes

two main types of the conception [of the Happy Otherworld], the Oversea, and the Hollow Hill type. . . . In the Hollow Hill type ("The Wooing of Étaín"), the wonderland is not figured as lying across the sea, but rather . . . within the *sid* or fairy hills. No special insistence is laid upon the immortality of its inhabitants, though this too is practically implied by what the story-teller relates concerning them, nor is the absence of strife singled out as a characteristic feature. In other respects both the positive and negative qualifications of this Elyisum correspond fairly to those of the other type. Women do not, however, play the same important part, there is no special portion of the land set aside for them, it is not the dames of Faery who come to woo mortal heroes, but a prince of the land who strives to allure thither a mortal maiden. (1:229–30)

He concludes that:

The vision of a Happy Otherworld found in Irish mythic romances of the eighth and following centuries is substantially pre-Christian; it finds its closest analogues in that stage of Hellenic mythic belief which precedes the modification of Hellenic religion consequent upon the spread of the Orphic-Pythagorean doctrines, and with these it forms the most archaic Aryan presentment of the divine and happy land we possess. (1:331)

In volume 2, while examining the concept of rebirth in Celtic literature, Nutt returns to this tale and gives a more detailed summary, entitled "The Étaín Birth-Story" (47–57). He describes it in three acts, thus:

A. Étaín was one of the two wives of Mider, lord of the *sid* (fairy mound) of Brí Leith. Her jealous rival wife, Fuamnach, succeeded in blowing Étaín out of Mider's land

and whirling her hither and thither through Ireland. At last sucked down by the force of the wind through the chimney of an Ulster chief, Étaín fell into the cup of the chief's wife, was swallowed by her, and in due course was born as a girl [and] . . . raised in great style. But one day he encountered a stately stranger singing a lay, alluding to the scenes through which Étaín had already passed. Whereupon he suddenly vanished. Meanwhile, Mider discovered the treachery, executed Fuamnach, and set off in search of Étaín.

   B. Eochaid Airem, High King of Ireland, had no wife. So he sent messengers the length and breadth of Ireland to find a wife worthy of him, and the choice fell upon Étaín. Now Ailill, Eochaid's brother, fell in love with Étaín, and Étaín was willing to satisfy his desire. To the arranged tryst came not Ailill, but a man in his shape, who admitted that he was in fact Mider, her fairy husband. He pressed her to come with him, but when she hesitated, he offered to duel with Eochaid for her.

   C. Mider induced Eochaid to game with him. The result of this was that Eochaid was tricked into wagering Mider's right to his arms about Étaín and the right of a kiss. Mider won, and despite the closed doors and the surrounding warriors of Ireland, Mider took Étaín with him, rising through the roof. The last that was seen of them were two swans winging their way to Síd-ar-Femain. Eochaid pursued them, and long after he was able to storm Mider's fairy palace and win back his wife. Thus his race inherited the enmity of the fairy clan. (2:47–53)

As we see, this version emphasizes Étaín's life before (and after) hers with Eochaid. This is not the case with de Jubainville's. His version of the story is very selective (176–82), but it features a prose translation of Mider's wooing song, the climax of all versions (and of Synge's transformation, as I argue here). He points out that Mider was inviting Étaín to a land she already knew well, and to his own home. Mider's song also "is the song which the messenger of Death sings to the woman he is bearing away to the mysterious sojourn of immortality." De Jubainville also focuses on the protracted duel between King Eochaid and his supernatural rival. When Mider beat Eochaid at chess, he demanded his wife. This the king countered by offering another game at the end of a year. Mider agreed "with ill grace" and disappeared. On his return, the same thing happened, and he was forced to return a third time. Thus, while Eochaid counted in anguish the days that Étaín remained to him, Étaín, while remaining faithful to her terrestrial husband, received many visits from the amorous god. On the final night, Mider was suddenly among them. Eochaid greeted him. "Here I am," said Mider. "I have already told thee," said Étaín, "that I will not go with thee until my husband yield me up to thee. If Eochaid gives me, I am willing." De Jubainville concludes with Mider's grasping Étaín around the waist, their rising into the air, and disappearance through the hole in the roof which served as a chimney. The warriors rose up ashamed of their impotence, and going out, they saw two swans flying around Tara, their long white necks united by a yoke of silver (182).

   Synge read at least two other versions of Étaín's story, Douglas Hyde's in 1899, and A. H. Leahy's in 1904–1905.[2] Hyde's brief version, which Synge had read in 1899, all but confines itself to Mider's lay, commenting that:

The ancient Irish pagans believed in the possibility of rebirth, and founded many of their mythical sagas on the doctrine of metempsychosis, and that they had a highly ornate and fully-developed belief in a happy other-world of Elysium, to which living beings were sometimes carried off without going through the forms of death. But it is impossible to say whether rebirth with life in another world, for those whom the gods favoured, was taught as a doctrine or had any technical significance attached to it by the druids of Ireland, as it most undoubtedly had by their cousins the druids of Gaul (104; Kiberd 55–56)

This is a concise summary of what the authorities that Synge had been reading—Kuno Meyer, Nutt, de Jubainville, and perhaps W. C. Wood-Martin—on the ancient Irish view of the survival of the personality after death. They agree that, through some process such as the transmigration of souls, metempsychosis, or metamorphosis, the Celts held that the individual personality survived bodily death. Nutt emphasizes the distinctions between what the Celts inherited from the "mythic fancy" of their predecessors and what they acquired from contact with Pythagorean religion. Thus, whereas the Irish Celts did not distinguish between soul and body, they tended to retain elements from a cruder pantheism, or even bodily metamorphosis, the southern Celts—perhaps due to their contact with Greek religion—conceived of metempsychosis as a process by which the soul survived the death of the body, subsequently inhabiting another one. Missing from all of these conceptions of an afterlife is any notion of eternal justice (Nutt 2:96, 122–23; Wood-Martin 251–52; de Jubainville 26–35, 197–99). The classic reference here is "Tuan Mac Cairill's Story to Finnen of Moville" (Nutt 2:285–301), although many tales, including "The Wooing of Étaín," imply the notion of a nonjudgmental spiritual order, which Synge found congenial.

Calling "The Wooing of Étaín," "the most extraordinary of all early Irish 'Wooings,' " Alwyn and Brinley Rees's comment applies equally to Synge's *Shadow*:

Eochaid did not marry a woman from another world; but although in mortal guise, the woman is essentially a being from another world. She is as mysterious as any fairy bride, for she has a complicated history of previous existences. Of all of this she herself has no conscious memory, and her husband, who has made a point of marrying "a woman that none of the men of Ireland has known before him," is unaware of the fact that he has a supernatural rival" (276).

Thus, unless *The Shadow of the Glen* was written by someone other than J. M. Synge, it must be seen as a transformation of "The Wooing of Étaín." The play is a redaction of the climactic scene in the long-drawn-out duel between terrestrial and supernatural forces. Similarly, Synge's dramatizes only the final and decisive last moves in a protracted game between Daniel Burke, Nora, and her lovers. Just as Étaín underwent metempsychosis, Nora has a complex nature, with identities and ties in two competing worlds. On the one hand, she has the security of her role as a strong farmer's wife, of "a man with a bit of a farm, and cows on it, and sheep on the back hills," at the price of a grinding routine required to maintain that condition "at the foot of the back hills, sitting up here boiling food for himself, and food for the brood sow, and baking a cake when the night falls" (Synge 3:49). But on the other, she is separated from her people, the *sídhe*, who are the permanent inhabitants of these same hills. As with Daniel Burke's wife, her lot is to be

looking out from a door the like of that door, and seeing nothing but the mists rolling down the bog, and the mists again, and they rolling up the bog, and hearing nothing but the wind crying out in the bits of broken trees were left from the great storm, and the streams roaring with the rain (49)

Nora's ennui arises, not for want of the city lights, but from a "divine discontent" for what these mists conceal from her. The Tuatha Dé Danann wear such mists—the *fé-fiada* of classic and folk literature—as "cloaks of concealment" from human eyes. As Étaín *rediviva*, Nora has genuine affection for her mortal and immortal consorts, for even in the midst of their final confrontation, and as she is about to depart with her fairy lover, she reaches out to Dan: "Let you be getting up into your bed, and not be taking your death with the wind blowing on you, and the rain with it, and you half in your skin" (55). Similarly, as Étaín was not willing to go with Midir until Eochaid agrees to cede her, so, too, Nora only leaves when ordered out of Dan's house.

Synge transmutes Midir into the Tramp, the mysterious stranger whose romantic pastoralism is a reflection of his predecessor's magnificent lay in praise of the Celtic Otherworld. Further, the three phases of the duel for Étaín's love are formally reflected in Nora's succession of three lovers: Patch Darcy, Michael Dara, and the Tramp. And just as Midir lost the first two rounds to Eochaid, so here, too, it is not until the third visitation that this emissary of the spirit world succeeds in bearing away his bride. Like Darcy, Nora's third visitant comes from the land of the immortal dead, the Tuatha Dé Danann or *sídhe*. Thus, the Celtic myth and its implicit doctrine of metempsychosis illuminate the mysterious links between Darcy and the Tramp, and between both and Midir. In this context, what are we to infer about Michael Dara? While at first he appears (to us, and evidently to Nora) to be potential lover, a counterpart of that "free spirit," Darcy, he soon reveals himself a counterpart of that settled man of the world, Daniel Burke. In this way, his development in the play complements Nora's.

Synge's adaptation of the myth to include such a figure as Michael Dara illuminates a number of finer points in the dramatic text. The mercantile marriage that John Butler Yeats saw as the social target in *The Shadow* had an ancient lineage, for each time that Étaín was married, she was purchased: first by Midir, by her weight in gold and silver; and later by Eochaidh Airem, when the bargain struck was seven *cúmal*, or female slaves (de Jubainville 177). It also gives a delightful illumination to Synge's naming of Nora's potential second husband of substance, Michael Dara (*dara* meaning "second"). He is, indeed, second in two complementary ways: as offering Nora either the material security of another Daniel Burke or the passionate spirit of another Patch Darcy. But his true metempsychosis is again revealed by another play on his name. De Jubainville's note on Eochaid Airem's name speculated that *airem* derives from the verb *aram*, "to count" (180).[3] Indeed, during Nora's plaintive speech revealing her loneliness of spirit, Michael Dara proclaims himself of the spiritual progeny of Eochaid Airem by counting the contents of Nora's stocking, her prospective bride-price! This revealing gesture sets him opposite Patch Darcy, who, as we have seen, "would walk through five hundred sheep and miss one of them, and he not reckoning them at all" (Synge 3:47).

Thus, as "The Wooing of Étaín" is an expression of the Celtic doctrines of metempsychosis and of an ideal otherworld—of the tragic tension between material and spiritual orders—so, under the appearances of a realistic problem play, Synge invested *The Shadow of the Glen* with some of his own theological speculations about the soul's survival of bodily death.

This recovery of Synge's larger sympathies now admits new light on the genesis, gestation, and title of *The Shadow of the Glen*. At the end of his Paris sojourn in the spring of 1902, and before he turned to the composition of this play, he wrote *Vernal Play* (3:189–93). The cast of characters—all with Old Irish names—is drawn from either de Jubainville or Nutt (Cermuid/Cermait: de Jubainville 210; Boinn/Goddess of the Boyne: de Jubainville 152; Niave: Nutt 1:150; Luchtaine/Luchtine: de Jubainville 101–3).

Vernal Play is set in the Wicklow hills, where it has been raining for three or four days. Pretending to be picking flowers, Étaín and Niave, two young girls, are searching the woods for sleeping shepherds. An old man seeks shelter from the rain, and praises the spirit of love in all of nature. By the second scene he has died, and is waked by the women. Étaín laments: "All young girls must yield to rage/ All firm youth must end in age." But they are consoled by the spirit of the place: "Hills as these/ Young men in dreams have walked on" (Synge 3:192). These dreams became, in time, the Old Man's buoyant vision. The silent carrion crows await.

Here is a cluster of themes and images that unmistakably link "The Wooing of Étaín" to *The Shadow of the Glen*: the pastoral setting, weather, Étaín's search for love, the natural images, the wake, Nora's lament, the dead dreamer, the vision that transforms the grotesquerie of bodily death, and so on. The next steps are the transformation of legend into peasant realism and blank verse into poetic folk idiom. Somewhere about here, and as April became May in 1902, the sources in his reading became fused with his personal conflicts—with his mother's religion, over Cherrie Matheson's rejection of him, over his health—and Synge the scholar became Synge the poet.[4]

Turning to *Dead Man's Deputy*, a fragmentary draft of *The Shadow* (Synge

3:256–57), we see that the most intensely developed portion of the play, its "epiphany," is a 300-word speech of the "stranger" ("T"), including:

Maybe it's not woman of the house I'll be calling you but woman of the hills, and you'll [be] listening to the herons and they calling out over the black lakes when you'ld think the stars would be lepping on the water each with each twist of the wind, and you['ll] be listening to the grouse and the owls and the larks.

The reverberations of Midir's wooing song, as cited by Nutt and de Jubainville are, again, unmistakable: the litany of nature images, and the epithet, "woman of the hills," an unidiomatic but revealing echo that Synge later erased.[5]

The manuscript of this play got its first public reading on February 2, 1903. The next month, it was presented to the Irish National Theatre Society actors, who liked it and approved a production. The evidence assembled by Ann Saddlemyer implies that by then, *Dead Man's Deputy* had become *In the Glen*, and then *In the Shadow of the Glen*, before finally becoming *The Shadow of the Glen* (Synge 3, app. B). The title of the first stage production was apparently *In the Shadow of the Glen* and although the *In* appeared in *Samhain* (its first publication, Dec. 1904, 34–44), Synge refers to it as *The Shadow of the Glen* (dated 11 Nov. 1904; Saddlemyer, *Theatre Business* 65, 67n). The first time the full text appeared under the title *The Shadow of the Glen* was the Elkin Mathews's Vigo Series no. 24 (1905), which evidently had Synge's authorization. Thus, although its title seemed uncertain for a long time—Lady Gregory refers to it as the "Wicklow play" or *The Shadow of the Glen* (see Saddlemyer, *Theatre Business*), Joseph Holloway attended a rehearsal of *In the Glen* (4 Sept. 1903), and Yeats referred to it twice as *The Shadow* in *Samhain* (Dec. 1904, 10, 13)—it should be noted that throughout the public controversy and in his private letters, Synge always referred to it as *The Shadow of the Glen*, leaving no doubt that this was his preferred title. Evidently, some time between the first production and the first printing (i.e., during 1904–1905), he removed the preposition. Considering this evidence, it is irritating to encounter continuously printings, commentaries, and productions that refer to it under a provisional title.

The Shadow of the Glen accommodates a range of ambiguities: the passage of natural time, the prefiguration of age and death, the biblical view of the Garden of Eden become a Valley of Tears, perhaps an ironical allusion to Wicklow as "the Garden of Ireland," but also the Tramp as Darcy metempsychosed, his ghost or "shadow." Of course, there is the radical perspective that Synge drew from "The Wooing of Étaín": contrasted with the eternal, permanent world to which the Tramp calls Nora, Daniel Burke's glen is itself but a shadow.

As Synge was reading these materials from ancient Irish tradition, he was at the same time visiting the Aran Islands and some of the remoter regions in the Wicklow mountains. On these visits he had the opportunity to see how elements of these beliefs in the supernatural and preternatural survived in the folk imagination. On the one hand, he understood that fairy beliefs in modern Ireland were survivals of the ancient cults of fertility and worship of the dead. According to Wood-Martin, for instance, native religion deified the dead, calling them the *sídhe*—after the places where their remains had been deposited, the hollows of the hills and mountains. Thus, the term was successively applied to places of burial, fairy palaces, and finally to the fairies themselves (1:253–54). Various writers (Nutt, de Jubainville, Wood-Martin) have identified these beliefs as historically connected to the romantic mythology featuring the Tuatha Dé Danann, although modified and distorted by Christianity (Nutt 2:232). After their defeat by the Milesians, the Tuatha Dé Danann withdrew into underground palaces where they remain. They occasionally emerge, in mortal or animal form (de Jubainville 150). The Church absorbed this lore into its scheme by identifying the *sídhe* as fallen or neutral angels, who had been deprived of the beatific vision (Nutt 2:206–11; Synge 2:56), and the Irish country people, especially in Irish-speaking areas, accepted these various beliefs, putting them to practical and pleasurable uses.

All his work shows how continuously alert Synge was to manifestations of these beliefs and customs among the country people of Ireland. Again and again he noted folk belief in the return of the dead to this world. In *The Aran Islands*, he recorded the story of a woman who "saw all the people that were dead a while back in this island and the south island, and they all talking with each other" (Synge 2:157). A man was reported to attend a fair in the company of his two deceased grandfathers "with the people buying and selling and they not living people at all" (182). An old man told him "continually of the fairies and the women they have taken," causing Synge to consider that "it seemed that there was a possible link between the wild mythology that is accepted on the islands and the strange beauty of the women" (54). Pat Dirane related to Synge his many personal experiences of the fairies (80–82): doing much mischief, including the abduction of two women—one recently married—and a child. To all appearances, Synge was informed elsewhere that the dead and the fairies are not easily distinguished from ordinary people (165). One needs to be wary of them, especially after nightfall (181). Similarly, in Wicklow, he heard reports of "queer things them nights on the mountains" (189) and the fear of the unnatural powers of tramps or strangers (203). In "The People of the Glens," Synge told of being regaled in the one breath by stories of the hardships of life, historical events in the community memory, and stories of the fallen angels that ride across the hills (216).

Turning back once again to *The Shadow of the Glen*, we can see that, from the point of view of folklore, there is much more here than a mock wake (*pace* Kiberd 168–74). Like *Riders to the Sea*, its companion-in-the making during those summer months of 1902, it features the theme of the revenant and investigates the relationship between the living and the otherworlds housing the living dead: Under Hill and Under Sea. Also like its counterpart, it features a theme widely found in fairy lore: the return of the dead to take a living person with them. In this way, *The Shadow* reflects a folk version of the classic tale of the

Tuatha Dé Danann, "The Wooing of Étaín." Let us look at some of the evidence.

Synge wrote this play for the original Irish National Theatre—its members drawn from the Gaelic League—an organization pledged to restore the Irish language and lore. This audience could be expected to appreciate Synge's terms of reference. Kiberd cited Máire Nic Shiubhlaigh's observation that "these audiences brought to any play on a Gaelic theme an accumulation of ideas drawn from literature and folklore" (174). The bitter public controversy may have, in the event, spoiled their appetite for regional cuisine. It should not have been lost on such an audience that the conditions are right for the appearance of the fairies or the dead: the action commences after nightfall, the kitchen has been made neat "*as if for a wake*," and the superstitious references to Daniel Burke's "black curse," the "dark mist," and the stage direction calling for "*a sharp light beneath his* [the Tramp's] *haggard face*" (Synge 3:37) for the first couple of minutes all establish the conventional numinous conditions for a fairy tale. But Synge knew that "nothing is more pleasing to fairies than a well-swept kitchen and clean water" (Nutt quotes from Jeremiah Curtin, 2:222), and their attraction to a cottage fireside (Stith Thompson's Folk Motif F-266). In the stranger's rejection of tea in favor of whiskey (2:45), we have an echo of a widely held view of their libation of choice (Ó hEochaidh 397). Moreover, Nora's reference to "the bits of broken trees were left from the great storm" (Synge 2:49) must have had a particular significance for the original audience of ninety years ago. The "Big Wind" of late February 1903—the worst since 1839—blew down thousands of trees all over Ireland. The folk memory associates such events with major disruptions in the fairy realms, as in this instance (see Cardozo 231).

Now, while the ostensible subject of the wake is Daniel Burke, the audience learns that Nora is in mourning for Patch Darcy. It was him she really loved, but he suffered a premature death some time within the past year. Moreover, since his remains were picked by carrion crows, he got neither a proper Christian burial nor a proper wake. The pre-Christian view of untimely or accidental deaths is that they are not real: in contrast to those who have lived into old age, those suffering such ends are deemed to have been "taken away" by the *sídhe*, and may reappear as ghosts, among the *sídhe*, or in some other form. Thus, however one looks at it, Darcy's spirit is not at rest. Of the wide persistence of fairy stories involving the recently dead, Máire Mac Néill observed:

A large number of them deal with untimely deaths, with children straying on the hills, wayfarers overtaken by storm and mist, with losses of cattle, failures of crops, houses in which families did not prosper and, most prominently of all, with the dangers of the sea. (Ó hEochaidh 20–22)

Thus, like the unnatural deaths of Michael and Bartley in *Riders to the Sea*, unnatural manifestations of Darcy's presence may be expected. By contrast with these deaths is that of Daniel Burke, the completion of which will be assured by his age, his wake, his burial in the Seven Churches, and his being "quiet a while" (Michael Dara's ironic euphemism) or "rotting below" (Dan's direct speech) (Synge 3:52–53). The Irish Christian tradition of the "month's mind," a Mass offered one month after decease, would appear to mark this point at which the body is deemed to have decomposed, or in folk terms, to have undergone the "second death." Under such auspices, we should expect Patch Darcy's return to complete his life and his death (Thompson E-422).

The Tramp does this by claiming Nora. From his arrival, this stranger boasts of having "seen great wonders" (Synge 3:37), implies that he is not "a living soul," and as one familiar with the distortions of the fog, he denies being "easily afeard," except of what turns out to have been Patch Darcy before his death (39).[6] In this way, he is the reverse of Michael Dara, who admits, "I do be afeard of the dead" (45). It seems odd that although there are several references to the rainy night and to the Tramp's coat, there are none to a wet coat! In fact, on the apparent pretext of mending it and protecting himself against evil, he borrows a needle and thread from Nora, which she takes from her own dress. These incidental actions are subtly ominous and require comment. One of the signs of a fairy is that he is impervious to rain (Thompson F-259.3); moreover, rather than drying his coat, the Tramp sets about a favorite fairy occupation of mending cloth (Thompson F-271.4–8). In requesting the needle, and in reciting the *De Profundis*, he is invoking two familiar protections against fairies (cited by Synge himself, 2:80, 180). But for whose benefit are these shows of proper deference to the *sídhe* designed? And who but Daniel Burke is the intended victim of the deception? Is he not in competition with Daniel Burke for his wife? Moreover, is Nora not now—without her needle—left unprotected against the *sídhe?* Moreover, when she then goes outside and whistles into the night, she is expressly summoning the powers of darkness (Thompson E-384.3, G-303.6.3.5, G-303.16.18).

The Shadow of the Glen may therefore be read as the dramatization of a "mature type" of revenant story from folk literature. In these stories, the visitant is only with difficulty discernible from the living; it returns to complete unfinished business, to reenact an important event, or even for death itself; this return involves a contest with the living in which it is usually unsuccessful. In Synge's version, this does not happen: whether as a dead man come to claim his lover (Thompson E-310) or a fairy mistress returning to her people (Thompson F-300), the play evidently expresses its author's ambition to "give the reality, which is the root of all poetry, in a comprehensive and natural form" (Synge 4:53).

Thus, when Synge offered Pat Dirane's story as "the source" for *The Shadow of the Glen*, he was offering chauvinistic and objective-minded critics what they wanted. They were in too much of a hurry to savor its archaism. However, to the private Synge, riven by conflicts about his own fundamental beliefs, brooding on the myths of ancient Ireland, and undergoing the culture shock from his encounter with the lives of the people of Aran, his play of apparent social liberation affords more complex and ambiguous satisfactions. Understood in this way as a technically brilliant mediation between surface realism, mythological structure, and folk elements, it is an expression of the romantic vision that permeates all of Synge's work.

NOTES

1. Nothing . . . in the literature is as primeval as that faith that Greeks and Irish held in common: a faith in an otherworld where the dead continue a life similar to their terrestrial existence with neither the hope of being rewarded for their virtues nor the anxiety of being punished for their misdeeds.

2. In his review of Leahy's *Historic Romances of Ireland*, Synge contrasted Leahy's poor translation of Étaín's song to Ailill with Hyde's treatment of Gaelic poetry in *The Love Songs of Connacht* (Synge 2:372).

3. The more conventional and likely meaning of *Airem* is "ploughman," or "tiller of the soil" (see Keating 2:120).

4. Mary King quotes an early draft of fictionalized autobiography entitled, "In the Valley of the Shadow of Death" (TCD MS 4350, f. 87; see King 68).

5. In Irish idiom, the *sídhe* are never referred to, much less addressed, directly, but rather in some phrase such as *uaisle na gnoc* ("gentry of the hills"). (Máire Mac Néill gives a list of terms; see Ó hEochaidh 26–27).

6. Taken literally, his remark to Nora, "There aren't two living souls would see the little light you have shining from the glass," means that apart from Michael Dara—who apparently does see her light—there is none!

WORKS CITED

Benson, Eugene. *J. M. Synge*. New York: Grove Press, 1983.

Best, Richard Irvine, and Osborn Bergin, ed. and trans. *Tocmarc Étaíne*. Dublin: Royal Irish Academy, 1938.

Cardozo, Nancy. *Lucky Eyes and a High Heart: The Life of Maud Gonne*. Indianapolis, Ind.: Bobbs-Merrill, 1978.

de Jubainville, Henry, d'Arbois. *The Irish Mythological Cycle and Celtic Mythology*, trans. R. I. Best. Dublin: Hodges Figgis, 1903.

Gantz, Jeffrey, trans. and intr. *Early Irish Myths and Sagas*. New York: Dorset Press, 1985.

Greene, David H., and Edward M. Stephens. *J. M. Synge, 1871–1909*. New York: Macmillan, 1959. Rev. ed. New York: New York University Press, 1989.

Hyde, Douglas. *A Literary History of Ireland*. New York: Scribner's, 1899.

Keating, Geoffrey. *Foras Feasa ar Éirinn* (The History of Ireland). 4 vols. Dublin: Irish Texts Society, 1901–1913.

Kiberd, Declan. *Synge and the Irish Language*. Totowa, N.J.: Rowman and Littlefield, 1979.

King, Mary C. *The Drama of J. M. Synge*. Syracuse, N.Y.: Syracuse University Press, 1985.

Kopper, Edward A., Jr. "The Shadow of the Glen." *In A J. M. Synge Literary Companion*, ed. Edward A. Kopper, Jr. Westport, Conn.: Greenwood Press, 1988, 25–37.

Maxwell, D. E. S. *A Critical History of Modern Irish Drama, 1891–1980*. Cambridge and New York: Cambridge University Press, 1984.

Murphy, William M. *Prodigal Father: The Life of John Butler Yeats 1839–1922*. Ithaca, N.Y.: Cornell University Press, 1978.

Ní Dhuibhne-Almqvist, Éilís. "Synge's Use of Folklore: 'The Loving Wife.' " *Béaloideas* 50 (1990): 141–80.

Nutt, Alfred. "An Essay Upon the Irish Vision of the Happy Otherworld and the Celtic Doctrine of Rebirth." In *The Voyage of Bran Son of Febal to the Land of the Living*, trans. and ed. Kuno Meyer. 2 vols. London: David Nutt, 1895–1897.

Ó hEochaidh, Seán, Máire Mac Néill, and Séamas Ó Catháin. *Síscealta Ó Thír Chonaill* (Fairy Legends from Donegal). Dublin: Comhairle Bhéaloideas Éireann, 1977.

Rees, Alwyn, and Brinley Rees. *Celtic Heritage: Ancient Tradition in Ireland and Wales*. London: Thames and Hudson, 1961.

Saddlemyer, Ann, ed. *The Collected Letters of John Millington Synge*. 2 vols. Oxford: Clarendon Press; New York: Oxford University Press, 1983–1984.

———. *Theatre Business: The Correspondence of the First Abbey Theatre Directors: William Butler Yeats, Lady Gregory, and J. M. Synge*. Gerrards Cross, U.K.: Colin Smythe; University Park: Pennsylvania State University Press, 1982.

Synge, John Millington. *Collected Works*. Vol. 2, *Prose*, ed. Alan Price. Vol. 3, *Plays*, ed. Ann Saddlemyer. 1962–1968. Reprint. Gerrards Cross, U.K.: Colin Smythe; Washington, D.C.: Catholic University of America Press, 1982.

Thompson, Stith. *A Motif-Index to Folk Literature: A Classification of Narrative Elements*. Bloomington: Indiana University Press, 1955.

Thornton, Weldon. *J. M. Synge and the Western Mind*. Gerrards Cross; U.K.: Colin Smythe, 1979.

Wood-Martin, W. C. *Traces of the Elder Faiths of Ireland: A Folklore Sketch*. 2 vols. London: Longmans, Green, 1902.

7

Of Holy Wells and Sacred Spells: Strange Comedy at the Abbey

Dan Casey

John Millington Synge's first full-length play, *The Well of the Saints*, opened at the Abbey Theatre on February 4, 1905, to a near-empty house. The playwright had outraged the Dublin theatre crowd with *The Shadow of the Glen* fifteen months earlier and and shocked them with *Riders to the Sea* only the year before. Surely, in Synge's unlucky hands, a play about a saint, miracles, and a holy well would fare no better than a play about a runaway wife taking to the roads with a tramp or one about an islander who had fallen from grace with the sea.

In spite of Yeats's staunch defense of his protégé and the international plaudits already afforded Synge's one-acters, the Dublin playgoers had apparently written him off. Donna Gerstenberger tells us that Yeats sized up the situation and wrote to John Quinn in New York after seeing *The Well of the Saints*, saying it would be "a hard fight in Ireland before we get the right for every man to see the world in his own way" (53). The Irish did not understand *The Well of the Saints*, and the *Playboy* riots were still to come.

It is true that Synge had a singular view of the world, that he had invented his own aesthetic. Like his contemporaries, he had read the classics and used classical models to reshape Irish drama. What was unique about Synge was the way he melded classic comedy and tragedy with realism and extended it to the Irish scene. The Irish were not ready for it.

Though *The Well of the Saints* is a black comedy with a deceptively simple plot, it has invited more critical controversy than others of Synge's provocative plays. Simply put, Martin and Mary Doul are an uncomely pair, a blind married couple spinning away endless hours in idle talk at a country crossroad while begging alms from occasional passers-by. Over the years they have been flattered by local villagers to believing themselves "the finest man and the finest woman in the seven counties of the east." Martin, however, distrusts "the seeing rabble below'' and wishes ''one hour, or a minute itself'' for the Douls to see themselves as the villagers see them and confirm the truth of their beauty. It is the story of Adam and Eve and the apple, and Martin's apple comes in the shape of a wandering friar carrying a can of holy water from the well of the saints. Desperate for a cure, Martin disregards Mary's qualms, and, to their grief, the blind couple are made to see.

What they see is, of course, their own ugliness and an Eden scarred by visible imperfections. The world of the imagination has suddenly given way, as they are plunged into a hellish reality of lies. At his cure, Martin mistakes Molly Byrne, a young local beauty, for his unkempt, aging wife, who has been said to be ''the great wonder of the west.'' When he finally sets eyes upon the real Mary Doul, he castigates her and casts her out. For her part, Mary is repulsed at her vision of Martin and cries, ''I'm thinking it's a poor thing when the Lord God gives you sight and puts the like of that man in your way'' (139). The Saint's miracle effects only misery and humiliation, and Martin and Mary quarrel violently before they go their separate ways.

Martin, now deprived of his blindness, is forced to labor long hours in the forge with Timmy, the smith, for a slave's pittance. From his inferno, he endures the jibes of the rabble and the torment of watching the ''almost elderly'' blacksmith raise a house on the hill in anticipation of his marriage to Molly Byrne. Driven by passion, Martin makes a last-ditch effort to win young Molly, which ends in rejection and despair. And Mary Doul's plight—roaming the roads and picking nettles for the Widow O'Flinn—is equally hopeless.

But blindness is (they realize) their salvation, so they embrace it when it returns. They struggle to restore their dignity and their relationship and to reconstruct a life in the imagination where illusion can outdistance reality, where dreams and human converse can sustain the soul. When the Saint returns and offers, this time, a permanent cure, Martin unceremoniously knocks the watering can from the friar's hand and responds to threats from hostile villagers by threatening them. Like Christy Mahon in Mayo, he opts for a life away from the villainy of Grianan and, with Mary, he plans to escape to the south of Ireland, where imagination can concoct its own reality.

Major critics have differed on the merits and the meaning of the play. Alan Price finds *Well* ''a profound work . . . [that] deals searchingly with serious issues, and, unblurred by morbidity, reflects, with some compassion, a melancholy vision of the human condition'' (138). But Gerstenberger disagrees with Price and has said that the play is a failure, because, in the final compromise—the Douls' self-inflicted exile—Synge is inconsistent with his own aesthetic (55–62). Robin Skelton is another critic who applauds the play, interpreting Martin and Mary's departure as a final triumph of the spirit over reality (130). Numerous dissenters, however, point to the unrelenting savagery of the dialogue and say that the intensity of the exchanges thwarts Synge's effort at comedy, or else they see *Well* as minor and developmental, only serving to move Synge closer to the perfection of *Playboy*.

Why is there such disagreement among the critics? Does the miracle of the cure compromise the integrity of *Well?* Is the play inconsistent with the play-wright's aesthetic? Is it "a melancholy vision of the human condition" or "a triumph of spirit over reality"? Is there, in fact, more in this play that is relevant to modern audiences and readers than critics have thus far suggested?

In *The Well of the Saints*, Synge explores the human condition as he plays the blind beggar and his blind wife off against villagers who are not blind but yet will not see. He reworks a classical, timeless theme in a classical mode, localizing and blending it to an Irish landscape and mindscape, and he explores social and metaphysical questions. There is even more to it than that, and a reconsideration of Synge's sources (especially *The Aran Notebooks*) and aesthetic, along with close critical reading of the text, may help resolve some problems of interpretation.

Eugene Benson has recounted that Synge, while at the Sorbonne in the late 1890s, was influenced by readings in medieval French literature and by the fifteenth-century French farce, *Moralité de l'aveugle et du boiteaux*, by Andrieu de la Vigne (93). In fact, the plot for *Well* derives directly from de la Vigne's comedy about a mutually dependent blind man and a cripple who are cured by a holy man using a relic of Saint Martin. In the end, the ingrate of a cripple curses the holy man because he has forever lost the services of his blind companion. Synge wrote *The Well of the Saints* in 1902 and 1903, during and after his Aran sojourns; he took artistic liberties with the plot and circumstances of de la Vigne's farce, shifting it first to the Arans, and then again to the "eastern world."

The Aran experiences and sketches flesh out the characters, incidents, and nuances in this and other works; and Synge's reflections on the Arans bring him closer to an aesthetic that, while not yet fully defined, suggests the development of a novel dramatic approach. What happened during his novitiate on Aran was that he was witness to a fisherman's requiem and heard the revenant tale of ghostly riders to the sea; that Pat Dirane, the *sgealai* of Inishmaan, gave him "He That's Dead Can Do No Hurt"; and that the oldest man on the island provided him with details of the infamous Lynchehaun murder story. Synge caught the pristine echo of a pagan death-ritual and the eerie laments of the requiem and the *caoine* and made of it a tragic masterpiece that could only be set on that "Island off the West of Ireland." He transferred Pat Dirane's tale to the Harney cottage in the Wicklow Hills and made *The Shadow of the Glen* from it. He removed the old man's tale of the patricide from Achill and the Arans to a *shebeen* in Mayo, and recreated it as *The Playboy of the Western World*.

But he also remembered Martin Coneely's miraculous Aran well at Teampall an Ceattrair Alainn (The Church of the Four Beautiful Persons), a church ruin with a well nearby where, it was remembered, blindness and epilepsy had been cured. The ruin and the well were shifted to "some lonely mountainous district in the east of Ireland, one or more centuries ago" (69), and Martin, the blind

storyteller, who led Synge to the well and recounted the miracle, was transfigured to become a virtual model for Martin Doul in the play.

Old Martin, or Mourteen, as he was known on the island, was, like so many
of the eighteenth-century poets and tellers of tales, blind, but not blind from
birth. Synge enlisted him as his sometime Irish teacher and came to appreciate
him for his innocence and perverse wit. Martin often confided in Synge and
once, standing outside a beehive hut, told him "what he would have done if he
could have come in there when he was a young man and a young girl along
with him" (130). Martin Coneely had a vivid imagination, and he reveled in
bawdy imaginings. Like the Martin Doul of Synge's play, he had curiosity,
vision, and passion.

Finally, in "The Vagrants of Wicklow," Synge reported that a man in his
nineties wed a woman of eighty-five. On their honeymoon, they quarreled heat-
edly, and in the end, he beat her with a stick and went off on the road alone.
He was later arrested and thrown in jail where, as punishment, his proudest
possession—his white hair—was shorn from his head. Synge reported:

All his pride and his half-conscious feeling for the dignity of his age seemed to have set
themselves on this long hair, which marked him out from other people of this district;
and I have often heard him saying to himself, as he sat beside me under a ditch: "What
use is an old man without his hair? A man has only his bloom like the trees; and what
use is an old man without his white hair?" (488)

In *The Well of the Saints*, Synge built on de la Vigne, but he also insisted on
being his own man. The blind man and the cripple become blind Martin and
blind Mary Doul; Martin Doul takes on the character of Mourteen Coneely;
Martin and Mary quarrel violently and part company; and, in the end, Martin
will find solace in letting his beard grow, "a beautiful, long, white, silken,
streamy beard, you wouldn't see the like of in the eastern world" (131). There
are, of course, other emendations that the playwright introduces in transforming
the medieval French farce for the Abbey stage.

The play is, we must also remember, historical—set in a "lonely mountainous
district in the east of Ireland one or more centuries ago" (69)—and Synge, the
skeptic, accepts the "historical fact" of the cure for the sake of the comedy.
He has, however, already isolated the events, not only by shifting the action to
the remote, "mountainy district," where there is a simplicity of life and of
belief, but also by moving it back in time to the eighteenth century, when the
belief in tales of miracles at holy wells was commonplace.

But Synge was obviously no believer. He put no stock in priests or in the
efficacy of organized religion, and though his aesthetic recognized a natural
exoticism and preternaturalism, he never credited the supernatural. Instead, he
set up a dramatic compromise that permits the farce to go forward: that Martin
and Mary are temporarily cured by the incorrigible peripatetic friar is Synge's
way of calling for his audience to suspend disbelief and his way of moving the

play to its final irony. The initial cure is, after all, only temporary. In the end, the Saint promises a permanent cure, but by virtue of Martin's defiance, no such miracle is forthcoming.

During the Aran period, Synge's head was teeming with myth, epic, and folktale. He was reviewing books on mythology and lore for the *Speaker*, writing essays on ancient Celtic literature, and participating in a Breton folk revival. *Riders to the Sea* itself relies on mythic allusions and bears witness to extraordinary happenings. In *The Well of the Saints*, the playwright says again that there is perhaps more to the ancient myths and pagan wells than there is to the foolishness of friars and the vacant promises of Christianity. In the popular imagination, holy wells with curative waters were, we must recall, the shared province of tutelary pagan deities and Christian saints.

That uneasy pagan-Christian syncretism between the old gods and the new saints of the well sets up tensions that revive the race memory and echo the colloquies of Oisin and Patrick in the colloquies of Martin and the Saint. Anthony Roche and Kate Powers have both explored those mythic parallels in their research. However, it is important to note that, without water from the pagan well, the Saint cannot manage a cure. Perhaps it is the water, and not the Saint. And Molly Byrne, handing the watering can to Martin, says innocently, "Wonders is queer things, and maybe it'd cure you, and you holding it alone" (130), and a moment later vests him with the Saint's cloak, saying, "The way we'd see how you'd look, and you a saint of the Almighty God" (131). But Martin wants no part of asceticism or bell-ringing sanctity.

The villagers put as much stock in the Saint, with his little bell, as in a magician with a traveling circus, and his coming excites as much attention as a public hanging. Mary Doul says of the friar and his bell, "You know, I'm thinking, by the little silvery voice of it, a fasting holy man was after carrying it a great way by his side" (130–31). Timmy the smith says, "Isn't it a fine, beautiful voice he has, and he a fine, brave man if it wasn't for the fasting?" (135). There is great interest in the saint, the water, and the cure, but an even greater interest in the sideshow that follows: first in Martin's mistaking Molly, Bride, and a third young beauty for his ugly aging wife; and then in the vicious exchange and breakup of Martin and Mary.

The Saint, oblivious to the havoc he has wrought, sounds vaguely like a televangelist-healer playing the circuit. Emerging from the church, he asks, "Are their minds troubled with joy, or is their sight uncertain, the way it does often be the day a person is restored?" (140). On being told they are "making a great fight," he separates them, utters a vacuous sermon, and hies off to Annagolan, Laragh, and Glenassil to spread more grief. In ways that continue to relate to modern times, the play is really comic.

Synge's Saint is insensitive and mindless, scurrying about and dispensing "God's little miseries." Martin says to him: "What was it I seen when I first opened my eyes but your own bleeding feet, and they cut with the stones? That was a great sight, maybe, of the image of God" (167). And on the Saint's second visit to Grianan, Martin begs him not to continue "making a great mess with the holy water" he brings with him (170), but the Saint heeds no one. He hurries the crowd into the church to witness the catastrophic marriage between the "almost elderly" smith and the young Molly Byrne. No wonder, on hearing the approach of the menacing bell, Mary Doul prays, "The Lord protect us from the saints of God" (162).

It is important, too, that Martin and Mary Doul—Doul means "blind" in Irish—were "sighted" as children. They are, in that sense, blind visionaries whose fantasies have, over decades, embellished and extended what they have recollected. But in a fit of pride, Martin, like Lucifer, is tempted to test the truth of his own prowess, and like Satan/Lucifer, he finds it is pride that fells him, though it cannot keep him down.

Despite his flaws, the brave Martin Doul emerges as the hero of Synge's play. He may be a dirty old man, but he has a touch of the artist and maybe a touch of the madness about him. Martin is, after all, a man who loves sensual women and longs to be free in nature. He is a dreamer of dreams, a risk taker with the self-determination and courage to rise above the disillusionment of the shabby world he encounters (Act I); escape the fires of his own private hell (Act II); and, in an ironic reversal, challenge and best the Saint at his own game (Act III). No longer "blinded by sight," Martin refuses to kneel down and become a victim. Like Milton's Satan, he would rather "reign in hell than serve in heaven."

Martin is a kind of poet who hurls fearful curses on dream wreckers, spoilers, and saints. He has little patience with small-minded villagers who have played him for a fool or trifled with his dreams. He tells Molly Byrne, "I was the like of the little children do be listening to the stories of an old woman, and do be dreaming after in the dark night that it's in the grand houses of gold they are, with speckled horses to ride" (149). But when he is awakened from the dream to experience the briefest moment of ecstasy, followed by abject disillusionment, he turns on the world. He excoriates Mary and the villagers for their lies, and then Satan himself for letting him see the lies.

Martin has awakened to a cold reality. Trapped in an isolated eighteenth-century mountain hamlet that is devoid of sense and sensibility, he rails against the assaults of Timmy the smith, who has enslaved him in his hellfire of a forge, and against Molly Byrne, who has denied him and who will soon become the smith's wife—but never the smith's lover. Together, they have conspired to deprive him of life and sexual love—to destroy him. The awful curse he utters conjures up fire and brimstone: it is a curse worthy of a damned archangel with his wits astray:

Yet, if I've no strength in me I've a voice left for my prayers, and may God blight them this day, and my own soul the same hour with them, the way I'll see them after, Molly Byrne and Timmy the smith, the two of them on a high bed, and they screeching in hell. . . . It'll be a grand thing that time to look on the two of them; and they twisting and roaring out, and twisting and roaring again, one day and the next day, and each day always and ever. It's not blind I'll be that time, and it won't be hell to me, I'm thinking, but the like of heaven itself; and it's fine care I'll be taking the Lord Almighty doesn't know. (156)

Martin lashes out with the fury of artist or madman and hurls the poet's curse.

It is, however, in the final scene, when Martin refuses the cure and banishes the Saint, that he reaches the timeless plateau of true heroism. It is like Oisin banishing Patrick—the old gods of the well banishing the new saints of the well. He says, "Go on now, holy father, for if you're a fine Saint itself, it's more sense is in a blind man, and more power maybe than you're thinking at all" (171). The Saint retreats, and Martin and Mary opt for that better life, "sitting blind, hearing a soft wind turning round the little leaves of spring and feeling the sun [i] . . . not tormenting our souls with the sight of the gray days, and the holy men, and the dirty feet is tramping the world" (172).

So Martin and Mary turn south, "where the people will have kind voices maybe, and we won't know their bad looks or their villainy at all" (172). They have seen too much of wickedness and deceit, and though they are blind and the way south is perilous, they will chance the journey or die trying.

Martin and Mary, in their final moment of triumph, choose poetic truth and the life of the imagination. They rise above the community in what Thomas Kilroy calls "a private moment of self-assertion, self-fulfillment, and self-knowledge. In effect saying: I am what I am. I can go my own way now. Alone. What you offer me I do not need. Keep it" (12).

Seamus Deane explains:

Synge's drama affirms and denies the value of the heroicizing impulse of the Revival. It produces the hero out of the "organic" community but leaves the community empty and exhausted. The glorious language is not a signal that all is well. Self-realization involves social alienation. Those who walk away from society and those who remain within it represent two kinds of value which are not reconcilable (58).

In Martin Doul's metamorphoses—from garrulous, carefree beggar to indentured Luciferian misfit and then hero–courageous figure—there is a gradual spiritual awakening and a gradual distancing of the artist-hero from the community. His choice—to shun the real world for the world of the imagination—is a conscious choice of physical blindness over spiritual blindness. It is, however, an heroic choice, a fact that is lost on the community. Mat Simon says: "It'd be an unlucky fearful thing, I'm thinking, to have the like of that man living near us at all in the townland of Grianan. Wouldn't he bring down a curse upon us, holy father, from the heavens of God?" (172). In effect, the hero has only one choice—to walk away.

The Well of the Saints is not so darkly pessimistic. It is black comedy that examines human relationships and the relationship of the artist to community, but it goes beyond to explore broader and more enduring social and meta-physical questions as well. There are comedy, irony, and sardonic humor here in good measure—in Mary's anticipation of the Saint from the ''little silvery voice'' of his bell, Timmy the smith's comments on the fasting friar, and the utterances of the insufferable Saint himself. Entering the church, the misan-thropic friar cautions the faithful, ''Stay back there, I'm saying, and you'd do well to be thinking on the ways sin has brought blindness to the world, and to be saying a prayer for your own sakes against false prophets and heathens, and the words of women and smiths'' (134–35). The comedy depends on that mock-ery and satire, and Synge uses both to good advantage.

In the end, ''The glorious language is not a sign that all is well'' (58). The epiphany is realized: Martin is confident and self-assertive—his rebellion has succeeded, and in that sense, the comedy has succeeded as comedy. Martin tells Mary, ''It's small joy we'd have living near them, or hearing the lies they do be telling from the gray of dawn till the night.'' Mary Doul agrees, though she recognizes the terrors that lie before them. She answers *despondently*:

We'd have a right to be gone, if it's a long way itself, as I've heard them say, where you do have to be walking with a slough of wet on the one side and a slough of wet on the other, and you going a stony path with a north wind blowing behind. (173)

They will escape the world of liars and grope their way south, ''where the people will have kind voices maybe, and we won't know their bad looks or their villainy at all'' (173). There is no security in the ''maybes,'' no sign that all is well. The uncertainty of a life in exile is an expression of the playwright's drastic realism coming through.

In this, his first full-length play, Synge, the consummate artist, refined his aesthetic and produced a work that anticipates and complements *Playboy* in theme and character, allusion and symbolism, and language and rhythm. More than that, he gave us a successful comedy that stands on its own merits. He accomplished what he set out to do. He championed the artist-hero over the community and allowed illusion to triumph over reality. He created a hero with near-mythic courage to challenge a Saint and have his own way. There are allusions to Lucifer and Oisin; there are also the ubiquitous symbols—the cir-cular journey, the broken wheel, the Saint's wondrous paraphernalia.

Synge's language is another triumph. He has, in *Well* as in other works, stylized the Irish idiom, offering the audience a heightened natural peasant speech; his is a unique poetic dialogue that draws on the idiom and, at the same time, echoes Irish nature poetry in its rhythms and nuances:

For I've heard tell there are lands beyond in Cahir Iveragh and the Reeks of Cork with warm sun in them, and a fine light in the sky. And light's a grand thing for a man ever was blind, or a woman, with a fine neck, and a skin on her the like of you, the way we'd have a right to go off this day till we'd have a fine life passing abroad through them towns of the south, and we telling stories, maybe, or singing songs at the fairs. (150)

This is not the Tramp of *Shadow*; it is Martin Doul the poet courting Molly Byrne in a style worthy of the Munster poets of yore. Synge's peasants speaking Synge's lines have presence, nobility, and spirit.

Synge himself is interestingly complex, and in some ways enigmatic, yet his work is approachable. As the master playwright in a theater movement that reached beyond Ireland to all modern drama, he is significant and central. He has, in *The Well of the Saints*, offered a unique comedy and a unique vision of rural Ireland that melds myth and realism without ever jarring. His work continues to give voice to poetic dialogue that ever suggests biblical and Shakespearean dignity.

Always the artist, Synge remains true to his aesthetic. He creates a stage realism in which tyrannical friars, bumbling blacksmiths, and flirtatious young women are made flesh and offered to audiences, which recoil in horror at their mirror likenesses.

Whatever the reception *Well* had at the Abbey, and whatever the differences among the critics, Synge's reputation is secure. On the basis of *Riders to the Sea* and *The Playboy of the Western World*, his genius is univerally recognized. That genius is, however, better understood in the light of the formative works, like *The Well of the Saints*, which has been less read and less played over the years.

WORKS CITED

Benson, Eugene. *J. M. Synge*. New York: Grove Press, 1983.

Deane, Seamus. *Celtic Revivals: Essays in Modern Irish Literature, 1880–1980*. London and Boston: Faber and Faber, 1985. Reprint. Winston-Salem, N.C.: Wake Forest University Press, 1987.

Gerstenberger, Donna. *John Millington Synge*. New York: Twayne, 1964.

Powers, Kate. "Myth and Journey in *The Well of the Saints*." *Colby Quarterly* 26(4) (1990): 231–40.

Price, Allan. *Synge and Anglo-Irish Drama*. London: Methuen, 1961.

Roche, Anthony. "The Two Works of Synge's *The Well of the Saints*." *Genre* 12 (1979): 439–50.

Skelton, Robin. *The Writings of J. M. Synge*. Indianapolis, Ind., and New York: Bobbs-Merrill, 1971.

Synge, John Millington. *The Complete Works of John M. Synge*. New York: Random House, 1936.

8

"Passing the gap": Reading the Betwixt and Between of Liminality in J. M. Synge's *The Well of the Saints*

Carolyn L. Mathews

Mary Doul: What place are we now, Martin Doul?
Martin Doul: Passing the gap.
Mary Doul: The length of that? Well, the sun's coming warm this day if it's late autumn itself.

The Well of the Saints 71

The curtain rises on J. M. Synge's *The Well of the Saints* with the blind protagonists groping their way past a gap in a stone wall. While this "gap near centre" (71) in the play's first act will *eventually* demand attention from some viewers, other questions emerge long before the audience is faced with making meaning of this bit of stage set. In the first scene, for instance, Mary Doul speaks of her "splendor" and "white beautiful skin" (71). The audience, faced with reconciling the couple's belief in their fine looks with their weather-beaten ugliness, will draw on knowledge they bring to the play: what they know of beggars, Ireland at the turn of the century, blindness, Synge as a playwright, comedy as a dramatic mode, and a myriad other points of reference in their repertoires, which are drawn from the world and from literature. They will quickly hypothesize, rightly predicting that the couple's belief in their own fine looks stems from words they have been told—from lies that will eventually complicate the storyline. The gap the audience notes between words and appearance, like their eventual worry over the literal gap there on stage, will bring them to questions that pulse at the very core of Synge's drama: How is meaning made? What is the relation of language to reality? How do individuals and their community either perceive or construct the world in which they live?

    The meaning that audience members make—whether viewers, critics, or readers—depends in part, of course, on their own point of situation within history.

Differences in cultural norms, thought systems in place, and former readings of *The Well of the Saints* contribute to the acute differences of opinion on this, perhaps the most problematic work within the Synge canon. Using Wolfgang Iser's ideas as a springboard, I examine, in the first part of this chapter, former assessments of the play. In investigating the break between criticism of the past and the near-present, I explore how traditional critical orientations, as well as contemporary approaches, influence readings. In the second part I deal with a gap left by all these assessments. While all critics have had to deal with the Douls' choice to remain blind at the play's end, they have focused almost entirely on the way this action comments on the theme of dream versus reality.[1] Such interpretations force a metaphorical meaning on the couple's choice and fail to account for it in any literal way. My reading of *The Well* considers place, body, and action as indicators of social arrangements.[2] The actions of Synge's protagonists must be explained in terms of the society that ultimately casts them out. Bringing to Synge's text the anthropological writings of Victor Turner, I comment on Martin Doul's recognition of his own power at the play's end: "It's more sense is in a blind man, and more *power* maybe than you're thinking at all," he says (149, emphasis mine).

From the day of its first production at Abbey, *The Well of the Saints* has "mystified critics," who have often formed contradictory opinions regarding the play's worth (Kopper, *Synge* xvii).[3] Two seemingly distinct kinds of response show themselves in the diverse interpretations that have appeared throughout the twentieth century. Early reactions, governed as much by sociohistorical context as by the work itself, demonstrate how cultural norms and events influence reception. The criticism of the last twenty-five years, on the other hand, depends more directly on the host of reader expectations derived from literary allusion, understanding of genre, and assumptions about qualities that distinguish "literature" from other writing. Although for convenience's sake I treat social context and literary tradition as discrete aspects of interpretation, literary judgments never isolate themselves from history.

The early reception of *The Well* strikingly illustrates history and culture at work in interpretation. A writer for Dublin's *Daily Express*, in 1906, explained that the Douls are driven from the village at the play's end because of Martin's irreverence in knocking the holy water from the Saint's hand (cited in Kopper, *Synge* 5), an interpretation obviously dependent upon Dublin's shared religious assumptions. Theatergoers' violent dislike of *The Well*, Kopper suggests, had as much to do with Synge's Protestant Ascendancy background as with the play itself, but Dublin audiences resented him, too, for his characterization of the Irish. No doubt, Synge's resurrecting of the "Stage Irishman at a time when Ireland was fighting for Home Rule" (viii) distressed many, but probably even more offensive than this supposed lack of national spirit was the bestial quality of Synge's character, Martin Doul. In light of the racism many English harbored, audience rejection seems almost a given. The sort of prejudice Dubliners had learned to abhor is voiced in Engels's *Condition of the Working Class in En-*

gland. Having no qualms about cleansing the English workers at the expense of the Irish, Engels wrote:

The Irishman allows the pig to share his own living quarters. This new, abnormal method of rearing livestock in the large towns is entirely of the Irish origin. . . . The Irishman lives and sleeps with the pig, the children play with the pig, ride on its back, and roll about in the filth with it. (106)

To an audience who had heard too often of a supposed link between the Irish and animality, Synge's use of the grotesque in his characterization of Martin Doul was simply too insulting. Synge's own response to the criticism appears in a letter he penned to Willie Fay, the actor who played Martin Doul in *The Well's* first production:

Tell Miss G.—or whoever it may be—that what I write of Irish country life I know to be true and I most emphatically will not change a syllable of it because A. B. or C. may think they know better than I do. . . . You understand my position: I am *quite ready* to avoid hurting people's feelings needlessly, but I will *not* falsify what I believe to be true for anybody. (quoted in Saddlemyer xxiv)

Left unfulfilled were theatregoers' desires to see only an idealized version of the Irish people; even worse, through his commitment to realism, Synge was willing to spurn this image, which was so necessary to their self-esteem. Early viewers and critics, reacting to what was as clearly a cultural event as a literary one, were—more often than not—what Iser would call "irritated recipients." Though they saw no alternative but to reject the work and its writer, by 1932, *The Well of the Saints'* "message" had evidently changed.[4] Judged twenty-seven years earlier as gruesome and unsympathetic, the play at this point received praise for its "passion, love of humanity, and a faith in the poetic ideal" (Foster 55). This latter review, which was written between the wars, presents a yearning distinct from that expressed in a 1943 piece, which admired the play for showing "the realistic conclusion that darkness with hope is infinitely better than clear sight with despair" (Foster 55).

While these production reviews show the influence of history on interpretation, the criticism of the past twenty-five years illustrates the importance of literary tradition. The critical dialogue over the play's meaning calls on knowledge about genre, other texts, and classical norms for judging wholeness—all in a quest to judge worth. Of course, no reader is separate from literary traditions, but as Raymond Williams has pointed out, tradition does not inertly register the past; rather, it directs the selection of certain meanings and practices, and excludes others. Such exclusion has been at work in the complaints lodged against *The Well*. In examining the commentaries on the play, there is no need to point out that New Criticism has a political stance, yet Iser's reminder about consistency building should serve to make us question *any* reading that measures worth in terms of a work's coherence.[5] In both complaints of inconsistency *or* praise of resolved "tensions," we are apt to learn as much about the critic as the work. As Iser has noted, when critics demand consistency—which is built by the reader and not contained in the text—they indulge in the worst sort of subjectivism: personal opinion disguised as objectivity. As a case in point, when Price reads Martin Doul as an artist of extraordinary perception, he is compelled to make the old man's actions those befitting a sensitive person. In order to see in Martin's interaction with Molly a wondrous ability "adequately [to] comprehend and appreciate a woman's beauty and love" (149), Price must dilute the sexual undercurrent of the scene, diminish the role of Mary, and discard Martin's more grotesque qualities. Obviously, critics who do not eliminate the same elements as Price arrive at alternate meanings.

The critics' drive for consistency takes several forms. Gerstenberger, noting that Synge attempted to "wring from the scenes an intensity that the situation does not entirely possess" (46), has shown a desire for harmony. Seeing dissonance between content and tone, finding the second act as particularly sprawling and without movement, and detecting problems in the scene in which Martin dresses in the Saint's cloak, Gerstenberger has accused the work of "artistic weaknesses" (46). Not able to harmonize the play's action with her thesis, she is left to suggest that the cloak scene is a "byplay that seems to be rather unnecessary stage business" (50). Such a drive for consistency has led other critics to measure the degree of resolution in Synge's bringing together of the most disparate of thematic elements. Price, for example, praises *The Well* as a thematically grounded work showing the "tension between dream and reality" (139). Skelton sees the play as an examination of illusion and truth, and he has applauded Synge's recognition of the Douls' right to their dream (91–103). Similarly, Thornton sees the play as an "exploration of the philosophical issues with the theme of abstraction and reality" (83), but he sees the confrontation as ultimately leading to a nihilism at odds with the worldview presented in *The Playboy of the Western World*. In his comparison, Thornton shows another means by which critics look for consistency. He and others have measured the degree to which *The Well* adheres to the notions expressed in other works in the Synge canon. Kopper, for example, lists *The Well*'s often-overlooked similarities with other works, including, among others, "an aversion to bodily decay ... and fear of the loss of love" ("Assessment" 219). Benson writes that *The Well*, like Synge's other works, shows "the outsider vs. society; the pagan vs. the church" (91). Analyzing dialogue, Barnett sees in the other plays language as "the exact imaginative tool for ... poetic harmony and subtlety," but she finds *The Well* lacking, with "much of the language ... both bitter and bad-tempered" (123).

Incompatible opinions could conceivably complicate efforts to place *The Well of the Saints* on solid footing with Synge's more widely read works. However, a capacity for presenting a range of meanings could actually promote its endurance. Any work, Iser points out, gives rise to a "network of possible connections'' (118), and the variety of meanings available make possible the work's communication amid shifts in popular culture, thought, political awareness, and involvement. While critics continue to neglect *The Well of the Saints* in favor of most of the other plays, recent commentaries show that today, *The Well* communicates to readers *more* fully than in the past. Current critical approaches have increased the receptivity toward this play, which may introduce us to unexplored areas of Synge studies. King, for example, uses Marxism and discourse theory to show that together, the Douls work out, ''through reciprocity, a mode of access to the past which makes it available for the construction of a positive present-and-future'' (124). And while Johnson's discussion of *The Well*, in the essay, ''Interrogating Boundaries,'' is brief, her use of ideas on transgression politics and the writings of Mikhail Bakhtin increases the ''fit'' between this play and others in the Synge canon. The agendas that King and Johnson have brought to their interpretations suggest that future readings will further decrease the asymmetry between text and readers.

In a sense, my own interpretation begins at a juncture where Johnson's leaves off. Observing the importance of community to an understanding of the play, Johnson has said that the old couple opt for the open road rather than accept the ''denial of their desire to remain blind on the edge of the settled community'' (''Interrogating Boundaries'' 144). This emphasis on community is one I share, but because Johnson continues to read the play within its established framework—as a contest between illusion and reality—she concludes that the Douls opt for a ''fantasy world instead of consensus reality'' and that ''the community cannot tolerate the kind of difference that favors blindness over sight'' (144). Set within a different framework, however, the play yields other meanings and the old couple's choice becomes a choice for power.

Victor Turner finds, in a range of cultural performances, the state of liminality. Whether these performances be rites of passage, a healing ceremony, dance, theater, carnival, or social drama, each entails a period when normal social arrangements pause.[6] As a gap in the social structure, a ''no-place'' betwixt and between two stable positions, liminality implies ''anti-structure'' where individuals share in an extreme collectivism that he calls *communitas*. While Turner's early work distinguishes between the brief, always transitional state of liminality and the outsiderhood of groups permanently set apart, both liminal personae and outsiders share in the extreme collectivism of *communitas*: both signify ''anti-structure.'' From the Latin for *threshold*, liminality manifests a spacial quality—locations set apart from the quotidian, workaday world; places of spectacle such as fairs, carnivals, festivals; sites of open-air performances, mummery, and dancing. A domain outside the usual seat of authority, liminality suspends day-to-day reality and provides ''privileged spaces'' where ''taboos are lifted, fantasies are enacted'' (*Performance* 102). Liminality shows itself in acts of ''anti-structure''—the jester's joking, the jazz musician's riffing, the storyteller's ad-libbing. Improvisational and playful, liminal situations can suggest the rule breaking of Mardi Gras, when "almost anything goes . . . [and] behavior is re-versed; the low are exalted and the mighty abased" (*Performance* 102).

The complexity of Turner's work—its capacity for interrelating place, body, actions, and social formation—makes it a fitting tool for interpreting Synge's play. Using geographic space as an indicator of social relations, Synge sets the first and third acts at a crossroads, but the second in the village. The Douls' move, which takes them from outside the social structure into its lower-most position and then back again, originates at "the crossing of roads" (*Well* 77)—the threshold into the village *and* out, a place on the brink. The meeting ground of social forces, place forms a symbolic link between topography and social class. Links between the material body and class emerge in similar fashion. Martin Doul, whose character can best be explained in terms of grotesque re-alism, flaunts his coarse sexuality, manifesting "lowness." With the hub of his being in his genitals, and displaying a low stature and "lowly" appearance, Martin's bodily lowness becomes an analogue for his position in the village.

In the play's first two acts, geographic space underscores the move from outsiderhood to low social status. The roadside in Act I, lying between the village and the fair of Clash, is free, not only of the peasant farmers' trafficking of goods, but also of the village's institutions. Placing stress on the "anti-structure" of the locale, Synge notes a "low loose wall at back" and "at left, ruined doorway of church" (71), details bespeaking order undone and culture eroded. Here, beyond the village with its controls, which typically bind persons to orderly behavior, rests the scene of an earlier murder and the bog that served as grave for the "old fellow going home with his gold" (77). And when Timmy the smith predicts a great "wonder," Mary reminds us again of rules suspended when she imagines the spectacle of "a man hanging by his neck" (77). Inhab-itants of this space where the nonrules of "anti-structure" reign, Martin and Mary have a "home" here: "It's ourselves have a right to the crossing roads," Martin says. Sharing in *communitas*, they wait on the threshold of the miracle that will take them from blindness to sight, and from "anti-structure" to struc-ture. Neophytes in the ritual, when they are born into life within the community, the pure water from the well of four beautiful saints initiates their passage into society's inferior positions. The second act, which is set in the village at Tim-my's smithery, stresses the world of work, production, domesticity, and eco-nomic dependence. Getting "a corner to sleep, and money with it" (103), Martin labors for the once-benevolent Timmy, but when he proves to be a poor worker, Timmy cruelly wields his authority as taskmaster, calling him "a lazy, basking fool" and needlessly forcing the old man to shed his coat, despite the "black wintery air" (103). The move from the crossroads' undifferentiated "anti-structure" into the village's hierarchy has yielded not even economic gains for Martin, who is left to lament, "It's more [gold] I got a while since, and I sitting blinded in Grianan, than I get in this place, working hard, and destroying myself, the length of the day" (103).

More at home in their homelessness than in the village, Martin and Mary unsettle assumptions about status: they turn culture on its head. Using the body grotesque to invert images of the body perfect, Synge is able to explore oppositions: human/animal, spiritual/physical, culture/nature, youth/age, truth/lie, and others. Martin, "with the fat legs on him, and the little neck like a ram," and Mary, with eyes like "two eyes in any starving sow" (97), are linked in the first two acts with animals. Becoming lower members of the (wo)man/animal hierarchy, they draw attention to humankind's baser traits. As the references to "grey mare" (97), "life of a pig" (103), or "rat's eyes" (131) fill the air, social relations become infused with the language of verbal abuse. Identified with nags, pigs, and rats, the Douls serve to remind those present of their own position. The couple, with a status so inferior that they call to mind animals, reaffirm for the villagers their own superiority. Because such reversals typify any culture's process of mapping out the lineaments of order, Synge's exploration of his own culture's poles of experience becomes an act of cultural self-definition.[7] First charting the boundaries of Ireland's social system but ostensibly challenging that system, *The Well* gives glimpses of a topsy-turvy, unfixed, mobile world.

Inversion marks the action early in the play when Molly returns from the fair with the Saint's bell and cloak. In a sort of ritual of status reversal, Molly gives the bell to Martin and then dresses him in the cloak. Her laughter—foolish, mocking, a "loud braying laugh" (73)—brings carnivalesque gusto to the scene. Paralleling customs that celebrate a "world upside down" when "kings become servants, officers serve the ranks, boys become bishops, [and] men dress as women" (Stallybrass 183), Martin Doul becomes Saint. This primary inversion is underscored by lesser ones, such as Molly's supposed holiness (83) and her allusion to "the archangels below" (85). In this scene and others, Molly—herself on the threshold of a role change by way of marriage—enjoys the short-lived power that her sexuality brings. Here, an implicit sexuality clamors beneath the surface of the scene, with Timmy suggesting that the holy water will be polluted by "the likes of [Molly]" and with Mary asking how Martin could be "bell-ringing with the saints of God" (87). Wedded, he is unchaste; sensual, he is the inverse of the ascetic Saint. The distance between the physical and spiritual becomes abundantly clear in Martin's fondling of the Saint's fine cloak while he speaks of touching young girls' faces. His lecherous sensuality swells to sacrilege in this scene of unholy touching that prompts the fantasy. While the inversions in this scene examine the binary structure that serves as the basis for thought, actions, beliefs, and social arrangements, the Douls, here and throughout the first act, function as low-Others—grotesques, as the polar opposite of ideal beauty. Turner's summation of rituals of status reversal is particularly fitting for mapping out power relations, for he sees such rites as nonthreatening, and indeed crucial, to the status quo: "Not only do they *reaffirm* the order of structure; they also *restore* relations between the actual historical individuals who occupy positions in that structure" (*Ritual Process* 177, emphasis mine). When Martin removes the cloak, the fasting and asexual Saint—by virtue of his contrast with Martin—appears all the more holy. Martin's

putting on of the Saint's robe is carnivalesque—public liminality being cele-
brated at the crossroads. But it is temporary and contained. The performance,
which playacts at reversal so that those present can come face to face with the
extremes of spirit and flesh, stays always beyond Martin's control. Passively
entering into *Molly's* game, Martin's grotesqueness stands as the butt of a joke,
posing no threat to anyone.

What holds true at this threshold leading *into* society, though, holds only
partly true once the sighted Martin moves into the village. Still low-Other, Martin can be the yardstick against whom Timmy measures his own achievements,
with Martin's "lazy, basking fool[ishness]" and his "life of a pig" in "a corner" (103) lying in stark contrast to Timmy's hard work and "house with four
rooms in it above on the hill" (111). Martin, though, does not remain fixed. In
the second act, in his scene with Molly, a more disruptive aspect of the grotesque
emerges. In Synge's examination of the poles of nature/culture, the disruptive
qualities of the grotesque serve to unsettle the self-possessed Molly. Martin
crosses the borders of acceptable behavior, and social class serves as a flag
marking the spot. When he confesses to Molly that he has been "lying down
across a sop of straw" fantasizing about her "laughing and making great talk
in a high room" (113), the gap between the appearance and intentions of the
two points up the grotesqueness of his desire. "Making love . . . with the good
looks of [Molly]," his "romancing" consists of fetishizing her "fine neck" and
skin (115) and the "fine sound [of her] voice." With sexually implicit flattery,
he tells Molly, "it's of many a fine thing your voice would put a poor dark
fellow in mind, and . . . it's of little else at all I would be thinking" (113). While
critics like Price have ignored this aspect of Martin's discourse, it is important
to remember that the sexual tension of this scene disturbed Dublin's first audiences, a point made clear in a review of a revival production. Of this second
show, a reviewer noted:

The wild beast nature of "Martin Doul" was artistically kept in check, and it made him
a far more agreeable personage. W. G. Fay made him a very repulsive old man overwhelmed with sensuality. Arthur Sinclair made him more of a dreamer with a longing
for the beautiful. . . . In fact, the play was lifted out of reality into the realm of fancy
where it should have been from the first. (quoted in Benson 103)

Correspondence between Synge and Fay shows Synge's insistence on the grotesque, beastly characterization, and in Synge's production notes, his awareness
of class distinctions directs his comments. In a note intended for the cast, Synge
wrote: "If it is possible—Timmy, Molly should be got to show that in *all their
relations* with Martin & Mary—friendly as they are—they feel *their own superiority*—for this reason Timmy's slapping Martin on back etc. is better left
out" (Saddlemyer xxiii; emphasis mine).

Martin's grotesqueness, which is shaded so as to encode his character with
Synge's social and political awareness, functions slightly differently in each of

the first two acts. While Act I sets up poles between Martin's sexuality and the Saint's spirituality, Act II sets up poles contrasting physicality (or nature) and culture. Using culture here in the anthropological sense (as the structure of social arrangements), I take my lead again from Turner, who notes that an important component of liminality is "an enhanced stress on nature at the expense of culture" (*Dramas* 252). Including grotesques as liminal personae, Turner says that symbols giving utterance to liminality relate to "biological processes, human and nonhuman, and to other aspects of the natural order" (252). The liminal situation symbolically snuffs out structure with animality, and in just such a snuffing, Martin Doul tries to lure Molly away from the village with his talk, which puts nature on display. Describing a carnivalesque life of storytelling on the open road and "singing songs at the fairs" (115), he dispenses with culture as he lauds nature: "Let you come on now, I'm saying, to the lands of Iveragh and the Reeks of Cork, where you won't set down the width of your two feet and not be crushing fine flowers" (117). Martin paints a utopia of permanent "anti-structure," a communitas at the expense of structured community.

Molly's rejection of Martin results from a disgust bred of class distinctions. Too "fine," "civil," and "well-reared" to be bothered with the like of him, she suggests that he take his attention to the "tinker girls . . . running the hills, or down among the sluts of the town" (123). Vacillating between haughtiness, discomfort, and fear, she shrinks from him when he begins to talk like "a man would be losing his mind" (117). Like the insane, Martin refuses to act and speak in socially acceptable ways, and in refusing the order of her world, he "show[s] the cracks in [the] over-all system" (Clement and Cixous 7). Seemingly mad, he throws social structure into relief through his failure to fit in. Contradictorily, however, he merges the incompatible. Martin is mystical man in the guise of a pig, spiritualizing the flesh with his poetry. With his desire of the old for the young—of the beast for the beauty—he is the antithesis of order, system, and structure. Forcing his interaction with Molly toward crisis, Martin performs what might be interpreted as the first phase of "social drama." In *breaching* societal rules, he is the "fool . . . open[ing] his mouth to a fine woman" (119), thereby transgressing class lines. The ensuing *crisis*—Molly's panic and Timmy's taking her side—causes *redress*. Timmy, wielding his hammer in a symbolic action that reaffirms structure, forces Martin out of the village. Act II ends with what Turner sees as a possible fourth phase in "social drama": the *recognition of schism* (*Performance* 35). In a powerful final image that articulates schism as it inverts hierarchies, Martin describes the animality in the sex act. Envisioning Molly and Timmy "on a high bed . . . screeching in hell," he imagines the two of them "twisting and roaring out, and twisting and roaring again" throughout eternity. And praying for his own damnation, he asks to be a voyeur standing aside and watching this hellish spectacle that would be "Heaven itself" (123).

In the play's final act, geographic space once again underscores social ties. Blind again and jobless, with even their inferior rank within the village stripped, the Douls meet at the crossroads, the place of "anti-structure," and once again, actions and the body take on political meanings. Deciding that a shared life is better than "sitting alone with no one at all," Martin and Mary reconcile their differences, reestablishing the equality so essential to communitas. When the villagers recognize the piteousness of their situation "after seeing a while, and working for [their] bread" (137) and bring the Saint again to offer them sight, the old couple ask to be left in peace. Too often read as a "preference for a lie and an apparent insistence upon illusion" (Gerstenberger 45), the Douls' choice to remain blind shows instead a preference for communitas, or "anti-structure"—a continuous statuslessness on the threshold. Choosing liminality over inferior status within the community, Martin asks the Saint to walk on and leave them in their "peace at the crossing roads, for it's best [they] are this way, and [they are] not asking to see" (139). This second plea for the right to peace at the crossroads sounds a belief in the harmony that comes only when hierarchies are suspended and poles collapsed.

A shift in the way bodies are used signals such a collapse of binaryism. While the Saint's presence in the first act stresses spirituality, Martin's comment near the play's end calls attention to the physical price of asceticism. In a declaration that serves to collapse the futile opposition between spirit and flesh, he says: "What was it I seen my first day, but your own bleeding feet and they cut with the stones" (141). Similarly, while the first two acts use the body grotesque to examine poles in meaning, the third act significantly diminishes this element. A comparison of the Act III drafts indicates Synge's probable conscious choice to lessen the animality of the characters. Rather than calling Mary "a dirty wrinkled old beast," as early drafts indicate, Martin instead calls her a "hag" (124–25). Deleted completely is a line from the first scene that has Martin ask, "What am I now but an old wretched whining crimpled hog?" (124). To eliminate the animal qualities that place the grotesque body at opposition with ideal spirit and beauty is to remove the Douls as mere low-Others. Less animal and more human, they fall into the middle ground, which partakes of both poles.

The action, which continues to mimic "social drama," shows the consequences of intermixing poles. No longer bestial beggars with no choice but poverty, but instead individuals choosing "anti-structure," Martin and Mary threaten order. Turner discusses societies' fear of disorder growing out of liminality:

The possibility exists of standing aside not only from one's own social position but from all social positions and of formulating a potentially unlimited series of alternative social arrangements. That this danger is recognized in all tolerably orderly societies is made evident by the proliferation of taboos that hedge in and constrain those on whom the normative structure loses its grip. (*Dramas* 13–14)

In the villagers' fear that Martin will "be bringing great storms or draughts on us maybe" (149), they articulate a terror of nature gone wild, a horror of disorder not constrained within culture.

In choosing blindness over sight, Synge's characters ultimately opt for the power to imagine alternatives. In the crevices of "anti-structure," seeds of possible social change nestle and alternatives breed. Liminality, Turner notes, is transitory. Communitas gives way to structure, and structure gives way to its return. "What is certain," he writes, "is that no society can function adequately without the dialectic" (*Ritual Process* 129). Synge, by showing liminality's "anti-structure," confirms the power of his protagonists. But he does more. Forcing his audience to test beliefs that are at odds with the status quo, he pulls them away from binaryism and fixed hierarchies and toward the communitas of the open road. In most cultural performance, Turner writes, a "cultural subjunctivity" prevails—the "supposition, desire, hypothesis, [and] possibility" (*Performance* 101). Such performances and works of art, he says, "incite men to action as well as to thought" (129).[8] Such is the liminal power of Synge's play "when the blind . . . see" (*Holy Bible*, Isaiah 29:18).

NOTES

1. Price, for example, has said that Martin Doul is representative of the artist who is "unable to grapple with the whole of existence, unable to create something vital and beautiful out of actuality, and consoles himself again with private fancies and dreams" (159–60). Thornton maintains that "the Douls' decision to preserve their blindness and elaborate their dreams . . . leave[s] no doubt that [they] are willing to build their lives upon a lie" (139). Gerstenberger sees their blindness as "more honest than that of the self-deceiving sighted world," but says that "their choice is one that denies the wholeness of the world" (53). Grene notes that Martin Doul is "a powerful spokesman for the imagination" but asserts that Synge "remained aware that the imagination is at once truth and illusion" ("Introduction" 26). Johnson sees the Douls as "liv[ing] out a fantasy" (144), and King has said that their blindness is a "new way of seeing" (131). Only Kopper has suggested that the substance of the play lies, not in the clash between dream and reality, but elsewhere:

The play must be seen, however, as essentially a contrast between the Establishment and the two outsiders. . . . Synge's ruthless presentation of the deficiencies of Martin and Mary, on the one hand, and of the Saint, Molly, and Timmy the smith[,] . . . on the other hand; his refusal to glorify either side; and his insistence upon the cruel Rabelaisian element in both partially account for the play's being viewed as a direct precursor of Beckett and Black Comedy. ("Assessment" 219–20).

My reading of *The Well of the Saints* takes a lead from Kopper.

2. *The Politics and Poetics of Transgression*, by Peter Stallybrass and Allon White, has been integral in the development of my thinking on *The Well of the Saints*.

3. Kopper's 1979 bibliographic reference guide, augmented by the 1990 supplement, provides the most extensive listing of the criticism on *The Well of the Saints*. Especially helpful is the annotated listing of newspaper accounts of the 1905 production. This early criticism faulted the play for its preoccupation with sex, its unfair portrayal of the Irish character, its grossness and gruesomeness, and its lack of "compassion" (5–7). Both Grene, in his introduction to the 1982 editions of *The Well of the Saints* ("Introduction" 23–25) and Thornton in his study (128–32) provide discussion of the play's early recep-

tion, as well as comments on later criticism. Foster, too, provides a review of the literature, but of particular interest are commentaries of theater criticism from a 1932 New York production, a 1943 London production, and a 1954 Irish company's revival of *The Well*. Ann Saddlemyer's introduction to *J. M. Synge: Collected Works*, Vol. 3, provides valuable history on the writing and production of the play (xx–xxvii), and Green and Stephens's biography, *J. M. Synge, 1871–1909*, provides correspondences concerning the play and information on the first production's cast (172–92).

4. In his discussion of the reasons why readers reject particular works, Iser wrote:

The more committed the reader is to an ideological position, the less inclined he will be to accept the basic theme-and-horizon structure of comprehension which regulates the text-reader interaction. He will not allow his norms to become a theme, because as such they are automatically open to the critical view inherent in the virtualized positions that form the background. And if he is induced to participate in the events of the text, only to find that he is then supposed to adopt a negative attitude toward values he does not wish to question, the result will often be open rejection of the book and its author. Even this reaction still testifies to the undiminished validity of this structure. (202)

5. For a discussion of political assumptions undergirding New Criticism, see Eagleton (47–53).

6. Turner defines social drama as a course of events with successive phases of public action. (For a discussion of social drama, see *The Anthropology of Performance* 33–71.)

7. Stallybrass and White have discussed symbolic inversion (16–24), using Barbara Babcock's *The Reversible World*. Babcock's definition appears on p. 39 of her text. Stallybrass and White write,

By tracking the ''grotesque body'' and the ''low-Other'' through different symbolic domains of bourgeois society since the Renaissance we can attain an unusual perspective upon its inner dynamics. . . . For the classificatory body of a culture is always double, always structured in relation to its negation, its inverse. ''All symbolic inversions define a culture's lineaments at the same time as they question the usefulness and the absoluteness of its ordering.'' (20)

See also Turner's discussion of status reversal in rituals in *The Ritual Process* (172–78), *Dramas, Fields, and Metaphors* (55–57), and *The Anthropology of Performance* (174–75).

8. Although Turner's discussion describes cultural processes as opposed to the overtly political, *action* as Turner uses it here suggests the possibility of political action. Liminality for Turner entails neither a radical nor conservative thrust, a stance somewhat in accord with the carnivalesque as it is viewed by Stallybrass and White, who write:

It actually makes little sense to fight out the issue of whether or not carnivals are *intrinsically* radical or conservative, for to do so automatically involves the false essentializing of carnivalesque transgression. . . . The most that can be said in the abstract is that for long periods carnival may be a stable and cyclical ritual with no noticeable politically transformative effects but that, given the presence of sharpened political antagonism, it may often act as *catalyst* and *site of actual and symbolic struggle*. (14; emphasis in original)

WORKS CITED

Babcock, Barbara. *The Reversible World: Symbolic Inversion in Art and Society*. Ithaca, N.Y.: Cornell University Press, 1978.

Barnett, Pat. "The Nature of Synge's Dialogue." *English Literature in Transition 1880–1920* 10(2) (1967): 119–29.

Benson, Eugene. *J. M. Synge.* New York: Grove Press, 1983.

Clement, Catherine, and Helene Cixous. *The Newly Born Woman.* Trans. by Betsy Wing. 1986. Minneapolis: University of Minnesota Press, 1988.

Eagleton, Terry. *Literary Theory: An Introduction.* 1983. Minneapolis: University of Minnesota Press, 1983.

Engels, Friedrich. *The Condition of the Working Class in England.* Trans. by W. O. Henderson and W. H. Chaloner. New York: Macmillan, 1958.

Foster, Leslie D. *"The Well of the Saints."* In *A J. M. Synge Literary Companion*, ed. Edward A. Kopper, Jr. Westport, Conn.: Greenwood Press, 1988, 51–60.

Gerstenberger, Donna. *John Millington Synge.* 1964. Rev. ed. Boston: G. K. Hall, 1990.

Greene, David H., and Edward M. Stephens. *J. M. Synge, 1871–1909.* Rev. ed. New York: New York University Press, 1989.

Grene, Nicholas. "Introduction." In *The Well of the Saints*, by J. M. Synge. Washington, D.C.: Catholic University of America Press, 1982, 1–26.

Iser, Wolfgang. *The Act of Reading: A Theory of Aesthetic Response.* 1978. Reprint. Baltimore, Md.: John Hopkins University Press, 1987.

Johnson, Toni O'Brien. "Interrogating Boundaries: Fantasy in the Plays of J. M. Synge." In *More Real Than Reality: The Fantastic in Irish Literature and the Arts*, ed. Donald E. Morse and Csilla Bertha. Westport, Conn.: Greenwood Press, 1991, 137–50.

King, Mary C. "Work and Vision: Language as Symbolic Action in *The Well of the Saints.*" In *The Drama of J. M. Synge.* Syracuse, N.Y.: Syracuse University Press, 1985, 105–32.

Kopper, Edward A., Jr. *John Millington Synge: A Reference Guide.* Boston: G. K. Hall, 1979.

———. *Synge: A Review of the Criticism.* Modern Irish Literature Monograph Series, 1. Lyndora, Pa.: Kopper, 1990.

———. "Toward an Assessment." In *A J. M. Synge Literary Companion*, ed. Edward A. Kopper, Jr. Westport, Conn.: Greenwood Press, 1988, 211–29.

Price, Alan. *Synge and Anglo-Irish Drama.* London: Methuen, 1961.

Saddlemyer, Ann. Introduction. In *J. M. Synge: Collected Works.* Vol. 3, ed. Ann Saddlemyer. London: Oxford University Press, 1968, xi–xxxi.

Skelton, Robin. *The Writings of J. M. Synge.* Indianapolis, Ind.: Bobbs-Merrill, 1971.

Stallybrass, Peter, and Allon White. *The Politics and Poetics of Transgression.* Ithaca, N.Y.: Cornell University Press, 1986.

Synge, J. M. *Plays, Book I.* Vol. 3 of *J. M. Synge: Collected Works*, ed. Ann Saddlemyer. London: Oxford University Press, 1968.

Thornton, Weldon. *J. M. Synge and the Western Mind.* Gerrards Cross, U.K.: Colin Smythe, 1979.

Turner, Victor. *The Anthropology of Performance.* New York: PAJ Publications, 1986.

———. *Dramas, Fields, and Metaphors: Symbolic Action in Human Society.* 1974. Reprint. Ithaca, N.Y.: Cornell University Press, 1990.

———. *The Ritual Process: Structure and Anti-Structure.* 1969. Reprint. Ithaca, N.Y.: Cornell University Press, 1987.

Williams, Raymond. *Marxism and Literature.* 1977. Reprint. New York: Oxford University Press, 1989.

9

"More Matter for a May Morning": J. M. Synge's *The Tinker's Wedding*

Robert E. Rhodes

Audiences of John Millington Synge's comedy *The Tinker's Wedding* learn early on that the priest in the play, while not entirely reprehensible, is Synge's satirical target and that a band of outcast, earthy tinkers is there to undo him. However, among other problems that seem to have made this the least successful of Synge's dramas, and which delayed its Abbey Theatre production until 1971, the central one has been the near certainty that a typical Irish Catholic audience would not sit still for such a priest at center stage. Rather than seeing him as a variation in need of correction, there is a good chance he would be seen as a scandal to the whole Irish priesthood or rejected as not an Irish priest at all. Even if an audience willingly suspended disbelief for the sake of the comedy and the satire, the problems the priest raises are compounded by the tinkers and some probabilities about an Irish audience's reactions to them, considerations that have received less attention than concerns about the priest and that, while not neglecting the latter, are worth a longer and more searching look than they seem to have had.

In addition to familiarizing non-Irish audiences with the position of the tinker in Irish life, such an examination serves at least two purposes, both of which suggest the continuing relevance of the play in the canon of Irish drama and in Irish life. First, the conflict between a settled community and an itinerant culture dramatized by Synge has been exacerbated in our time by a growing tinker population still largely in conflict with an ever more respectable settled society. Second, a close look at the tinkers in Synge's play and tinkers in real life reveals that Synge, like many other twentieth-century Irish writers, tended to romanticize his tinkers for the sake of admonishing the Irish bourgeoisie.

For a priest—for anyone at all, some might argue—to be bested by tinkers is simply not all right, because in most Irish contexts, tinkers (however attractively packaged they might be, as Synge's sometimes are) are beyond the pale. This becomes even more problematic and difficult to sort out if we recognize that effective satire requires a norm, understood by and agreeable to an audience, from which the object of satire has deviated. The only norm here—the alternative to the priest's ethos—is the world of the tinkers; and there is only a very slight chance that a typical Irish audience would admire them and hold them up for the priest's emulation.

All this means that to an Irish audience, "tinker" usually signified, and continues to signify, something more ominous than a dictionary meaning: "a travelling mender of metal household utensils." To Synge, and many other Irish writers who have shared his romantic disposition toward Ireland's marginal peoples, tinkers have been instrumental in posing an alternative to conventional and respectable ways of life. To an Irish audience, however, "tinker" has ordinarily been a code word for a complex of characteristics anathema to their worldviews—characteristics, whether rightly perceived or misconstrued, that must be understood for a right perception of why an ordinary Irish audience would likely respond negatively to the tinkers as well as to the priest, with a resultant confusion about ends and means.

To suggest how ingrained and widespread are negative attitudes towards tinkers, we can consider the following examples from literature (which of course do not necessarily represent the authors' opinions of tinkers). In Eugene O'Neill's 1957 play, *A Touch of the Poet*, it is 1828, just outside Boston, and Nora Melody ponders the Thoreauvian life of her daughter's lover: "I'll never get it clear in my head," she says, "what he's been doing this past year, living like a tramp or tinker" (28). A century later, on Chicago's South Side, Weary Reilly's mother—of James T. Farrell's Studs Lonigan trilogy—trades lies with Studs's mother about their wayward sons: "Sure, he's a sensible boy," says Mrs. Reilly of the ne'er-do-well Weary, "and he knows full well that the curse of God has been put on the likes of them, the tinkers that's always to be seen in that poolroom" (191). To the lips of both anxious mothers springs the word— "tinker"—that would have been as automatic in Dingle or Dublin as it was with Boston or Chicago's Irish; transplanted, they can still conjure up illusions of superiority merely by evoking the dreaded epithet for someone else.

They have only copied literary characters at home in Ireland. In Synge's own *Playboy of the Western World*, for example, one of the reasons why Pegeen fears being left alone is that there are "ten tinkers . . . camped in the east glen" (63), and the first uneasy words she says to Christy are, "You're one of the tinkers, young fellow, is beyond camped in the glen?" (67). In James Joyce's "Ivy Day in the Committee Room," Mr. Henchy characterizes Tricky Dicky Tierney as a "mean little tinker" (123) because Tierney, a politician, may—or just may not—pay those soliciting votes for him. In Patrick Kavanagh's "Pegasus," the poet offers his soul—"an old horse"—for sale at fairs, to the Church, then to the state, next to business, and finally, out of desperation, to tinkers, who, though they are not buying either, are still at the bottom of the social scale (59–60).

More recently, although the word *tinker* never appears in Richard Murphy's poem "The Glass Dump Road," it is difficult to avoid the conclusion—with such lines as "the caravan/ Parked where three roads forked beside a mound/ Of broken bottles near a market town," and "A camp-fire in the ditch was dying out," for example—that the man who kneels "naked/ Over a naked child/ Offering her his penis to play with like a toy" is a tinker (115). In John B. Keane's play, *The Field*, the brutish and land-hungry "The Bull" McCabe, murderer of William Dee, has a ready-made scapegoat when asked if he knows who killed Dee:

Well, now, I'm damned downright glad you asked me that, because I have a fair idea. The wits was often frightened out of me, too, many a night, not knowing the minute a band of tinkers would break out from a bush and hammer my brains out. Try the camp of the Gorleys and if it isn't one of the Gorleys, try the McLaffertys, and if 'tisn't one of them 'tis sure to be one of the Molligans. Don't they kill one another, not to mind killing a Christian. (73)

As recently as February 1993, William Trevor's short story, "Timothy's Birthday," features Eddie, who "referred to the tinker encampment, and said it was a bloody disgrace, tinkers allowed like that. 'Pardon my French,' he apologized when the swearword slipped out" (146); it is a toss-up whether he meant "bloody" or "tinker."

To be sure—and to be both fair and accurate—authors themselves seldom share the negative views of their fictional characters toward tinkers. For example, if Richard Murphy's "The Glass Dump Road" is harrowing, his "The Reading Lesson" is understanding in its depiction of a fourteen-year-old tinker boy "learning the alphabet," whose hands "will grow callous, gathering sticks or scrap;/ Exploring pockets of the horny drunk/ Loiterers at the fairs, giving them lice" (107). Similarly, tinkers come in for a bad few minutes in John B. Keane's *The Field*, but in his drama, *Sive*, they are the instinctive and compassionate chorus commenting on the greed and materialism that lead to Sive's death:

Oh, come all good men and true,
A sad tale I'll tell to you,
Of a maiden young, who died this day.
Oh, they murdered lovely Sive,
She would not be a bride,
And they laid her dead, to bury in the class. (111)

In their exile from the settled population, Cahal and the tinker woman, Maire, in Walter Macken's novel, *The Bogman*, are a later reincarnation of similar characters in Thomas MacDonagh's poignant poem, "John-John." Here, a settled woman who has married a tinker man says:

> The neighbors' shame of me began
> When first I brought you in;
> To wed and keep a tinker man
> They thought a kind of sin;
> But now this three year since you're gone
> 'Tis pity me they do,
> And that I'd rather have, John-John,
> Than that they'd pity you.
> Pity for me and you, John-John,
> I could not bear. (55)

Bryan MacMahon is virtually the tinkers' laureate in his novels, *Children of the Rainbow* and, especially, *The Honey Spike*.

In approaching Synge's *The Tinker's Wedding*, then, with its conflict between a priest, who should be the exemplar of the putative virtues of the settled community, and tinkers, who are wayward and outcast, it is well to remember, not only the possible range of literary versions of tinkers, but that, on balance, even when they are negative, they may be less negative than parallel versions of some settled community. Further, much of the time it is some characters whose vision is negative, and not the authors, who are quite likely to reproach a smug and vaunting respectability by showing the tinkers' world as an acceptable alternative, and sometimes even a superior one. Frequently authors develop their satire by selecting details both from observation of tinker life and from a kind of received mythology of tinker life vis-à-vis that of the settled population.

It is worth considering the real-life disharmony that makes its way into Synge's play. Observation and common sense tell us that tinkers and settled community share the blame for their separation. As what is probably Ireland's smallest but most visible native minority, tinkers have been scrutinized by social scientists, who have chronicled a cycle of cause and effect: deprivation and resultant craftiness, followed by increased alienation from the settled community, succeeded by more mischief by tinkers and an ever-widening breach.

So it was, in June 1960, that a Commission on Itinerancy was established by the Irish government and charged with inquiring into the problem of "itinerancy"; more particularly, it was charged with promoting the absorption of itinerants into the settled population and, pending that, with reducing the disadvantages of itinerant life to both communities. (It is worth noting that while the government's commission used the term "itinerant" and the people these days speak of themselves as "travelers" or "traveling people," as do a number of quasiofficial bodies, the term "tinker" still has the widest currency and is invariably the word used in literature.) The *Report of the Commission on Itinerancy*, which is, by the way, an unusually readable piece of work for a document issuing from any government commission, was issued in August 1963, and it left no doubt that assimilation was its solution (though both settled population and tinkers might have other ideas), and that it could be accomplished by a series of slow, flexible, but quite explicit stages. The commission also seems to have inferred from available statistics that assimilation would be hastened by the natural attrition of the tinker population—an inference, however innocently drawn, that would have fired the indignation of the author of *A Modest Proposal*.

A December 1960 census undertaken by the commission recorded 1,198 itinerant families consisting of 6,591 persons; and citing a declining number of itinerants since earlier surveys, the commission concluded "that the number of itinerants in the country has not varied greatly in the past 20 years and that, contrary to statements otherwise, their numbers have decreased in recent years" (35). However, as reported in the *Irish Times* in an article by Mary Maher on October 16, 1978, the most recent report by the National Council for Travelling People found 1,953 itinerant families, 755 more than in 1960, with 854 families still on the road. To what might have been the astonishment of the government's commission, the *Times* report observed:

In proportion to their numbers, travellers are establishing new households at four and five times the rate of the settled community. . . . It's not impossible that by 1988 . . . there will be perhaps 4,700 travelling families in Ireland, a population of roughly 23,000, nearly four times what it was in 1963. (12)

Under the auspices of the Economic and Social Research Institute, David B. Rottman and associates issued, in July 1986, a report titled, *The Population Structure and Living Circumstances of Irish Travelers: Results from the 1981 Census of Traveller Families*, with the news that in 1981 there were 2,432 traveller families of about 14,821 persons, with 5,946 individuals—or 42.1 percent—of all travellers still on the road (23). It is interesting to intersect these figures with an observation from the commission's 1963 report, which is typical of its thesis that assimilation must, and will, occur:

While it is appreciated that difficulties and objections will be met in early years from many members of the settled population, it is not considered that there is any alternative to a positive drive for housing itinerants if a permanent solution of the problem of itinerancy, based on absorption and integration, is to be achieved. (62)

How that "permanent solution" chills—and suggests in its official tone what the conflict between tinkers and the settled community has been.

It is revealing to contrast that formal insistence on integration with a rather scanty, but somehow telling, survey taken in "Ballybran" in County Kerry and reported in 1979 by Nancy Scheper-Hughes in her *Saints, Scholars, and Schizophrenics: Mental Illness in Rural Ireland*. On a "Village Occupations Hierarchy Scale,'' forty-eight secondary school students ranked tinkers dead last (the doctor came first) (51–52). Moreover, if it is thought that Dubliners might be more tolerant than their ''down-country'' cousins, Michael MacGreil's monumental 1977 study, *Prejudice and Tolerance in Ireland*, revealed that Dubliners have precious little tolerance and are far from ready for absorption. For example, on an overall scale of acceptability of seventy distinct groups, tinkers ranked fifty-sixth; excluding various racial and political groups, only criminals, drug users, and drug pushers ranked lower (233).

All of this more-or-less objective material about a real-life gulf reflects, and helps explain, the ease with which literary characters slip into mere name calling and suggests why writers have frequently used tinkers in their romantic quest to poise what they may only imagine to be the free and instinctive life of tinkers against the repressions of settled life. Thus we come to *The Tinker's Wedding*, where the most extreme conflict in Synge's plays—often comical, to be sure, but still charged with mutual animus—works itself out. Rosemarie A. Battaglia summarized the plot this way:

> The play consists of two acts. The setting is in Ballinaclash in Wicklow. . . . The characters are Michael Byrne, a tinker; Mary Byrne, his mother, an old woman; Sarah Casey, a young tinker woman; and a priest. Both acts take place at a roadside near the village. It is the month of May. Briefly stated, the play consists of a confrontation between the tinkers and the priest, both of whom represent a separate world. Sarah, who has been the longtime companion of Michael and who has borne him children, now wants to be married by a priest to be legitimized as the wife of Michael Byrne. Sarah expresses a longing for the world the priest represents to her, a world she does not know but which Mary describes mockingly. . . . A bargain is struck between the tinkers and the priest, who agrees to marry Sarah to Michael, provided he receive payment of a gallon can, the product of the tinkers' work, and ten shillings. The bargain is abrogated because Mary has traded the gallon can for a bit of drink and places three empty bottles and straw in its place. When the priest returns the next day to perform the ceremony, his anger is provoked when the empty bottles fall from the bundle supposedly keeping the can. The priest refuses to marry the couple, throwing the ten shillings on the ground. The contract has been ruptured, and the tinkers gag and tie the priest in sacking. . . . The tinkers fear discovery by peelers to whom the priest begins to shout, and the priest is then unbound and ungagged by them. At his freedom he promises not to inform on them. Sarah places her intended wedding ring on the priest's finger and the tinkers gather up their things. The priest, now free, utters a Latin malediction and the tinkers scatter. (62)

Clearly, this priest, who is no apple of God's eye, strays some distance from the priestly ideal into an unacceptable stereotype; on the other hand, the tinkers, despite some comical and energizing antics, virtually epitomize the tinker archetype, then as now. Thus, while Synge's aim is doubtless to contrast cultures for some corrective purpose, Irish audiences probably would have seen it as a contrast between equally unattractive alternatives, and so, perhaps, only confusing, or even pointless.

Critics generally agree on the central conflict but, naturally enough, differ widely on its intensity and significance. For instance, Weldon Thornton straight-forwardly observed that "the dramatic and psychological interest of the play grows largely out of the interplay of two cultures poised against one another" (19), while Battaglia made it all a bit, well, rarified in contending that "the entire aim of Synge, in form and meaning, then, in *The Tinker's Wedding*, is to destroy abstract Western categorical modes of thought, feeling, and behavior in a dramatic enactment that creates a solution to his own inner drama" (66)— which perhaps lays too heavy an onus on so slight a vessel.

Synge began *The Tinker's Wedding* in the summer of 1902. Since he was simultaneously working on *The Shadow of the Glen* and *Riders to the Sea*, the latter a stipulated masterpiece, *Tinker's* is not mere apprentice work. Rather, the fact that Synge worked with it through several versions, revising characteriza-tions of the priest, the tinkers, and their interactions until it was published in 1907, argues for a struggle to find appropriate expression for what he knew was a chancy enterprise that, on balance, does not succeed. She was speaking of another play, but Lady Augusta Gregory, an astute enough observer of the Irish drama scene, was, as reported by Ann Saddlemyer, on the mark when she said, "a priest on the stage is risky" (xv). This is risky enough with any priest, but it is volatile when he is a bit of a rogue to begin with and then mixes it up with renegade tinkers who, all in all, get the better of him—and this the scenario for a theater that had already heard alarums over other threats to Irish household gods in Yeats's *The Countess Cathleen* and Synge's own *The Shadow of the Glen*.

Here, then, is a priest who is not entirely blameworthy from the perspective of several decades later. For instance, he plays the role he should play in wanting to marry Sarah and Michael so that Sarah will not be like the unrepentant Mary. Similarly, his fear of the bishop and his envy of the free and easy life of the tinkers resonate for those weary of endless rounds of onerous duties. Still, he is compounded mostly of images of the fat and drinking—if not jolly—friar and the fat, avaricious, and hypocritical priest. As Michael says of him: "It's often his reverence does be [at the doctor's house] playing cards, or drinking a sup, or singing songs, until the dawn of day" (13), and he may have an un-seemly interest in watching the girls. Joining the tinkers with some reluctance and resignation to their pleas, he makes a toast and drinks with them and, as the verbal violence that accelerates and escalates between them passes over into physical violence, he lays angry hands on Michael.

Ann Saddlemyer traced a paper trail of letters strewn by Yeats and Synge between 1905 and 1908 that attests to their awareness of this new threat to propriety; for example, Yeats: "too dangerous for the theatre to present"; Synge: "they say it is too immoral for Dublin"; Synge: "it is thought too immoral and anticlerical" (xiii–xvi). Furthermore, Synge's persistent discomfi-ture is reflected in two prefaces (there were also other drafts). One, unpublished;

dated November 20, 1907, and reported in a note by Ann Saddlemyer, amounts to a sort of apology to Ireland's Catholic priests:

I do not think these country clergy, who have so much humour—and so much heroism that everyone who has seen them facing typhus or dangerous seas for the comfort of their people on the coasts of the west must acknowledge—will mind being laughed at for half an hour without malice, as the clergy in every Roman Catholic country were laughed at through the ages that had real religion. (3–4)

Since Synge's particular priest has neither humor nor heroism, his praise of Irish priests has a hollow ring to it and appears directed less at priests whom he might offend than at audiences in order to forestall the potential hostile reaction implied in the letters.

The concluding paragraph of the published ''Preface'' takes up and varies from the draft version:

In the greater part of Ireland . . . the whole people, from the tinkers to the clergy, have still a life, and view of life, that are rich and genial and humorous. I do not think that these country people, who have so much humour themselves, will mind being laughed at without malice, as the people in every country have been laughed at in their own comedies. (3)

Gone are the Irish priests' courage and their non-Irish confreres' willingness to be laughed at. Added are the Irish tinkers, who are placed at the antipodes of the priests. We cannot be sure that Synge meant to include with the priests' lives the tinkers' lives, their view of life as ''rich and genial and humorous,'' and the fact that they were willing to be laughed at. It is no matter, however, because one suspects that there is no way that Synge was going to worry that tinkers, who would never read nor see the play to begin with, would be offended (or, given their real-life ghettoization, would be offended if they could read or see it). Nor would most actual readers and audiences worry about offense given to tinkers. On balance, the purpose here is the same as for the draft version— to forestall the outrage of those who would, for the most part, agree with Daniel Corkery's assessment:

Only a coarse-grained hobbledehoy could relish either the character-drawing of the priest or the general shindy in which *The Tinker's Wedding* ends. . . . To judge by his passing remarks on them, the priests he met with in his travels he seemed to like; it is nevertheless true that no one reared in an Irish Catholic household would dream of creating a similar figure, unless of course he were, like Liam O'Flaherty, a mere sensationalist, for he would know that such a character would not be accepted. (150–52)

What is the source of Synge's priest? We will never know for sure, nor will we know if leaving him nameless was Synge's device for rendering him as a type. Synge's Anglican background—several of his kin had been Anglican clerics and some, bishops—and the loss of his own religious faith when he was about fourteen may have left him with some indifference, but probably no animosity, to the religion of his Catholic countrymen. He may well have not etched his portrait of the priest with intended malice; on the other hand, as some have thought, he may have written out of an ingenuous lack of understanding of the Irish Catholics' depth of feeling about their faith and—for public consumption, at any rate—their attachment to their priests. As Vivian Mercier has observed, "I don't suppose any Irishman today would accuse Synge of malice. At most he can be blamed for lack of empathy or lack of tact" (88). Still, Synge's treatment of priests elsewhere is different enough to note.

Synge's two other plays in which action and characters are about contemporaneous with the lives of their first audiences—*Riders to the Sea* and *The Playboy of the Western World*—have off-stage priests whose roles have some bearing on the plays' themes. Commentators customarily note that *Riders*' concluding tableau enacts Synge's vision of Aran's blend of Christianity and paganism, and they sometimes note that the characters' repeated, pious ejaculations such as, "The son of God forgive us," "By the grace of God," "God spare his soul," and "God speed you," for example, are at odds with the total absence of the island priest who, when mentioned at all, is always "the young priest," and so doubly distanced from the islanders' ethos by his particular faith and by his youth. Thus, for instance, when Nora says to Kathleen, "Didn't the young priest say the Almighty God won't leave [Maurya] destitute with no son living?" Maurya, who has overheard her, replies, "It's little the like of him knows of the sea" (21).

Perhaps Irish Catholic audiences of *Playboy* were appalled to learn, in Act III, when Michael James and his cronies return from Kate Cassidy's wake, that there were "flows of drink" and that "there were five men, aye, and six men, stretched out retching speechless on the holy stones" (151). However, Father Reilly, who may be supposed to have frowned on these didoes, like the young priest, never appears on stage either. Furthermore, like Mrs. Grundy, whose priggish views are made known only by other characters saying, "What would Mrs. Grundy say?" and "What would Mrs. Grundy think?" he is the voice of conventional morality, as represented on stage by the timorous Shawn Keogh, Pegeen's betrothed, who says (*with plaintive despair*), " 'I'm afeard of Father Reilly, I'm saying' " (65).

Neither the young priest nor Father Reilly has done anything wrong, except perhaps by omission. It is just that they represent attitudes and beliefs irrelevant to situations as understood by other characters, and probably by Synge as well. As such, they are only disembodied voices from the wings, as, in a way, are other Irish priests in some fiction of about the same period who were not on so public a display as a stage. Father Purdon in *Dubliners'* "Grace," for example, is James Joyce's venal urban priest, and Father Madden, of "Julia Cahill's Curse" from *The Untilled Field*, is George Moore's power-abusing and repressive rural priest. However, as Lady Gregory might have observed, here in *The*

Tinker's Wedding, Synge's priest is literally at center stage, at the very heart of evolving action and absolutely relevant to whatever point Synge wants to make by putting him up against the tinkers, who are just what Irish audiences would have expected them to be. Where did the tinkers come from?

Shortly after Synge's death, Yeats wrote of his friend: "He loves all that has edge, all that is salt in the mouth, all that is rough to the hand, all that heightens the emotions by contest, all that stings into life the sense of tragedy" (326–27). Thus, Synge wrote of the Irish "folk"—the Aran Islanders; those in the Congested Districts, West Kerry, and the Blaskets; the dwellers in Wicklow's glens; the habitués of a Mayo *shebeen*. Moreover, he wrote of Wicklow's "vagrants," a term he sometimes used and that Harold Orel used in his 1972 essay, "Synge's Concept of the Tramp":

John Millington Synge's fascination with tramps—with the character of the vagrant—is obvious enough. . . . Synge . . . did not differentiate between tinkers and gypsies and other travellers. Others may have called these people by the generic term "tramps," but Synge blanketed them with the name "vagrants." (55)

Did he really mean for there to be no distinction? After all, in his letters to his beloved, Molly Allgood ("Maire O'Neill"), he regularly signed himself, "Your old Tramp," "The Tramp," "Your old Tramper," "J. M. Tramp," "Ever your Tramp," and so on, but never "Your old Tinker" or "Your old Vagrant."

In 1975, Nicholas Grene contended that although Synge tended to blur distinctions between tramps and tinkers in his Wicklow pieces, they were in fact different, with the distinction being shown between the admirable tramp of *The Shadow of the Glen* and the tinkers of *The Tinker's Wedding*. Grene has argued, for example, that the tramps had always been lone wanderers, whereas tinkers were members of families. Additionally, as "agriculture laborers" and "professional drovers," tramps could be an accepted part of a rural community, while tinkers "were always genuine outcasts [with] an age-old reputation for dishonesty." Furthermore, the "mutual suspicion and dislike" between tinkers and settled population "could, on occasion, ignite into open conflict" (88–89). A careful rereading of the Wicklow pieces supports the distinction, which is an important one.

For instance, in "People and Places," one old tramp (like most tramps Synge encountered) has "the humour of talk and ideas of a certain distinction." Tramps are admired as "vigorous men and women of fine physique." They rarely commit crimes, and Synge had never seen one "drunk or unseemly," and if treated with "tact," they are "courteous and forbearing" and marked by "freshness of wit" (195–97). In "The Vagrants of Wicklow," Synge's tramps are distinguished by "vitality" and "an occasional temperament of distinction," and he observed that their way of life conferred on them "many privileges," including "good humour and fine bodily health" (202). Finally, for example, also in "The Vagrants of Wicklow," Synge contended that

In all circumstances of this tramp life there is a certain wildness that gives it romance and a peculiar value for those who look at life in Ireland with an eye that is aware of the arts also. In all the healthy movements of art, variations from the ordinary types of manhood are made interesting for the ordinary man, and in this way only the higher arts are universal. (208)

On the other hand, though Synge sometimes looked favorably on tinkers—for example, in "People and Places," an old tinker woman and "two beautiful children, are a precious possession for any country" (199)—much more frequently, the contrast with tramps leaves them wanting. In one tinker camp in the same essay, for instance, Synge noted piles of "hay and sacking and harness that is literally crawling with half-naked children" (198). On another occasion, reported in "At a Wicklow Fair," Synge spied "the usual camp of tinkers, where a swarm of children had been left to play among the carts while the men and women wandered through the fair selling cans and donkeys" (227–28). Soon after, in the same piece, Synge noted that "before [a ballad singer] had finished a tinker arrived, too drunk to stand or walk, but leading a tall horse with his left hand, and inviting anyone who would deny that he was the best horseman in Wicklow to fight him on the spot" (229).

The germ for Synge's play is to be found in "At a Wicklow Fair," where he reported—that is, he did not know from personal observation—the anecdote told him by a herdsman about a tinker who has just left their company:

That man is a great villain. . . . One time he and his woman went up to a priest in the hills and asked him would he wed them for half a sovereign, I think it was. The priest said it was a poor price, but he'd wed them surely if they'd make him a tin can along with it. "I will, faith," said the tinker, "and I'll come back when it's done." They went off then, and in three weeks they came back, and they asked the priest a second time would he wed them. "Have you the tin can?" said the priest. "We have not," said the tinker; "we had it made at the fall of night, but the ass gave it a kick this morning the way it isn't fit for you at all." "Go on now," says the priest. "It's a pair of rogues and schemers you are, and I won't wed you at all." They went off then, and they were never married to this day. (228–29)

If we add to this the following passage from "The Vagrants of Wicklow," we have virtually the material Synge brought from his prose writings to the composition of *The Tinker's Wedding*. In this passage, too, Synge reports what someone else has told him about tinker matchmaking and a breach in conventional sexual morality:

One time I seen fifty of them gathered above on the road to Rathdangan, and they all match-making and marrying themselves for the year that was to come. One man would take such a woman, and say he was going such roads and places, stopping at this fair and another fair, till he'd meet them again at such a place, when the spring was coming on. Another, maybe, would swap a woman he'd had with one from another man, with as much talk as if you'd be selling a cow. It's two hours I was there watching them from the bog beneath, where I was cutting turf, and the like of the crying and the kissing, and the singing and the shouting began when they went off this way and that way, you never heard in your life. (204)

Whatever Synge's intentions, it is a fairly good guess that he meant to draw a paradigm of Irish "tinkerhood" from a variety of sources—personal observation, the reports of others, and the body of tinker lore from which other writers down to our own time have drawn—and that he knew that, so far as his audience was concerned, there would be little disbelief to suspend. Here is the gist of it, and a good deal continues to hold true.

To begin with, there is appearance—details at which an audience would have nodded, saying that Synge had them just right. For example, the tinkers' clothing is ragged, and Mary accuses Sarah of actually washing her face. Playing both the shrewd tinker game and the poor mouth, Sarah wheedles and whines when she first approaches the priest. His life experience leads him to expect her to beg; she does not, but it comes to the same thing because she wants him to marry her and Michael for nothing. He refuses, but Sarah gets the best of the bargain when he agrees to accept ten shillings and a gallon tin can. Later, the priest threatens to tell the peelers (police) that the tinkers have stolen hay and a black ass; and at one point, Sarah and Michael go off to steal Tim Flaherty's hens. The truth is not in their mouths, but larcenous trickery is in their souls. For example, the can that is part of the deal is temporarily put in a sack but is then stolen—to sell to pay for porter—by Mary, who, as we have seen, substitutes three empty porter bottles and straw. Indeed, drink drives Mary, a right old reprobate who is drunk or near to it for most of the play. She probably characterizes the priest right enough as "droughty," but it is she who tempts him with drink and leads him, reluctantly, to join and drink with her.

On the subject of the play's title, Michael's opening speeches are delivered "gloomily," "grimly," and "glumly" (by contrast, when Sarah first approaches the priest, it is "eagerly"). He is worried that Sarah will be "dragging [him] to the priest this night" (7), but he is also worried that, if they do not set the sacred seal on their long-illicit union, she, who rather fancies herself, will run off with rich tinkers or with another tinker man, the legendary and flashy Jaunting Jim, who, Sarah reminds Michael, has named her "the Beauty of Ballinacree" (11). In an ironic twist on maternal solicitude, Michael declares that his mother would not want him to marry, and Mary repeatedly shows that he is right. Finally, for example, Michael resents making a wedding ring, symbol of what he wants to avoid, because it takes him away from making cans, symbol of what he wants to cleave to.

Sarah's attitudes toward, and motives for, marriage are mixed, but on the whole, they appear frivolous. For one thing, they often seem the merest whim, an antic disposition teased out by a May change of the moon; indeed, an early alternative title for the play was *Movements of May*. For example, she says that it is spring and that she has been having "queer thoughts" (7), and Mary warns Michael: "Oh! isn't she a terror since the moon did change" (31). On a more serious level, Sarah says she wants the church's blessing on her union, not from any profound conviction of its moral and spiritual efficacy, but for the show of respectability. Additionally, there is an intimation that she and Michael have already had one or more children. In the first two minutes, Michael says to her: "You to be going beside me a great while, and rearing a lot of them, and then to be setting off with your talk of getting married, and your driving me to it, and I not asking it at all" (7), which may be why Sarah wants marriage. Either way, her loose living arrangement and possible willingness to dissolve even that to run off with Jaunting Jim led Corkery to brand her a "doxy" (147), an epithet with which audiences probably would have agreed. While Sarah sometimes seems to weaken a bit in face of opposition from Mary and Michael, early in Act II she is all ferocity about getting married, and she delivers ultimatums to the priest. Still, and almost as much by whim as her sudden earlier passion to marry, she reverts to type, puts the wedding ring on the priest's finger, and joins the others in punishing him.

As to knowledge about priests and church, Sarah is innocent of what will actually happen in church should she and Michael come to that. Again, her concern is with appearances; for instance, she tutors Michael on dress and conduct: "You'll find a kind of a red handkerchief to put upon your neck, and a green one for myself," and "let you not forget to take your hat from your head when we go up into the church. I asked Biddy Flynn below, that's after marrying her second man, and she told me it's like of that they [regular churchgoers] do" (29).

Mary is more antagonistic than Sarah to priests and the church, and her theme song, which is sung when she enters and exits in Act I, is "The Night before Larry Was Stretched":

> And when we asked him what way he'd die,
>   And he hanging unrepented,
> "Begob," says Larry, "that's all in my eye,
>   By the clergy first invented." (17)

And with "heathen" as Mary's motif, her views carry the day. Tinkers, she tells the priest, neither know prayers nor need priests, and she adds that as a young woman, she, too, had nothing to do with them. Further, she avers, all that she knows about church she has learned from Biddy Flynn, Sarah's mentor in such matters. Under Mary's influence, even the avid prospective bride comes to harangue and insult the priest, saying, for example, "I'm thinking the ten shillings in gold is a good price for the like of you, and you near burst with the fat" (43). Mary herself retreats into superstition, such as yelling at Sarah that Sarah is a "weathered heathen savage," who "quenched the flaming candles on the throne of God the time [her] shadow fell within the pillars of the chapel door'' (33).

Finally, rounding off Synge's catalogue of Irish tinker transgressions is the strong current of violence or threat of violence that runs throughout the play, born of the tinkers' inherent lawlessness and the tensions between their world and the priest's and fueled by an atmosphere in which drink sets free what few inhibitions remain.

Among the tinkers themselves, violence is always near the surface and often spills over. Sarah, for example, surprisingly—but perhaps not, given the marked passion with which she pursues her whimsical determination to marry—sometimes seems the most unbridled. She is no blushing bride-to-be. Act II reveals these few examples from among many: In addition to several threats to strike Mary, Sarah takes after her with hammer-and-tongs or, in this case, hammer-and-bottle. She pushes Mary, who declares she would feel safer with the peelers than with Sarah; another time, Mary hides behind the priest to escape Sarah; yet again, she declares she would feel safer in church than within Sarah's reach—all these fears from Mary, who is the most renegade of them all, tell us something about Sarah's fierceness.

In Act II, it is, finally, the priest against whom the accumulating and accelerating violence is aimed; this may account for Synge and his associates' greatest fear about an audience's reaction, that a priest, however blemished, is deeply humiliated by outlaw tinkers. Forgetting her fury against Mary for thwarting her wedding plans, Sarah turns on the priest and roars: "I've bet [beaten] a power of strong lads east and west through the world, and are you thinking I'd turn back from a priest? Leave the road now, or maybe I would strike yourself" (43). Then, in rapid succession, Michael threatens to beat the priest, who loses his temper and shoves Michael, who in turn runs at him, reins in hand, while Mary, calling for Michael to knock the priest down, claps a hand over his mouth. After Michael pulls him down, he is gagged with the sack that had held the tin can, tied, and put in some sacking, and Michael threatens to put him in a bog hole so that "he'll not be tattling to the peelers" (47). Saved by the approach of the peelers and an oath not to tell them of the day's mischief, the priest is released, Sarah puts the wedding ring on his finger, and she declares to him: "It'll be a long day till I go making talk of marriage or the like of that" (49). True to his oath, the priest does not tell the peelers, but he does intone against the tinkers "*a Latin malediction in a loud ecclesiastical voice,*" while the tinkers flee, "*leaving the priest the master of the situation*" (49).

But is he the master of the situation, or is Synge's stage direction the sop his "Preface" seems to be, to mollify indignation at the treatment of the priest? During his physical trial, the priest is also subjected to the further humiliation of having to listen to Mary's sermon (which is perhaps Synge's own) on the lessons of the day, and it is likely that this reproof lingers longer than the priest as "*master of the situation,*" a stage direction, after all, that no audience would see any more than the "Preface":

Be quiet, your reverence. What is it ails you, with your wrigglings now? It is choking maybe? [*She puts her hand under the sack, and feels his mouth, patting him on the back.*] It's only letting on you are, holy father, for your nose is blowing back and forward as easy as an east wind on an April day. [*In a soothing voice.*] There now, holy father, let you stay easy, I'm telling you, and learn a little sense and patience, the way you'll not be so airy again going to rob poor sinners of their scraps of gold. [*He gets quieter.*] That's a good boy you are now, your reverence, and let you not be uneasy, for we wouldn't hurt you at all. It's sick and sorry we are to tease you; but what did you want with meddling with the like of us, when it's a long time we are going our own ways— father and son, and his son after him, or mother and daughter, and her own daughter again—and it's little need we ever had of going up into a church and swearing—I'm told there's swearing with it—a word no man would believe, or with drawing rings on our fingers, would be cutting our skins maybe when we'd be taking the ass from the shafts, and pulling the straps the time they'd be slippy with going around beneath the heavens in rains falling. (47)

This speech will appeal to those (including many other writers of a similar bent and similar goals, both earlier and more recently) who propose an idealized version of tinkers' lives, and it may represent Synge's romantic view of the gulf between the free and easy tinkers and the complacent and materialistic priest, but it does not fully accord with the facts of the play as Synge has set them out. For instance, the priest does not seek out the tinkers; rather than the priest interfering with their way of life, they interfere with his when he seeks to avoid them. Further, whatever attractions these tinkers may sometimes have, they do not accord with Synge's essentially dim view in the Wicklow pieces, so there is a kind of selectivity being exercised—legitimate, to be sure—for the sake of a satiric point.

To understand better how Synge drew, not only on his personal observations and the reports of others in the Wicklow essays, but also, quite probably, on a kind of received lore about tinkers, it is worthwhile to see what some other twentieth-century Irish writers have done with the same resources and, often, with similar intentions. Frequently, the tinker is simply a foil—sometimes comic, sometimes social, sometimes moral—to the settled community; very often, indeed, the tinker seems to serve as a symbol with which to reproach the settled population and as an emblem of some illusory and elusive freedom, which in real life may carry a terrible price. Three fairly fluid categories—there are others—will illustrate these generalizations.

In the first category, the tinker, a social outcast, is a ready symbol of both the antithesis of the "Big House"—in the secular realm having something of the putative authority of the clergy in the spiritual order—and its fall. Serving as vehicles of revelation in two examples are more or less romantic encounters between a member of a Big House and a tinker.

Jennifer Johnston's novel, *The Gates*, offers a paradigm of Irish social classes. Major Frank MacMahon and his niece, Minnie, reside at the Big House of Gortnanee, County Donegal, in about 1970. Big Jim Breslin represents the middle class, and the Kellys are tenants. Kelly is a brutal, lustful sot. His wife is a tinker, and their son Kevin declares: "I hate her, too. Dirty tinker, snivelling in corners" (106). However, she is here not simply to represent the lowest social order; Minnie uses her to demonstrate the problems of rigid class distinctions and, perhaps, to forecast their end. When Minnie (the child of a son of the Big House and a Catholic shopgirl) shows interest in Kevin (the child of a tinker and a tenant), Ivy, the housekeeper, tries to keep her in her place. Look, says Minnie, "How do you know my mother wasn't a tinker, too?" and while the Major writhes in distress, she adds: "So don't pull the class angle on me. Maybe I'm finding my own level" (146).

Sean O'Faolain's short story, "Midsummer Night Madness," is set in County Cork during the Black-and-Tan period. The story's narrator, John, is on a military mission to decrepit Henn Hall, the Big House of the ancient libertine, Alexander Henn, to learn why Stevie Lang, the local Irish commandant, who is billeted at Henn Hall, has not been active for several months. Recalling his youth near Henn Hall, John wonders if old Henn still has his pick of fashionable women. "Perhaps," John thinks,

the travelling tinker-women would have to suffice? But thinking of the big Red House, with its terraced lawns, and its cypresses and its views, and its great five-mile estate wall, all built by the first Henn . . . , I could not believe that even such a house would fall so low. (5)

Arriving at Henn Hall, however, John discovers that not only is there a tinker woman—Gypsy Gammele—in residence but that she is with child by Stevie Lang and shows a marked fondness for old Henn. Stung into action by John, Stevie and his men burn out another Big House family, the Blakes, and Stevie threatens to burn Henn Hall, too, unless Henn marries the pregnant Gypsy. Much of O'Faolain's point seems to be that Stevie, who should represent the aspirations of a new and more just Ireland, can prove his patriotism only by burning out helpless old people and by forcing Henn, a Big House relic, to marry a pregnant tinker—the ultimate degradation, apparently, for an Anglo-Irish aristocrat. Having touched bottom, Henn nevertheless salvages more than the feckless Stevie: "I'm going to marry her," says Henn. "She's as good as the next, and better than some, even though she *is* only a tinker's daughter. Besides," he adds, "if it's a boy 'twill keep the family name alive" (34).

In *The Tinker's Wedding*, Mary's substitution of the empty porter bottles for the can is a stunt to achieve her own ends and suggests a second category: the tinker as trickster, flimflam man, or hustler, someone we are invited to be amused by because of his cleverness, and sometimes expected to admire, and perhaps applaud, because he confounds authority and power figures by a combination of duplicity and naivete. It is less that the tinkers are themselves admirable or better than the settled community than that their creators have made them, on the whole, more likable than their strawman adversaries. Patrick

Boyle's "Myko" and Seumas O'Kelly's "The Can with the Diamond Notch" are short stories that illustrate these points.

Patrick Boyle's character, Myko, is a publican, a funeral undertaker, and an infamous skinflint; he also hates tinkers. Naturally, then, we are not surprised to learn that when old Maggot Feeney, head of "a notorious band of tinkers" (89), dies, his son, Cracker, seeks out Myko to make funeral arrangements. The adversaries are doomed to clash, and a week's maneuvering with the body brings the long-dead Maggot to Myko's back shed, where, smelled out by Myko, he will have to be buried by him. Myko's amused curate explains to him the final indignity:

The Feeney clan'll be doing a pilgrimage . . . to old Maggot's grave every year . . . and tinkers from every art and part . . . will be lined along the bar counter . . . drinking and fighting and smashing bottles and glasses . . . to do honour to the decent man that buried the Maggot Feeney. (98)

The power figure in Seumas O'Kelly's "The Can with the Diamond Notch" is Festus Clasby, gombeen-man. Large and powerful, self-righteous and authoritarian, inspiring awe and reverence, at the end of the story, "His soft velvety eyes were suddenly flooded with a bitter emotion and he wept" (29)—because he has been utterly outwitted and stripped of goods by yet another band of tinkers, led by Mac-an-Ward, the Son of the Bard, who is spare, nimble, and imaginative. O'Kelly expects us to applaud the deflation of so powerful a figure as this particular gombeen-man by so clever and charming a tinker, and doubtless we do applaud, because it is a comical story and O'Kelly has made his stock figure overripe for plucking. Twenty percent of the story, at its opening, goes to a detailed elaboration of a figure—Festus—who could instead have been characterized as economically as the tinker, had O'Kelly's purpose been only to introduce him as the tinker's adversary. However, Festus, a caricature, is O'Kelly's target; he does not want us to miss this, and he relies on a stylized tinker to bring him down. True, Mac-an-Ward has the tongue of a poet, but so bloated with hubris is Festus that a witty child could have reduced him to tears.

The third category finds women playing a role analogous to the male trickster: that of the woman tinker as sexual temptress and as a symbol of mystery, romance, and liberation, of whom Synge's Sarah is a rather pale version. These women are voluptuous and promiscuous. O'Faolain's Gypsy Gammele is dark and aggressive; already pregnant, she and Stevie make love in John's presence, and she dallies with old Henn. The eighteen- or nineteen-year-old tinker who lures Denny, the sexton, in Bryan MacMahon's "The Cat and the Cornfield" is "mature [,] . . . wild and lissom" (140); she has "wild fair hair and a nut-brown complexion," and when she spies Denny "her eyes [gleam] with puckish pleasure" (141). A tinker in Liam O'Flaherty's short story, "The Tent," has two wives, "both of them slatterns, dirty and unkempt, but with [a] proud, arrogant, contemptuous look in their beautiful brown faces"; the golden-haired one of the pair, the story's temptress, is six feet tall, "surpassingly beautiful, in spite of her ragged clothes and the foul condition of her hair" (110), and of soft body, but, to the stranger to whom she is about to yield, she "bare[s] her teeth in a savage grin and pinion[s] his arms with a single movement" (113). The tinker woman in William Cotter Murray's novel, *Michael Joe*, has, like all her sisters in these stories, dark skin, and her dark hair is "slightly matted, unkempt, uncombed"; her voice is "sensuous, lingering, half-wheedling, half-caressing"; her walk is the "walk of another race of women from warmer climates" (211). Her sloe-colored eyes frisk, look "frankly and directly," and then stop "playing the looking game and [start] playing the burning one" (212).

In these stories, the men who are tempted are, or have been, figures of moderate circumstances and respectability: a military man and a seedy aristocrat, a church sexton, a recently discharged sergeant-major, and a moderately successful shopkeeper, respectively. In three of the four stories—excepting O'Faolain's—the men are tempted beyond the ordinary, narrow circumstances of their lives and brought to the brink of what might be liberating sexual consummation, which is then denied them. All are caught and punished: the sexton mildly by the parish priest; the former sergeant-major by the tinker husband, who easily bests him in a fight; and Michael Joe McCarthy, the shopkeeper, by the tinker husband, who knocks out the two front teeth and leaves him bleeding copiously.

These men have further reactions to these encounters. The sergeant-major, who may be supposed to have had some experience with women, fails utterly to penetrate this mystery and marches off crossing himself and crying, "Almighty God!" every two yards. Denny, the middle-aged sexton, reaches the epiphany of knowing he is trapped; with images of a "known road stretching before his leaden legs" and of his "soul . . . as a pebble trapped in a wire mat of despair," he hears the distant sound of the tinker woman's harness bells as "a recessional song of adventure" (148). Murray's Michael Joe has the profoundest reaction, the deepest urge—it is sexual very probably, primitive certainly, and far from his shopkeeper's world. As the tinker woman sings to him in *shelta*:

There was something personal and impersonal about the song, both at the same time. He felt she was talking to him, singing it to him in what was like the voice of some animal or bird. The Sheela gave the song that touch of darkness. But at the same time, he felt himself being drawn into a world where he could not recognize himself. A world where he was a wild, roaming, animal, the world outside, her world where all the rules and laws and order were gone, and he was only himself, as if he were the first man born into the world and without guidance, and thrown entirely on his blood and what it told him to do. (213–14)

By no means does the intersection of the real and the fictional tinker woman cover all the cases where tinker life objectively observed and tinker life imagined cross—a review of the 1963 *Report of the Commission on Itinerancy*, George

Gmelch's *The Irish Tinkers: The Urbanization of an Itinerant People* (1977), *The Report of the Travelling People Review Body* (1983), and David B. Rottman and associates' *The Population Structure and Living Circumstances of Irish Travellers: Results from the 1981 Census of Traveller Families* (1986) is a good starting point for what cannot be done here—but it is illustrative of kinds of comparisons that might be made for the sake of further understanding what writers have frequently done with the same body of material and why.

Synge's Sarah is not as brazen as the tinker women of O'Faolain, MacMahon, O'Flaherty, and Murray, but her actions and her attitudes fairly put her in about the same camp. If she is not as voluptuous as the others, she remains, as do they, splendid symbols for the allure, mystery, and romance of a liberated life. Doubtless, there are sexual irregularities in tinker life as in any other; but Synge and the others seem to have departed somewhat from tinker norms for the sake of the symbol. For example, Gmelch observed that despite increasing strains on tinker marriages because of the dislocation of traditional tinker sex roles, "adultery on the part of Traveller women is not common" (121). Moreover, both Gmelch (125) and the commission report stressed the high value placed on premarital chastity, with the report observing: "All authorities are satisfied that itinerants have a high standard of sexual morality, and there is no evidence of promiscuity or a tendency towards indecency or immodesty" (90). Thus, even allowing for some exaggeration by the government commission, at least some of the literature suggests that writers have either had mild erotic fantasies of their own or created a type of tinker woman to chastise the strait-laced nature of the settled population.

In Bryan MacMahon's "The Cat and the Cornfield," there is a moment of classic confrontation that epitomizes the mystery at the heart of the meetings of tinker and settled community and those of the tinker and writer. Denny, the middle-aged, black-clad sexton asks the nubile, tartan-shawled girl: "Do you never tire of the road?" and she flashes back: "Do you never tire of being fettered?" Then MacMahon adds, "Both sighed fully and deeply" (142).

WORKS CITED

Battaglia, Rosemarie A. *"The Tinker's Wedding."* In *A J. M. Synge Literary Companion*, ed. Edward A. Kopper, Jr. Westport, Conn.: Greenwood Press, 1988, 61–67.

Boyle, Patrick. "Myko." In *At Night All Cats Are Grey and Other Stories*. New York: Grove Press, 1969, 89–98.

Commission on Itinerancy. *Report of the Commission on Itinerancy*. Dublin: Stationery Office, 1963.

Corkery, Daniel. *Synge and Anglo-Irish Literature*. 1931. Reprint. Cork: Mercier Press, 1966.

Farrell, James T. *Studs Lonigan*. New York: Avon Books, 1977.

Gmelch, George. *The Irish Tinkers: The Urbanization of an Itinerant People*. Menlo Park, Calif.: Cummings Publishing Company, 1977.

Grene, Nicholas. *Synge: A Critical Study of the Plays*. New York: Macmillan, 1975.

Johnston, Jennifer. *The Gates*. London: Hamish Hamilton, 1973.

Joyce, James. "Ivy Day in the Committee Room." In *Dubliners*. New York: Compass Books, 1958, 118–35.

Kavanagh, Patrick. "Pegasus." In *Collected Poems*. New York: W. W. Norton, 1964, 59–60.

Keane, John B. *The Field*. Cork: Mercier Press, 1966.

———. *Sive*. Dublin: Progress House, 1959.

MacDonagh, Thomas. *The 1916 Poets*. Dublin: Allen Figgis, 1963.

MacGreil, Michael. *Prejudice and Tolerance in Ireland*. College of Industrial Relations, Research Section, 1977.

Machen, Walter. *The Bogman*. London: Pan Books, Ltd., 1972.

MacMahon, Bryan. "The Cat and the Cornfield." In *Irish Stories and Tales*, ed. Devin A. Garrity. New York: Washington Square Press, 1961, 140–48.

Maher, Mary. "News Focus: Travellers." *Irish Times*, 16 Oct. 1978, 12.

Mercier, Vivian. "*The Tinker's Wedding*." In *A Centenary Tribute to John Millington Synge 1871–1909: Sunshine and the Moon's Delight*, ed. S. B. Bushrui. London: Colin Smythe, 1972, 75–88.

Moore, George. "Julia Cahill's Curse." In *The Untilled Field*. London: T. Fisher Unwin, 1903, 201–20.

Murphy, Richard. *High Island*. New York: Harper and Row, 1974.

Murray, William Cotter. *Michael Joe*. New York: Popular Library, 1965.

O'Faolain, Sean. "Midsummer Night Madness." In *The Finest Stories of Sean O'Faolain*. New York: Bantam Books, 1959, 1–34.

O'Flaherty, Liam. "The Tent." In *Selected Stories of Liam O'Flaherty*. London: New English Library, 1970, 108–14.

O'Kelly, Seumas. "The Can with the Diamond Notch." In *Irish Short Stories by Seumas O'Kelly*. Cork: Mercier Press, 1969, 7–29.

O'Neill, Eugene. *A Touch of the Poet*. New Haven, Conn.: Yale University Press, 1957.

Orel, Harold. "Synge's Concept of the Tramp." *Eire-Ireland* 7(2) (Spring 1972): 55–61.

Rottman, David B., A. Dale Tussing, and Miriam M. Wiley. *The Population Structure and Living Circumstances of Irish Travellers: Results from the 1981 Census of Traveller Families*. Dublin: Economic and Social Research Institute, July 1986.

Saddlemyer, Ann. "Introduction." In *J. M. Synge: Collected Works*. Vol. 4, *Plays, Book II*, ed. Ann Saddlemyer. London: Oxford University Press, 1968, xi–xxxiii.

Scheper-Hughes, Nancy. *Saints, Scholars, and Schizophrenics; Mental Illness in Rural Ireland*. Berkeley: University of California Press, 1979.

Synge, John Millington. "At a Wicklow Fair," "People and Places," "The Vagrants of Wicklow." In *J. M. Synge: Collected Works*. Vol. 2, *Prose*, ed. Alan Price. London: Oxford University Press, 1966, 193–201, 202–8, 225–29.

———. *Letters to Molly: John Millington Synge to Maire O'Neill*, ed. Ann Saddlemyer. Cambridge, Mass.: Belknap Press of Harvard University Press, 1971.

———. *The Playboy of the Western World*. In *J. M. Synge: Collected Works*. Vol. 4, *Plays, Book II*, ed. Ann Saddlemyer. London: Oxford University Press, 1968, 51–175.

———. *Riders to the Sea*. In *Collected Works*. Vol. 3, *Plays, Book I*, ed. Ann Saddlemyer. London: Oxford University Press, 1968, 1–27.

————. *The Tinker's Wedding*. In *Collected Works*. Vol. 4, *Plays, Book II*, ed. Ann Saddlemyer. London: Oxford University Press, 1968, 1–49.

Thornton, Weldon. *J. M. Synge and the Western Mind*. New York: Harper and Row, 1979.

Travelling People Review Body. *Report of the Travelling People Review Body*. Dublin: Stationery Office, February 1983.

Trevor, William. "Timothy's Birthday." *New Yorker*, 22 Feb. 1993, 143–49.

Yeats, William Butler. "J. M. Synge and the Ireland of His Time." In *Essays and Introductions*. New York: Macmillan, 1961, 311–42.

10

"Cute Thinking Women": The Language of Synge's Female Vagrants

Jane Duke Elkins

The wanderer or traveler as a predominant character type in J. M. Synge's drama has received some attention from scholars. Generally, scholars agree that Synge's wanderer moves outside settled society, that his presence creates conflict for the Irish peasantry, and that his lifestyle, as presented onstage, has surprised, and even shocked, audiences.[1] The wanderer is also called the tramp, vagrant, beggar, tinker, and traveler.[2] Because the term *vagrant* denotes a wanderer and has connotations of the excluded or outcast, I primarily use that term but do make recourse to the other synonyms.

The vagrant may seem, in the popular mind, to be the lonely, degenerate hobo, but in *The Shadow of the Glen, The Well of the Saints*, and *The Tinker's Wedding*, Synge pairs the vagrant with a female companion and, in the latter play, forms a family consisting of a mother, her son, and his female partner. Synge treats the women vagrants—Nora Burke in *The Shadow of the Glen*, Mary Doul in *The Well of the Saints*, and Mary Byrne and Sarah Casey in *The Tinker's Wedding*—in as much detail as he does the men. These female vagrants are liberated from the social constraints usually placed on Victorian women, for the female vagrants, except for Nora Burke before her decision to travel, are not bound to a fixed home life with its responsibilities of cleaning house, cooking meals, and tending the garden and livestock. Nor must these women worry, while they accompany other travelers, about social conventions of ''proper'' female behavior. The female vagrants can express attraction to men unabashedly and indulge in pastimes previously reserved for men, like drinking in pubs or attending such events as fairs without chaperones or escorts, as Mary Byrne does in *The Tinker's Wedding*, for instance.

The freedom of these female vagrants constrains them, however, in other ways. They live very uncertain, tenuous lives. Although living outside the bounds of society frees them *from* the social conventions placed on Victorian women, their lifestyle fails to free them *for* the construction of alternative, autonomous, and meaningful existences. Instead, these women are bound to male companions who may not respect them and whose "road," whether smooth or rough, the women must follow. In these three plays, the female traveler's desire to stabilize her life is primarily accomplished through strong imaginative language, which sometimes undercuts itself and shows the instability of her life. While Nora Burke demonstrates an appreciation for the Tramp's language, she employs her own to cut the domestic ties binding her to Dan; similarly, Mary Doul and Sarah Casey use language dramatically to create ideal roles for themselves, and Mary Byrne's language makes her a folk artist.[3]

In *The Shadow of the Glen*, Nora Burke becomes a tramp only at the end of the play. She exemplifies a woman at a transitional point between a settled and a roving life. At the beginning of the play, she is the Irish peasant wife involved with domestic duties. Although her immediate job is to arrange her husband's burial, she mentions the other domestic duties of the cottager's wife—including watching sheep, drawing turf, sewing, and fixing meals. She is the Irishwoman bound to household work and isolated from society. Ironically, Nora chose servitude as Dan Burke's wife in hopes of attaining financial security although she regrets that practical decision now:

I do be thinking in the long nights it was a big fool I was that time . . . for what good is a bit of farm with cows on it, and sheep on the back hills, when you do be sitting, looking out from a door the like of that door, and seeing nothing but the mists rolling down the bog, and the mists again, and they rolling up the bog, and hearing nothing but the wind crying out in the bits of broken trees were left from the great storm, and the streams roaring with the rain.[4]

In this speech, the words, "you do be sitting," convey her sense of being held captive. The cottage door forms a threshold of and for change, a symbolic boundary between the two lives, which Nora has not yet crossed.[5] This doorway frames Nora's view of nature and implies that cottage life has shaped her vision detrimentally.

Nora's description of the landscape expresses her internal emotional state— loneliness, emptiness, and despair. Her inability to see any future for herself is signified by the pervasive mists, which cloud any prospect of the countryside. The wind "crying" and the "streams roaring with the rain" emphasize her emotional distress, and "the bogs," along with the rain and mists, suggest depression, while "bits" and "broken trees" indicate Nora's impression that the world is fragmented or disorganized. Her description to Michael of this lonely life anticipates her willing departure with the Tramp, although her enraged husband instigates the exodus.

Nora predicts a rough road still ahead of her with the Tramp: "What good is a grand morning when I'm destroyed surely, and I going out to get my death walking the roads?'' (28) and ''I'm thinking it's myself will be wheezing that time with lying down under the Heavens when the night is cold'' (29). However, besides offering an end to Nora's isolation, the Tramp pictures a life more congenial than Nora's cottage life, for the new one contains beauty and pleasure as well as pain and ugliness. Together, Nora and the Tramp will still be ''feeling the cold and the frost,'' but they will also hear the wild bird's music, including ''fine songs'' of herons, grouse, owls, larks, and thrush (29). Although she does not construct this scene herself, Nora is able to project herself sympathetically into the Tramp's conception of their life together, and thus she can sever her marriage bonds.

Yet, Nora's last speech is significant for her deployment of negative, critical language so as to make departure seem the best possible outcome for her. This speech is directed to Dan Burke and comprises the last words about their marriage:

You think it's a grand thing you're after doing with your letting on to be dead, but what is it at all? What way would a woman live in a lonesome place the like of this place, and she not making a talk with the men passing? And what way will yourself live from this day, with none to care for you? What is it you'll have now but a black life, Daniel Burke, and it's not long, I'm telling you, till you'll be lying again under that sheet, and you dead surely. (29)

Hammering out one rhetorical question after another, all of whose answers are ''no way'' or ''nothing,'' Nora sounds like a prosecuting attorney condemning a criminal. Her purposes in this speech are to justify her own fate and to curse her husband's. A question like ''What way would a woman live in a lonesome place . . . and not [be] making a talk with the men passing?'' on the one hand attempts to exculpate Nora's past involvement with men and present a willingness to desert her husband. On the other hand, the question aims at making Dan jealous and attacking his self-confidence by insinuating that his attractions were insufficient to keep Nora interested. In this respect, Nora acts like two of the other women vagrants in Synge's plays, Mary Doul and Sarah Casey.

In most respects, however, Mary Doul, in *The Well of the Saints*, differs from Nora Burke. Unlike the cottager leaving the settled life for the first time, Mary Doul has begged for food and money along the road for a long time. She is aged and blind, not young and pretty like Nora, yet Mary's husband has remained with her and helped her find food and shelter. Mary Doul wants Martin's company and whatever protection he can provide, for she fears abandonment. Periodically, each member of the couple refers to the sound of the other's voice, sometimes derisively and sometimes with appreciation. By listening for each other, they relate to each other, and therefore, spoken language has a greater intensity for them both as speakers and auditors than it would for sighted persons.

Like Nora Burke, Mary Doul curses using language destructively in order to express anger and defend herself. Mary Doul curses not only her husband, but also any peasant who offends her. Toward Martin Doul, her verbal abuse extends to physical violence although, in some cases, she (not he) is the aggressor. When, after receiving sight, Martin criticizes her appearance, Mary accuses him of being cured by the devil, driven crazy by lies, and capable of fathering only "a crumpled whelp" or "things [that] would make the heavens lonesome above, and . . . scar[e] the larks" (73); her cursing next erupts into the threat of hitting him: "Maybe if I hit you a strong blow you'd be blind again." (73). When Mary exhibits anger in physical terms again, her outburst is unprovoked by Martin:

MARTIN DOUL: . . . The heavens is closing, I'm thinking, with darkness and great trouble passing in the sky. [*He reaches* MARY DOUL, *seizes her with both hands— with a frantic cry.*] Is it the darkness of thunder coming, Mary Doul? Do you see me clearly with your eyes?

MARY DOUL: [*snatches his arm away, and hits him with an empty sack across his face.*] I see you a sight too clearly, and let you keep off from me now.

Striking verbally or physically is Mary's defense mechanism: "Let you keep off from me now" conveys her sense of being trapped. Her redundant "off from" refers to, and combines, a more general physical distance with a sexual one, while "keep," which is a verb of bonding as well as maintaining, renders ambiguous that distance between the couple. Strong language constructs a verbal defense of Mary Doul and attempts to free her from external constraint. At these moments, her responses indicate her awareness that physically she is weaker than, and dependent on, the folks around her.

For instance, Mary Doul turns from suddenly attacking Martin to curse Molly Byrne, who has insensitively labeled Mary as "an old wretched road woman" (83), while at the same time applauding Mary's defense of herself against Martin. Mary retaliates by portraying Molly, whose name ironically is a nickname for "Mary," as merely a younger version of herself:

When the skin shrinks on your skin, Molly Byrne, there won't be the like of you for a shrunk hag in the four quarters of Ireland. . . . It's them that's fat and flabby do be wrinkled young, and that whitish yellowy hair she has does be soon turning the like of a handful of thin grass you'd see rotting, where the wet lies, at the north of a sty. (89)

This description acts like a curse not only because it forecasts Molly Byrne's future, but also because Mary bases her prophecy on the natural progression from youth to age. Mary Doul's judgment of Molly Byrne is less subjective than Nora Burke's assessment of her husband because the old beggar's curse will come true, while the lonesome "black life" predicted by Nora in *The Shadow of the Glen* is offset for her husband by the fact that Michael remains to drink whiskey with Dan after Nora leaves.

While Mary's curse on Molly Byrne may be intended simply as revenge for being called an ugly old woman, Mary's characterization is empirically more true than any of her own self-portraits: Mary's fancy-color descriptions of herself. Mary Doul's depiction of Molly as aged underscores the transience of beauty and youth and makes golden hair and plump cheeks, though as apparent as wrinkles and baldness, seem superficial criteria for praising people. While Mary Doul's self-praise is comic both because it is untrue and because she persists in her folly, her imaginative capability for seeing herself as beautiful paradoxically enables her to continue living and to keep Martin as a faithful companion. At the start of the play, Mary rationalizes that her cracked voice comes from "sitting out all the year in the rain falling" (59); but the "white beautiful skin" promoted by exposure to the rain more than compensates for a cracked voice. In praising her skin, Mary Doul, of course, shifts the "beautiful" from the aural to the visual, a mode of perception unavailable to either beggar. Whereas Mary dismisses any correlation between sight and sound, Martin tries to reconnect the two when he says of Molly, "It should be a fine soft, rounded woman, I'm thinking, would have a voice like that" (60). Mary refutes his claim both by denying Molly's beautiful voice and by asserting that Molly's "sweet" tones make no sense.

Nevertheless, Mary's language describing herself creates beautiful word pictures of "the wet south wind ... blowing upon us," "white beautiful skin," and "fine skin" which verge on poetry. Besides these word pictures, Mary formulates elaborate, if ultimately fallacious, arguments to support her "views" of herself. She appeals to sighted persons' authority to corroborate that she is "the beautiful dark woman" of Ballinatone, although her later assertions— "they're a bad lot those that have their sight, and they do have great joy, the time they do be seeing a grand thing, to let on they don't see it at all" and "the seeing is a queer lot" (60, 61)—contradict the earlier appeal. Mary thereby entangles Martin in arguments that attempt to elevate herself above him and the other peasants. Rather than horrifying, Mary's various stratagems for making herself "look" good, which are obvious to the audience but not readily apparent to Martin, are comic, even commendable, because of her audacity and persistence. Mary Doul's assertion of her physical beauty relegates her internal sense of self-worth only to external features, and ultimately masks any other view of herself that Mary might have. Even after she receives sight, Mary Doul never admits to being ugly. In Act II, Martin's reference to Mary seeing herself "when you looked down into a well, or a clear pool, maybe" only elicits Mary's retort that "I seen a thing in them pools put joy and blessing in my heart" (88). Although the audience may reasonably think, as Martin does, that Mary is deluded about her appearance, in reality she is trying to reshape her experience to project the best possible picture of herself. In anticipating her future appearance with a "face would be a great wonder when it'll have soft white hair falling around it, the way when I'm an old woman there won't be the like of me surely in the seven counties of the east" (88), Mary's prophecy inverts the kind of negative language leveled against Molly earlier. As a means of offsetting threats to her existence, Mary thus manipulates language both negatively and positively in her own self-interest.

Moreover, Mary's positive view of herself as an old woman wins Martin's approval: "You're a cute thinking woman, Mary Doul, and it's no lie" (88). Her insight prompts him to "look" for beauty in himself, in "a beautiful, long, white, silken streamy beard, you wouldn't see the like of in the eastern world" (89). He defines himself by claiming this feature as uniquely his own. His hyperbolic stringing of one adjective after another shows him competing with Mary to be the most beautiful beggar. Further, as did the Tramp for Nora in *The Shadow of the Glen*, Mary employs poetic language to envision the nature surrounding the beggars as congenial and beautiful:

There's the sound of one of them twittering yellow birds do be coming in the springtime from beyond the sea, and there'll be a fine warmth now in the sun, and a sweetness in the air, the way it'll be a grand thing to be sitting here quiet and easy, smelling the things growing up, and budding from the earth. (89)

Whether or not her "vision" is empirically accurate—how does a blind woman know that a bird is yellow, for instance—is not at issue. As Martin has claimed, Mary is a "cute thinking woman," and her imagination forms a fine world for the beggars. Her vision is "true" in allowing the beggars to project beauty, pleasure, and hence contentment into their surroundings. Martin exclusively prefers this poetic vision to actual sight, whereas Mary ultimately capitulates to the community's desire that the beggars have their sight restored.

Martin's preference for blindness indicates that he is more idealistic than Mary, while Mary's gradual concession to having sight restored points to another reason for her poetic speeches to Martin. Martin seeks to avoid such painful sights as the priest's bleeding feet, the harsh skies, the abject mongrels, and Molly's wicked grin. Martin's inability to see brings him, as for the speaker of Keats's "Ode to a Nightingale," "finer sights" of

sweet beautiful smells do be rising in the warm nights and hearing the swift flying things racing in the air, still we'd be looking up in our own minds into a grand sky, and seeing lakes, and broadening rivers, and hills are waiting for the spade and the plough. (94)

Although Mary agrees with Martin, she nevertheless accepts Mat Simon's argument, "If you had your sight you could be keeping a watch that no other woman came near to [Martin] at all" (95).

Since Mary has designed her language throughout *The Well of the Saints* to steer Martin's interest toward her and away from Molly and the other peasant girls, Mat's advice appeals to her as means of really "watching" Martin; she would willingly abandon poetic "sight" in language if actual eyesight could take over its function. Mary's conformity to the community's expectations depends on her insecurity about Martin's faithfulness, her fear of separation from him, and her awareness of the beggars' precarious life. She expresses her grasp of the beggars' situation in her last speech, which comprises one of her most negative statements in the play:

We'd have a right to be gone, if it's a long way itself, where you do have to be walking with a slough of wet on the side and a slough of wet on the other, and you going a stony path with a north wind blowing behind. (99)

This picture modifies the earlier word pictures and indicates that Mary conceives of the beggars' life in ways other than her earlier landscape descriptions.

Like Mary Doul, Sarah Casey and Mary Byrne, the two female vagrants in *The Tinker's Wedding*, demonstrate complex views of tramp life and have different attitudes toward it. Both women in *The Tinker's Wedding* are also accustomed to the life of the beggar. Like Mary Doul, Sarah is trying to hold on to her male companion Michael Byrne; but unlike Mary Doul, the younger Sarah is not married to Michael. This uncertain relationship forces her to play two extreme, even contradictory, roles—the eager bride and the "vamp." Sarah's predicament further explores the conflict experienced by Mary Doul, but in contrast to Mary Doul, Sarah Casey is physically attractive and must also contend with fears of growing old and ugly.[6]

Sarah plays the role of eager bride by waiting for the Priest to pass by the tinker's camp on his way home and by urging Michael to finish making her wedding ring. Michael corroborates Sarah's anticipation: "You to be going beside me a great while, and rearing a lot of them, and then to be setting off with your talk of getting married, and your driving me to it, and I not asking it at all" (35). That he and Sarah have lived together "a great while" and reared many children raises questions about Sarah's motives for marriage. The grounds for Sarah's desire to wed are unclear, and she evades Michael's questions. Why she eludes his probings might range from a desire to hide her motives to the possibility that she herself fails to comprehend them fully.

Sarah's strange behavior is further complicated by her acting like a flirt as Michael keeps seeking explanations. When he asks her what she has to gain, she says, "I'd have a right to be going off to the rich tinkers do be traveling from Tibradden to the Tara Hills; for it'd be a fine life to be driving with young Jaunting Jim" (36). Sarah mentions joining Jim three more times in this conversation and refers to the peelers "talking love to me in the dark night" and their praise of her as "the Beauty of Ballinacree, a great sight surely" (37). Sarah's words here echo Mary Doul's quotation about sighted men's praise, and like Nora Burke, Sarah describes Michael's life without her as "lonesome" (37). Sarah switches from being the expectant bride to playing the woman chafing to escape a boring lover. Her previous attitude, along with the stage direction that she must speak "teasingly" (36), makes this sudden change in her behavior seem like a pose.

Perhaps Sarah deliberately threatens to leave, anticipating Michael's response either because she has offered to leave previously or because, having never broached the subject before, she knows it will surprise Michael. Changing from bride to flirt, however, reveals Sarah's inherent conception of her relationship with Michael—which depends on one person selfishly controlling the other. Michael is being coerced into marriage, and his recognition that he is being forced leads him to interrogate Sarah and compel her to give reasons. Instead of growing angry, Sarah reconstructs the situation so that marriage seems unnecessary for her. Thus, she entices Michael to view marriage as advantageous for him and a way of keeping Sarah. She effectively blackmails Michael, ensuring his emotional investment by giving him an ultimatum: either marry her or she will leave tomorrow for Jim. Her ultimatum, though, implies that she is less secure in the tinker's present living arrangement than she admits, perhaps because she knows that Michael could leave her as easily as she could leave him.

Dropping the "vamp" role at the Priest's arrival, Sarah resumes the role of bride-to-be, but she appears also as a shrewd, nearly corrupt businesswoman, bargaining with the Priest over the ceremony. First, she begs him to perform the rites not just for free but with the gift of "a little small bit of silver to pay for the ring" (39). With a ring already made, Sarah misrepresents the truth, sacrilegiously turning the wedding into barter by which she will profit. Moreover, she conducts the "deal" with extreme reverence, almost obsequiousness, so that one critic claims she is really flirting with the Priest. While it is not clear that Sarah is sexually attracted to him, she does get the Priest to agree to marry the tinkers.[7] The pious phrases with which Sarah loads her speech include her constantly addressing the Priest as "your reverence" or "holy father," her attributing of good weather to "the grace of God," and her contrasting of herself to Mary Byrne, "an old wicked heathen" (42). In arguing that the Priest should protect her from Mary Byrne's fate, Sarah presents herself as a woman trying to reform her ways. The sincerity of this desire to reform is undercut when Sarah initiates a raid on Farmer Flaherty's hens after the Priest departs (44). Sarah, thus, conceives of marriage as morally unrelated to her other behavior. Her view of the institution of marriage is completely pragmatic.

In fact, even when Mary points out the marriage's fruitlessness, Sarah treats it as a business deal: "If it's wise or fool I am, I've made a good bargain, and I'll stand to it now" (50). Sarah seems to have invested the ritual with a guarantee that it may not have, while she ignores its moral and religious value. When the Priest refuses to perform the ceremony, Sarah insists on the completion of the "deal" anyway. Ironically, her obsession with the wedding as absolutely necessary is isolated from any real practical benefit it may have for her life. Her extreme outrage and violent temper indicate an irrational attachment to the *idea* of marriage as necessary for her self-protection.

When Sarah tells the Priest that he cannot leave until he marries the couple, she demonstrates the same kind of strong anger as Mary Doul in *The Well of the Saints.* Like Mary Doul's aggressiveness, Sarah's bullying reflects not so much an inherently bullying nature as an irrational response generated by her need for self-preservation. Because Mary Doul and Sarah exist outside the bounds of society, they can express their feelings in ways unacceptable for women within society. Their vagrant life forces these women to think for themselves and negotiate the "business" of their lives, but the absence of law and conventional standards of behavior keeps them constantly in uncertainty and unpredictability. Sarah thinks to escape this fate through marriage—a "bonding" that, she thinks, will prevent Michael from leaving her. Mary Doul knows, though, that marriage fails to shield the female vagrant from the "slings and arrows" of a tinker's "outrageous fortune."

Sarah Casey's inherent dissatisfaction with the tinker life contrasts with Mary Byrne's full embrace of life on the road. Mary Byrne has no regrets for her choice of life, takes no care about the morrow, and neither toils nor spins. She is, therefore, different from both Sarah and her son, Michael. Although Michael shows no interest in society's institutions, he does attempt to work for a living by hammering tin. Indeed, Mary is almost an "outsider" within her own group. The tinker family is the site of instability in Mary's life. Her uncertain relationship with the other tinkers is implied by her numerous entrances on- and exits off-stage and her wanderings on-stage during the play.

Of all the female vagrants in these plays by Synge, Mary Byrne most closely approximates an "artist" who modifies her harsh life with song and story. Mary also cleverly and strategically manipulates language, much as Mary Doul does; Mary Byrne's "reasoning" everywhere is false but presented with such Falstaffian complexity, wit, and insistence that she wins the audience's sympathy. The audience hears Mary "singing tipsily" (39) before seeing her stagger onto the stage, a jug of whiskey clutched in her hands. The first song she sings tells of Larry the criminal, who refused to repent at his death because penitence was "by the clergy first invented" (40). This phrase implies that penitence is without divine origin and serves the clergy, not the sinner; therefore, the real "sinner" is the clergy, and not Larry.

The next song Mary herself interrupts by admitting to Sarah "it's a bad, wicked song" (41), but Mary's reason undercuts the gesture toward refraining from immorality. She says that she will wait to finish the song until the Priest leaves, thus making her "morality" contingent on circumstance. She continues to stab at the clergy's ethics when she disclaims that she could further corrupt him; but, simultaneously, she urges the Priest to drink whiskey, rationalizing, "Aren't we all sinners?" and promising, "We won't let on a word about it till the Judgment Day" (40). Then she warns him against refusing the whiskey, for to do so would reveal his hypocrisy. Finally, when Sarah speaks to the Priest privately, Mary reads the worst possible meaning into their talk, her interpretation saying more about her own moral decay than about Sarah's or the Priest's behavior.

Mary so entangles morality with immorality that she appears less than rational. She seems well-intentioned and good-hearted, but naughty—like a child who confuses right with wrong. Although her confusion partly results from being drunk, it also may come from senility, a form of second childhood. The absence of any remorse for taking the tin can to buy more whiskey reinforces this impression, as does her helplessness, in Act II, in deciding how to hide from Sarah: Mary starts for the fair, veers to the church, and then encounters the Priest, who blocks her entry (50–52).

Despite her corruption and instability, Mary Byrne realizes the demands of tramp life on her. She articulates these to Sarah Casey; Mary states what the future inevitably entails for the female vagrant and argues that marriage will not provide security from loneliness or old age.[8] Mary Byrne argues from her experience wandering the streets, talking to tramps, and observing fine ladies. Although the vagrant life corrupts, it also educates. Its lesson, however, is that life is rough. Rather than succumbing to despair, Mary accepts this fate and scorns its power over her ability to have a good time, while, simultaneously, she sees death as a welcome end to misery.

Along with singing and drinking, Mary deploys storytelling in order to assuage discomfort and misery. Of course, at its worst, her capability for shaping tales is mere lying, but Mary also offers a story to Sarah as a way of mitigating, and hence controlling, loneliness.[9] In Act I, after the Priest departs, Mary settles herself by the fire and starts singing but is too hoarse to continue. She then begins a story. Her change from song to story indicates that Mary can keep herself entertained and also entertain others. She offers to tell Sarah ''the finest story you'd hear any place from Dundalk to Ballinacree, with great queens in it, making themselves matches from the start to the end, and they with shiny silks on them the length of the day, and white shifts for the night'' (43). Although unaware at this point of Sarah's plans to marry, Mary has already intuited part of what Sarah craves—stability, love, and comfort—for the story's characters are ''great queens'' who control their own fates by ''making themselves matches'' and who have wealth and comfort, signified by the ''shiny silks'' and ''white shifts.''

Although Mary's story may provide Sarah with a temporary escape from the immediate problems of tinker life, the folk tale is only as much practical ''use'' in solving the problems confronted by the tinker women as Sarah's plan to marry. Rather than trying to live her ''story'' as Sarah does, Mary Byrne acknowledges the ''story'' as an imaginative creation, enhancing, but not necessarily changing, tramp life. While Sarah thinks to change her manner of life by marriage, she nevertheless maintains it by raiding the nearby farm for food. Sarah's rejection of Mary's story speaks to the younger woman's inability to find other ways, besides forcing Michael to marry, to solve the problem of loneliness. After the couple leaves to steal the hens, Mary Byrne resolves to go to the pub, not just for drink, but to seek human companionship as well.

Although in these three plays the female vagrant varies from character to character, all the women tramps react to constraints that their lives place on them. These pressures include loneliness, a precarious dependence on their fellow travelers' whims, and the changes that nature and the settled community wreak on their lives. As Nora Burke's situation proves, however, problems are not limited to the vagrants' lives, and she moves from domestic hardship to a life that promises freedom and companionship along with ill-health and poverty. *The Shadow of the Glen* stops short of demonstrating what life on the road is like for a woman, but *The Tinker's Wedding* and *The Well of the Saints* do illustrate it. Like her husband, Mary Doul is handicapped by her blindness and life as a beggar, yet these fetters paradoxically force her to excel in exercising her imagination, which in turn enables her to manage the anxiety, if not to transcend the reality, of her existence. Similarly, Mary Byrne of *The Tinker's Wedding* shows an imaginative faculty for creating worlds through language in which criminals are heroic, clergy are con artists, and "great queens" wear beautiful silks and marry at will. Sarah Casey counters Mary Byrne's "poetic" vision with dramatic posing. The younger woman acts out the contradictory roles of bride and vamp in an effort to maintain Michael's allegiance. The exigencies of their lives—the absence of order provided by customs and conventions— force the vagrant women in Synge's plays to rely on imaginative language, both poetic and dramatic, in order to survive. While the female vagrant's life is foreign to that of most women, either past or present, nevertheless, the language of Nora Burke, Mary Doul, Sarah Casey, and Mary Byrne points to how, as Feste's song at the end of *Twelfth Night* suggests, with our "little tiny wit" we "must make content with [our] fortunes fit,/ Though the rain it raineth every day."

NOTES

1. To my knowledge, two article-length studies exist: Paul F. Botheroyd, "The Year of the Travellers: Tinkers, Tramps and Travellers in Early Twentieth-Century Irish Drama and Society"; and Harold Orel, "Synge's Concept of the Tramp." Botheroyd argued that most critics have previously not dealt with the subject because of its "touch[iness]" with the Catholic Church, cites such sociological studies on the tramp as George Gmelch's *The Irish Tinkers: Urbanization of an Itinerant People*, and notes other Irish plays presenting the traveler figure. Orel's article points to Synge's prose studies of Irish peasantry, like "The Vagrants of Wicklow," and characterizes the tramps as "truly children of Nature" (61). Besides Orel's and Botheroyd's studies, W. Thornton's *J. M. Synge and the Western Mind* notes two polarized character types in Synge's plays: "the sedentary, practical, safe . . . and the itinerant, imaginative, venturesome one" (106). Brenna Katz Clarke, in *The Emergence of the Irish Peasant Play at the Abbey Theatre*, identifies the traveler as one of the "outsider" figures in Irish drama (126–27).

2. In *The Irish Tinkers: Urbanization of an Itinerant People*, George Gmelch noted that the terms "tinkers" and "travelers" are used interchangeably; although the Irish government calls them "itinerants," "travelers" are the name by which they know themselves (4); Nicholas Grene, in *Synge: A Critical Study of the Plays*, criticized Synge's tendency "to blur distinctions between one type of vagrant and another" (88).

3. Ann Saddlemeyer's "Synge and the Nature of Woman" usefully comments on Synge's personal friendships with women and his sympathetic treatment of women in his dramas, while Bonnie Kime Scott's "Synge's Language of Women" has drawn critical attention to Synge's concern with how women express themselves verbally.

4. J. M. Synge, *Plays*, 25. Italicized portions of Synge's quoted dialogue indicate my emphases.

5. Thomas J. Morrisey, in "Synge's Doorways: Portals and Portents," drew my attention to the psychological import of Nora's speech. For another stylistic study of this speech's syntax, see Mary C. King's chapter on *The Shadow of the Glen* in *The Drama of J. M. Synge*.

6. Thornton describes Sarah as in a "life-crisis" of confronting old age and sees Mary, implicitly, as an authority who "is aware of aging and hardship"; she "has reconciled herself to life as the tinkers know it, and she accepts it fully" (119). My interpretation of *The Tinker's Wedding* generally follows this reading.

7. Mary C. King, in *The Drama of J. M. Synge*, suggested that Sarah is both physically attracted to the Priest and admiring of his speech (90).

8. See Thornton 119–23.

9. Bonnie Kime Scott argues that, in this sense, Mary tries to "soothe" her own loneliness (182), but that she comforts Sarah as well.

WORKS CITED

Botheroyd, Paul F. "The Year of the Travelers: Tinkers, Tramps, and Travelers in Early Twentieth-Century Irish Drama and Society." In *Studies in Anglo-Irish Literature*, ed. Heinz Kosok. Bonn: Herber Grundmann, 1982, 162–75.

Clarke, Brenna Katz. *The Emergence of the Irish Peasant Play at the Abbey Theatre*. Ann Arbor: University of Michigan Press, 1982.

Gmelch, George. *The Irish Tinkers: The Urbanization of an Itinerant People*. Menlo Park, Calif.: Cummings Publishing, 1977.

Grene, Nicholas. *Synge: A Critical Study of the Plays*. Totowa, N.J.: Rowman and Littlefield, 1975.

King, Mary C. *The Drama of J. M. Synge*. Syracuse N.Y.: Syracuse University Press, 1985.

Morrisey, Thomas J. "Synge's Doorways: Portals and Portents." *Eire-Ireland* 17(3) (1982): 40–51.

Orel, Harold. "Synge's Concept of the Tramp." *Eire-Ireland* 7(2) (1972): 55–61.

Saddlemeyer, Ann. "Synge and the Nature of Woman." In *Woman in Irish Legend, Life and Literature*, ed. S. F. Gallagher. Totowa, N.J.: Barnes and Noble, 1983, 58–73.

Scott, Bonnie Kime. "Synge's Language of Women." In *A J. M. Synge Literary Companion*, ed. Edward J. Kopper, Jr. Westport, Conn.: Greenwood Press, 1988, 173–89.

Synge, John Millington. *Plays*, ed. Ann Saddlemeyer. Oxford: Oxford University Press, 1969.

Thornton, Weldon. *J. M. Synge and the Western Mind*. New York: Barnes and Noble; Gerrards Cross, U.K.: Colin Smythe, 1979.

11

Synge's *Deirdre of the Sorrows*: Defamiliarizing the Myth

Eileen J. Doll

John M. Synge's final play, *Deirdre of the Sorrows*, which was left unfinished at his death in 1909, has been studied less than most of his previous plays for reasons of some importance: the lack of a truly definitive text, since the work-in-progress at Synge's death did not completely satisfy him, and critical complaints that certain elements of the play are not well motivated or integrated.[1] For many years the work was dismissed with more biographical than critical attention; as Donna Gerstenberger explains, "The concluding act of Synge's own life seems to have prevented his last play until recent years from receiving the kind of attention it deserves as drama in its own right" (85). Notwithstanding these obstacles, *Deirdre of the Sorrows* remains relevant to modern readers and spectators; it is important as a culmination of the author's work, a piece dealing with universal and timeless truths, a strong and beautiful comment on women and their role in society, and a successful attempt to defamiliarize and demythologize Irish saga material. Some of these aspects have been discussed previously by other critics, but no one has brought together all of the elements in order to analyze the total impact of this play. It is precisely through Synge's use of the myth and archetypal figures that he is able to subvert the audience's expectations, defamiliarizing, and subsequently elevating, the traditional, local Irish topic to a new and universal level.

Even though he himself, in a letter to Leon Brodzky in 1907, called the work "an experiment chiefly to change my hand" (*Letters* 2:102), *Deirdre* can be studied as an interweaving of various threads in Synge's dramatic canon. His last play picks up an interest from his student days—Celtic saga material—and transports it to the rural settings of his other plays. It likewise deals with themes such as love, death, unrelenting destiny, old age, and self-determination, with which we are familiar from the earlier works. The play asserts the universality of these themes, transcending, just as in Synge's earlier pieces, the local settings. Rather than the love, death, and tragedy of a particular saga figure—or of the particular author, for that matter—this play demonstrates how these problems apply to all human beings. Indeed, as Harold Orel claims,

The play will impress most readers as something other than a comment on Synge's impending marriage, a study of the natural landscape of Ireland, or a criticism of beautiful women. . . . It is a play marked—as no other in Synge's canon is—by a recognition of the cruel, inexorable quality of passing time. (310)

As literary topics, these themes are far from new; the originality resides in Synge's treatment of them, and most of the critical attention the play has received until recent years has been, if not biographical, an analysis of this originality. Nearly always using a comparative approach, the critics have contrasted Synge's use of the oldest, Gaelic versions of the Deirdre myth to the more romanticized treatments of his contemporaries (especially Yeats and A. E.), and then proceeded to underscore the universality of Synge's themes through comparison of his play to Shakespeare's *King Lear* or *Antony and Cleopatra*, or the ancient Greek tragedies, thereby placing his work in the ranks of great literature.[2] Declan Kiberd additionally sees the human, universal quality of Synge's play as part of the author's understanding and incorporation of the folk tradition into all of his works: "The folk tellers delighted in describing Deirdre's minute and credibly human response to her difficult plight. . . . Like the folk storytellers, Synge grasped the relationship between the heroic world of the ancient legend and the peasant Ireland in which the story still lingered" (191).

Much recent criticism of Synge's plays in general, and of *Deirdre of the Sorrows* in particular, however, has focused on the issues of the feminine and female roles within society. As Bonnie Kime Scott has observed, "Synge's sympathetic depiction of female characters has led a number of critics to the theme of woman as victim of social and geographical entrapment" (174). The discussion of feminism in *Deirdre* is linked to the demythologizing of the mythological figure of Deirdre and the other saga characters. Reed Way Dasenbrock studies the Deirdre myth and Synge's manipulation of it, concluding that in *Deirdre of the Sorrows*, Synge "inaugurated what was to become an important current in modern Irish literature, the conscious demythologizing of Irish mythology" (142). Other critics analyze how Synge used the Deirdre myth to underscore the female plight in a patriarchal society, without actually discussing demythification.[3] Only if we take all of these factors into account, however, will the full impact of Synge's manipulation of the Deirdre myth become evident: stereotypes are destroyed, archetypes are made individual and personal, and the heroic is undercut. Then, when the demythologizing is complete, Synge reinstates the myth, albeit now on a new plane and with a new meaning.

We know that Synge was conversant with numerous versions of the Deirdre legend, including the oldest ones.[4] The earliest extant version of the Deirdre story dates to about 1160 and is found in the Book of Leinster.[5] That story begins before Deirdre's birth, when she cries out from her mother's womb during a feast. The prophecy given to explain the scream is that Deirdre will be so beautiful that kings and champions will woo her and she will cause great destruction, including the exile of the three sons of Usna and of Fergus. The warriors want to kill the child, but the high king, Conchubor, decides instead to rear her apart until he can marry her. Deirdre longs for a handsome young man to love, and the satirist Lavarcham shows her Naisi, with whom she falls in love. Deirdre steals out to Naisi one day when he is alone, but is rejected by him; she leaps at him, grabbing his ears, and tells him to take her with him or he will suffer shame and mockery. The three brothers and Deirdre pass from one king to another, ending in Alban, where the king's steward sees Deirdre and tries to woo her for his king. When they flee Alban, the Ulstermen ask Conchubor to relent and take the brothers back—they should not "die in a strange land because of a bad woman" (262). Fergus and others (the guarantors) are detained on the way to Emain Macha, and as a result, Eogan is able to kill the three brothers. Deirdre is taken, hands tied, to Conchubor. Fergus and the others discover the treachery, destroy Emain Macha, and then flee into exile. For one year, Deirdre is with Conchubor, but she does not laugh, smile, or eat or sleep sufficiently. She continually grieves for Naisi and his brothers, and finally Conchubor sends her off to Eogan, whom she most hates. She is behind Eogan in his chariot when Conchubor makes a crude, sexual joke, causing Deirdre to dash her head on a great rock that she sees nearby. Synge's work utilizes other sources as well as this, and his story line does not begin until shortly before Conchubor comes to claim Deirdre as his bride, but much of the Book of Leinster can be found in his play.

Synge employs the saga characters and the bare settings and descriptions of the mythology, especially as found in the oldest forms, to create the ambiance of his play and to build certain expectations in his audience. The only furnishings—a tapestry frame, a high chair of state, a stool, a large press, and a heavy oak chest—while realistic in a cottage in the woods and dramatically motivated, become important symbols of fate and of Deirdre's assumption of her destiny in Act I. This is consistent with the Book of Leinster version, which only mentions objects that pertain directly to the story line and action. As Scott observes, Synge's Deirdre uses the symbols of the female-dominated domestic realm to express her own desires and reject the life of Emain Macha: "Clearly, Synge is sensitive to women's symbolic systems and their nonverbal powers of communication through domestic arrangements" (180). The legend, the realistic yet symbolic settings, the three women on stage with the needlework, the impending storm, and the poetic language immediately evoke mythological time and space, removing the play from quotidian reality. The three women may be interpreted as the classical Fates, working on the tapestry of the destiny of Deirdre, the sons of Usna, and king Conchubor, or as the three faces of the moon, living in the natural world and guiding the hunters (the sons of Usna) to their door.[6]

The contrast between Synge's earthy, realistic, even naturalistic treatment of the legend and the dreamier, more romanticized or distanced versions of his contemporaries reveals his attempt to defamiliarize the contemporary Deirdre symbol. Synge returns to the oldest, most brutal versions of the myth in order to achieve this end. At the same time, he imbues his saga characters with motivations, feelings, and reactions that are much more human and individual than the formulas found in the legends themselves. For those familiar with the legend from nineteenth-century sources or from the renderings by Lady Gregory, A. E., or Yeats, the treatment by Synge is surprising: the language is plain, not regal; the characters are human, motivated by personal desires and self-interest; and although the ending is foretold, the lovers' quarrel and bitter words prevent them from preserving their perfect love through an early death. For those familiar with the earlier versions of the legend, the language and brutality are not shocking; rather, the surprise lies in Synge's use of inner motivation rather than superstition, premonitions, and *geas* (the oaths of the medieval period), along with the ironic quarrel of Deirdre and Naisi by the grave. All of these surprises subvert the audience's expectations, defamiliarizing the myth and causing a reevaluation of its meaning. By undercutting the heroic myth figure, Synge also undercuts and destroys the usual female archetypes and stereotypes embodied in Deirdre.

A woman traditionally had a subordinate role in rural society (and, of course, even in the "civilized" society of the playwright's time). Her subordination included the right of her parents or other authority figures to choose her husband and plot her housewifely destiny. Even if destined to be a queen, as in Deirdre's case, the woman was not consulted about her own desires. When Synge's Deirdre is reprimanded by King Conchubor for her rustic manners in Act I, she responds, "I have no wish to be a queen" (191). Against her will, then, Deirdre has been raised to be the bride of an older king. As a woman, she must respect the imposed authority's plans for her within this patriarchal society. In addition, Deirdre is doubly subordinate, for she also holds a lower position in the societal hierarchy and must submit to the orders of the high king. The woman's role within the structure of rural Ireland in Synge's day was equally subordinate, something Synge had observed during his travels and wanderings. By choosing to use the older versions of the Deirdre legend in particular, and through his specific manipulations of the myth, Synge underscores the parallel of powerlessness of women in both societies. In the saga, Deirdre's only recourse is escape from the kingdom, although remaining under the "protection" of men (the sons of Usna), or suicide. In his work, Synge calls attention to the patriarchal restrictions and the expression of choice of a male partner by the female saga character. The Deirdre of the medieval manuscripts had no real choice in her life, for she was part of a prophecy of doom and her actions were all previously decided by powers beyond her control; she rebels, but her rebellion acts to fulfill the prophecy and seal her fate. The rural Irish woman of 1909 similarly had no choice in her destiny. The realism of Synge's play situates us simultaneously within the patriarchy of the story and that of the contemporary society. Synge additionally removes the pre-Christian sense of doomed fate in terms of Deirdre's actions, however, thus making them more humanly motivated; his Deirdre contemplates, makes choices, and acts accordingly. As used by Synge, the figure of Deirdre, which is already an archetype of the rebellious woman, furthers that archetype. At the same time, however, Synge's Deirdre helps to defamiliarize the patriarchal society's stereotype of the female's "proper station" *because* she is rebellious. Through her active participation in deciding her fate, Deirdre reverses the traditional role of submissive woman, thereby breaking that stereotype.

She also embodies another archetype—the femme fatale or siren, who seduces men and brings them to disaster. In this guise she may be viewed additionally as the moon deity in one of her phases or the sovereignty goddess of native Irish tradition, who, according to Máire Herbert, embodied the physical land governed and dominion over the land, a goddess "who is often depicted as taking the initiative in the mating game" (16).[7] This nonpassive Deirdre again reminds us of the early myth in which she both leaps at the reluctant Naisi and dashes her head against a rock. By combining the femme fatale and rebellious woman archetypes with the traditional subordinate female stereotype, the figure of Synge's Deirdre functions as a constant contradiction: the oppressed female, whose liberty is usurped by the male king and who rebels, set against the earlier, pre-Christian sovereignty goddess of matriarchal days who initiates the action in this play. Neither facet–the sovereignty goddess herself or the rebellious albeit oppressed female—poses any problem or offers any real threat to society as long as she remains in the mythological world. But if these female figures are simultaneously demythologized, as in *Deirdre of the Sorrows*, then the archetype shifts its referent in time and becomes a new figure: that of the rebellious woman of contemporary society who is able to break the stereotype and obtain her own desires before authority imposes its desires on her, thus thwarting authority. This representation diverges significantly from the archetype of the seducing female, for the focus is different and the impact more dangerous.

The play demonstrates this subversion of expectations at various points. Deirdre deliberately changes her role by changing her clothes and putting out the riches Conchubor had sent only *after* he leaves: "I'm going into the room to put on the rich dresses and jewels have been sent from Emain" (*Plays* 199). When Naisi and his brothers enter the house, the older women try to hide the fact that Deirdre lives there, but she comes in and takes command of the situation. It is Deirdre who, rather than being the obedient betrothed who meekly submits to Conchubor's will, summoned Naisi, and who now causes him to take her part: "It isn't many I'd call, Naisi" (209). After some convincing by Deirdre and a consideration of the probable fate that awaits them for going against the king, Naisi promises to take Deirdre away. Like a siren, Deirdre has lured Naisi away from a trouble-free life of hunting to a short, intense life of loving her, to be followed by foretold disaster. We expect this union and flight, but Synge

intensifies the expectations of doom by presenting the femme fatale–siren archetype at this point in the play. Like a siren, Deirdre has a charming voice,
which metaphorically grabs her lover by the ears, as Naisi notes: "And it is
you who go around in the woods, making the thrushes bear a grudge against
the heavens for the sweetness of your voice?" (207).[8]

In Act II, it is again Deirdre who makes the decision to return to Emain
Macha, even though their return means probable death. Since Deirdre's fate
holds no surprises for those conversant with the legend, it is her decision to
return that distinguishes Synge's heroine from her previous manifestations.
Synge adds a very human motivation to his play: Deirdre fears the loss of
intensity in her love with Naisi, which is threatened by coming age and time
itself. The bigger surprise in Synge's play comes in Act III, however, when
Deirdre and Naisi are brought to bitter words and loss of love before the very
grave they have chosen in order to save their sweet love. Some critics interpret
Deirdre's harsh words as a heroic prompting to force Naisi to leave her and
manfully defend his brothers, creating for him a death worthy of him; others
condemn them as too brutal and unnecessary. Whatever the motive, the words
and resulting action defamiliarize the story and demythologize the characters,
removing them from their mythological formulas. All the expectations built up
in the previous scenes are now subverted. The mythological—or what we conceive as the mythological—suddenly becomes real, and the heroic is undercut
since the saga characters are not able to live up to their heroic plans.

Synge subsequently closes his drama with the ritual of the keen. The proud,
sorrowful Deirdre, who keens her dead lover and stabs herself, enacts the ritual
that closes the circle of prophecy and freezes the action on the stage. Through
the final liberating/condemning act of suicide, Deirdre foretells the same sort of
frozen repetition through time: "And because of me . . . there will be a story
told of a ruined city and a raving king and a woman will be young forever"
(267). Of course, our continued interest in her legend and Synge's version of it
attests to the truth of her prophecy. The use of ritualized action to close the
work not only projects the action back into the realm of mythological time and
space but also underscores the suggestion that the new archetype is different.
Deirdre's choices were made in a mythological world that became, at least
momentarily, demythologized. By humanizing and defamiliarizing the heroic,
the demythification process is established. The heroic is undercut by the inadequacy of humanity to live up to the myth. As Deirdre reminds us, "By a new
made grave there's no man will keep brooding on a woman's lips" (253). The
only way that Deirdre can be free of the patriarchal oppression of Conchubor
is to remain in the mythical realm: she must die to "live on." She preserves
the myth only through her choice to be excluded from society; inclusion in this
particular society would mean total submission of her will. The demythologizing
of the heroic ultimately results in a new heroic act, Deirdre's suicide. Her choice,
however, is between two grim realities, neither one completely satisfactory. True
liberation exists only outside of reality.

Synge achieves at least two effects with the demythification of the Deirdre legend: showing the myth in its earlier, more brutal, and natural form to debunk the contemporary glorification of Irish national heroics, and bringing home in a much more intimate, personal way the enduring messages held within the myth itself. As Dasenbrock notes, Synge appreciated the myth for its original purposes and in its original guise, and felt that "the time had come to show the Irish some of the truth about their own mythology," for they had no idea what it was really like (142). In addition, Deirdre, a figure with the potential to symbolize various facets of Irish womanhood, when demythologized, carries a somewhat different message. She becomes more human, modern, universal, and archetypical of woman, thereby for once destroying the stereotyped of woman held by the majority of Irish and Continental society of the time. Weldon Thornton feels that Synge was successful at imbuing Deirdre with a psychology like the people he knew, "for he broke through the stereotyped attitudes toward the myth to produce a distinctive portrait of Deirdre and a complex interpretation of her relationship with Naisi" (153). But Synge is equally successful in breaking through the stereotyped attitudes toward the role of women in general through his demythification of the figure of Deirdre. Although Deirdre, of course, ultimately rests in the grave with the others, not able to avoid her "destined fate," she has been able to make her own decisions within the limits of that destiny, thus creating for herself the intense joy of fulfilled living on an equal status with her chosen mate. Deirdre's final words demonstrate the same idea: "It was sorrows were foretold, but great joys were my share always, yet it is a cold place I must go to be with you, Naisi. . . . It's a pitiful thing, . . . yet a thing will be a joy and triumph to [the] ends of life and time" (269).

Synge utilizes the archetypal seducing female figure, the demythologized Deirdre figure, and the pre-Christian Deirdre figure to destroy the traditional, subordinate female figure. After destroying the stereotype, the playwright closes with ritualized action to reelevate the action to a more universal plane. This ritual finale is a tremendously effective dramatic recourse. *Deirdre of the Sorrows* achieves its effect on the spectator or reader by means of the technique of demythification followed by remythification, causing us to consider the Deirdre figure in a new light, as a destroyer of the female stereotype both on and off the stage. These techniques and the ensuing message continue to speak to us today. The play criticizes the traditionally accepted female stereotype: society has blinded itself to reality by accepting the myth as truth, and the playwright strips the myth away momentarily to uncover the reality. If we add to this the further social implications of traditional society as rooted in the stereotype of the submissive female, then the reality becomes more than problematic. Synge's Deirdre becomes the new archetype of what women everywhere should be able to do, and yet she reminds us at the same time that all humanity is condemned to the limits of mortality: Deirdre's wonderful story will be told forever, but to ensure that it will be, Deirdre herself must die.

NOTES

1. See especially Donna Gerstenberger, Nicholas Grene, and Harold Orel. All three critics see the play as not totally successful, but with moments of great beauty and interest.

2. See especially Alan Price (195–215), who also extends the comparisons to "some of the great monodies in the Bible" (205); Toni O'Brien Johnson; and Declan Kiberd.

3. See Lorna Reynolds, Ellen S. Spangler, and Ann Saddlemyer. Another issue that David Cairns and Shaun Richards have discussed in great detail in relation to *The Shadow of the Glen* and *The Playboy of the Western World* would also apply to *Deirdre of the Sorrows*. This is their interpretation of the discourse of colonialism and Celticism in Ireland during the late nineteenth and early twentieth centuries. They see the colonial view of woman (emotional, otherworldly, and therefore ineffectual) as a reason for the conceiving of the masculine Gael and the strong nationalist protests to Synge's female characters. Since the patriarchal structure of the rural Ireland of the time upheld the imposed English concept of the socially and sexually submissive female and the nationalists regarded the Irish-speaking countryman as the "true Irishman," the concept of the feminine was crucial to Home Rule. Synge's women characters broke this pattern, and were therefore dangerous to the nationalist cause.

4. Kiberd and Johnson make the most convincing and exhaustive analyses of this issue.

5. My paraphrase is based on the translation by Jeffrey Gantz in *Early Irish Myths and Sagas*. I have retained Synge's spelling for the character and place names.

6. See Spangler's study of the moon symbolism as a feminine image.

7. Spangler addresses the various possibilities of the moon deity in the figure of Deirdre, and Herbert discusses the sovereignty goddess, ultimately rejecting this as a possible interpretation of Deirdre.

8. It is interesting to note that Synge makes Deirdre the singing "siren" rather than Naisi, whose singing in the Book of Leinster attracts Deirdre and causes an uprising. This role reversal underscores the fact that Deirdre takes on various characteristics normally associated with the male figure.

WORKS CITED

Cairns, David, and Shaun Richards. "'WOMAN' in the Discourse of Celticism: A Reading of *The Shadow of the Glen*." *Canadian Journal of Irish Studies* 13(1) (June 1987): 43–60.

Dasenbrock, Reed Way. "J. M. Synge and Irish Mythology." In *A J. M. Synge Literary Companion*, ed. Edward A. Kopper, Jr. Westport, Conn.: Greenwood Press, 1988, 135–43.

Gantz, Jeffrey, trans. *Early Irish Myths and Sagas*. Intro. by Jeffrey Gantz. Middlesex, U.K.: Penguin, 1981.

Gerstenberger, Donna. *John Millington Synge*. 1964. Rev. ed. Boston: G. K. Hall, 1990.

Grene, Nicholas. *Synge: A Critical Study of the Plays*. Totowa, N.J.: Rowman and Littlefield; London: Macmillan, 1975.

Herbert, Máire. "Celtic Heroine? The Archaeology of the Deirdre Story." *Gender in*

Irish Writing, ed. Toni O'Brien Johnson and David Cairns. Philadelphia: Open University Press, 1991, 13–22.

Johnson, Toni O'Brien. *Synge: The Medieval and the Grotesque*. Irish Literary Studies 11. Gerrards Cross, U.K.: Colin Smythe, 1982.

Kiberd, Declan. *Synge and the Irish Language*. Totowa, N.J.: Rowman and Littlefield, 1979.

Orel, Harold. "Synge's Last Play: 'And a Story Will be Told for Ever.'" *Modern Drama* 4 (1961): 306–13.

Price, Alan. *Synge and Anglo-Irish Drama*. London: Methuen, 1961.

Reynolds, Lorna. "Irish Women in Legend, Literature and Life." In *Woman in Irish Legend, Life and Literature*, ed. S. F. Gallagher. Irish Literary Studies 14. Gerrards Cross, U.K.: Colin Smythe, 1983, 11–25.

Saddlemyer, Ann. "Synge and the Nature of Woman." In *Woman in Irish Legend, Life and Literature*, ed. S. F. Gallagher. Irish Literary Studies 14. Gerrards Cross, U.K.: Colin Smythe, 1983, 58–73.

Scott, Bonnie Kime. "Synge's Language of Women." In *A J. M. Synge Literary Companion*, ed. Edward A. Kopper, Jr. Westport, Conn.: Greenwood Press, 1988, 173–89.

Spangler, Ellen S. "Synge's *Deirdre of the Sorrows* as Feminine Tragedy." *Eire-Ireland* 12(4) (1977): 97–108.

Synge, John Millington. *The Collected Letters of John Millington Synge*. Ed. by Ann Saddlemyer. 2 vols. Oxford: Clarendon Press, 1983–1984.

——. *Plays, Book II*, ed. Ann Saddlemyer. Oxford: Oxford University Press, 1968. Vol. 4 of *Collected Works*. Gen. ed., Robin Skelton. 4 vols. Oxford: Oxford University Press, 1962–1968.

Thornton, Weldon. *J. M. Synge and the Western Mind*. Irish Literary Studies 4. New York: Barnes and Noble; Gerrards Cross, U.K.: Colin Smythe, 1979.

12

"Stimulating stories of our own land": "History Making" and the Work of J. M. Synge

Heidi J. Holder

The works of J. M. Synge, while maintaining their place in literary and dramatic studies, often seem in danger of losing their true artistic and political edge. Synge's interest in the Celtic Revival and his troubled relations with Irish cultural nationalism have been amply discussed. But if one considers the debate over Ireland's cultural history and the attempts, during the Celtic Revival, to define an artistic canon and describe its purpose, another source for the power of his works becomes evident.

The Irish were in a unique position in the nineteenth and early twentieth centuries: they faced the problem, and the opportunity, of creating their own cultural history. Simultaneous with the growth of Irish literature in English was the perplexing recovery of an enormous body of "lost" materials from the Old and Middle Irish. Irish cultural nationalists hotly debated the proper way to translate and "frame" these materials for public consumption and political effect. The rise of the Gaelic League and the growth of assorted nationalist organizations and clubs led to assertions, by such activists as Douglas Hyde, that a specifically "Irish" culture had to be fostered for the sake of the moral, artistic, and political health of the Irish people. In short, the past was to provide a kind of model, one that would determine the future of Ireland. This tight linking of an understanding of the past with the political and cultural circumstances of the moment made Irish history, and particularly literary history, a hotly disputed territory.

That this "storytelling" task is fraught, in Synge's plays, with the possibility of danger and disillusionment reveals both his enthusiasm for, and his scepticism at, contemporary ventures in literary politics. While his characters do indeed create their histories and identities, their efforts prove to be profoundly antisocial, most obviously in Synge's best-known work, *The Playboy of the Western World.*

The great debate over the proper construction of the Irish canon and the qualities and boundaries of Irish literature was, in large measure, a debate over the *purpose* of Irish culture: what was it supposed to *do* for Ireland? Judging from the arguments set forth by such prominent cultural nationalists as Charles Gavan Duffy, Douglas Hyde, D. P. Moran, and Arthur Griffith, it was supposed to accomplish extraordinary things. The Irish people were to be transformed by a proper understanding of their own history and the qualities of their culture.

This "transformative" view of Irish cultural history had as its basic premise the notion that the Irish people were degraded, ignorant, and in perpetual danger of sliding further behind other European nations. The description of the Irish to be found in the writings of Irish nationalists was not flattering; in fact, these images of Ireland come perilously close at points to resembling the stereotypes and caricatures of anti-Irish propagandists: the modern Irish are depicted as ignorant, as "gloomy and resentful," their native good qualities "perverted" (Duffy, Sigerson, and Hyde 46). These images are carefully contextualized as a result of Anglo cultural-political aggression; however, they are used so frequently that they reveal a lingering and powerful worry that the Irish were *indeed* devolving into stereotypes. Sir Charles Gavan Duffy's lectures display this sense of inferiority, relentlessly comparing Ireland to other European nations and repeatedly making the point that the Irish are unique in lacking knowledge of their own history, lag behind Europe economically and culturally, and are in danger of becoming, at best, pale imitations of Englishmen—the hopeless sort of non-Irishman that D. P. Moran would sarcastically refer to as a "West Briton."

Douglas Hyde echoed this sense of the Irish as being deeply degraded when he spoke of the "failure" of the Irish people to maintain a vital culture and society:

If we take a bird's-eye view of our island to-day, and compare it with what it used to be, we must be struck by the extraordinary fact that the nation which was once, as every one admits, one of the most classically learned and cultured nations in Europe, is now one of the least so; how one of the most reading and literary people has become one of the *least* studious and most *un*-literary, and how the present art products of one of the quickest, most sensitive, and most artistic races on earth are now only distinguished for their hideousness. (cited in Duffy, Sigerson, and Hyde 118)

The pro–"Irish Ireland" newspapers such as D. P. Moran's *Leader* and Arthur Griffith's *United Irishman* constantly threatened their readers with cultural, economic, and political destruction if they did not quickly follow the "Celtic" path to improvement, to the restoration of the glories of the Irish nation. If on the one hand Ireland had the potential to be, as Padraic Pearse put it, "the saviour of idealism in modern intellectual and social life, the regenerator and rejuvenator of the religion of the world, the instructor of nations'' (221), on the other hand its alternative path was clearly to realize all the stereotypical attributes that had been its burden. Tom Garvin has discussed the ways in which the Gaelic League, with its promise of a moral revival that would accompany the revival of the Irish language, addressed such widespread anxieties about status. In this view, Celtic culture became a tool for solving social anxieties about *place*. Garvin asserts that this ''status resentment'' leads to ''the attempt to devise a counter-culture'' (87–88). This making of an alternative Celtic culture, and its concomitant program for a national renewal that would restore Ireland to its proper place as an advanced and cultured nation, can be seen clearly in the plans set forth by such a cultural nationalist as Charles Gavan Duffy.

In the summer of 1892, Charles Gavan Duffy was invited to participate in the Irish Literary Society. He gave a lecture in July entitled ''What Irishmen May Do for Irish Literature,'' and his arguments therein brought him into immediate conflict with Yeats. Duffy's lecture, and another, ''Books for the Irish People'' (given the following June), show the relentless utilitarianism of his views of cultural history. Duffy repeatedly emphasized that Ireland would *profit* from the study of its past; it would become ''wiser, manlier, more honest, and what is less than any of these, more prosperous'' (17). Despite the low rank accorded here to prosperity, it is a constant theme for Duffy, along with his preference for the study of representative virtuous Irishmen (a tactic that would replace ''bad'' Irish types with ''good'' ones):

Big books of history are only for students, they are never read by the people. But they will read picturesque biographies, which are history individualised, or vivid sketches of memorable eras, which are history vitalised. A dozen lives of representative Irishmen would teach more of the training and growth of Ireland than a library of annals and State papers. . . . How profitable it would be if the best men of this time would contribute each of them a study to a gallery of representative Irishmen. (26)

In these two lectures Duffy presented a classic attempt at canon formation, which would be strongly opposed by the likes of Yeats and Synge, who have been made ''canonical''—as Duffy's own candidates for that status (Roger O'Moore, Luke Wadding, Patrick Sarsfield) decidedly have not. Seamus Heaney, in considering the conflict over the Irish Library between Yeats and Duffy, sums up the latter's position:

The utilitarian soul that lay behind such sentiments could never please the romantic poet, whose vision of Ireland was at this time magical and legendary, and not at all in sympathy with the kind of economic realism that made Duffy's mind tick and his pen deliver sentences like the following, one of my favourite declarations by an Irish writer. ''When I met in France, Italy, and Egypt the marmalade manufactured at Dundee, I felt it as a silent reproach.'' (1–2)

Nationalists such as Duffy saw culture as a tool that would help achieve Ireland's advancement, and this obsession with Ireland's place among nations—with how well Ireland competed in areas from art to athletics to industry—made the creation of an Irish canon and a coherent cultural history an essentially practical exercise. The end of such a project was to be the elevation of the Irish race to a properly lofty position. This mundane approach to the wealth of Irish culture that was being uncovered, adapted, translated, and popularized was ripe for satire, and opponents such as Synge were indeed pondering the best method of attack.

That Synge was paying careful attention to these developments is clear in his letters and manuscripts; it is also apparent—more subtly, however—in his plays. Synge was certainly more knowledgeable than many cultural nationalists in the Celtic materials that were the object of much debate. He studied Irish language and literature in France with the eminent Henri d'Arbois de Jubainville, learned modern Irish himself in the west, and carefully read and reviewed new translations and adaptations as they were published. What is initially striking about Synge's work as a reviewer is his resolute avoidance of polemic, of participation in the cultural-nationalist disputes. His review in The *Speaker* (7 June 1902) of Lady Gregory's highly influential version of *Cuchulain of Muirthemne* carefully noted its value and its limitations. Synge did suggest that the text

should go far to make a new period in the intellectual life of Ireland. Henceforward the beauty and wonder of the old literature is likely to have an influence on the culture of all classes, and to give a new impulse to many lukewarm Irishmen who were unsympathetic toward their country because they were ignorant of her real tradition. (*Collected Works* 2:367)

That said, Synge went on to compare the text favorably with previous, inadequate translations and adaptations; he closed with a warning that Gregory had omitted certain "barbarous" features of the text, and that "readers who take more than a literary interest in these stories" and "students of mythology" must look to the original texts and other versions for a more accurate account of such features as the battle rages of Cuchulain. Gregory herself, in her preface, told her readers, "I have left out a good deal I thought you might not care about for one reason or another" (xvi).

Synge, while doing the reviewer's job of presenting the merits and flaws of the particular work, argued only that the work would have an *intellectual* effect on readers: it would go far to educate the Irish about their literary heritage. He did *not* take what seemed at the time the inevitable next step of connecting the work to any sort of larger plan; even Yeats—who could hardly be called a friend to the cultural nationalists—had argued in his introduction to Gregory's text, "if we will but tell these stories to our children the Land will begin again to be a Holy land" (xvii). Synge's careful avoidance of the rhetoric of transformation and his refusal to argue for the wider uses and effect of culture are notable in his other reviews of such works as the *Poems, Songs, and Keenes of Geoffrey Keating* (1900), the *Foras Feasa Ar Eirinn* of Keating (1902), and A. H. Leahy's volumes of *The Heroic Romances of Ireland* (1905, 1906). It is particularly striking in this case because Cuchulain was to become such a highly politicized figure. Padraic Pearse would devise a whole educational curriculum at his St. Enda's school for the purpose of creating an "Ireland teeming with Cuchulains" (Stephen MacKenna, "Memories of the Dead," unpublished pamphlet quoted in Thompson 77).

Both as a critic and a playwright, Synge persistently refused to involve himself directly in political matters. Just as he withdrew, in 1897, from Maud Gonne's nationalist organization *L'Irlande Libre* (see *Collected Letters* 2:47), so he would continue to turn away from the temptation of direct engagement in political debate. Despite his genuine interest in Irish culture and Irish nationalism, Synge chose to make his own politics known in a more oblique manner than was usual at the time. This preference becomes clear if we look to some of the sketches and scenarios that Synge did *not* develop into completed dramas. *The National Drama: A Farce*, for instance, reveals the goings-on in a club room, where various "types" of Irishmen debate the correct qualities of a national theater, eliminating one by one such models as Molière, Shakespeare, and Ibsen. The scenario offered much in the way of unsubtle satire:

FOGARTY: The National Drama of Catholic Ireland must have no sex. That's certain sure, Mr. Chairman.

JAMESON: With the help of God we'll make Ireland in this matter a glorious exception from the Catholic countries of the world. (*Collected Works* 3:223)

This piece also offers up Synge's vision of a nationalist-approved Irish library as one of the characters, a middle-class Catholic gentleman, peruses the approved works on the clubhouse shelf:

The Whole History of Hungary for Beginners, by an Eminent Writer. The Re-afforestation of the sea-shore. The Five Parts of Father O'Growney, being the complete Irish course needed for a patriot. How to be a Genius, by a Gaelic Leaguer. The Pedigree of the Widow of Ephesus. The Complete Works of Petronius and Boccaccio, unabridged. The Plays for an Irish Theatre, abridged and expurgated by a Catholic critic. Controversial Ethics for the use of Editors, by a doctor of Louvain. Fairy Tales for all Ages. The Dawn of the Twilight, and the Autumn of the Spring. The Encyclopedia Celtica, a brief statement of the facts of the Universe for Irishmen, being very useful for all who are awaiting the foundation of a University of Orthodox Science and Art. . . . What at all will I read, Mr. Murphy? You've no Novels. (221)

Another pair of scenarios, written slightly earlier, carry the projected title *Deaf Mutes for Ireland* and offer a "practical" solution to the problem of the dominance of the English language in Ireland.[1] This first scenario well conveys the thrust of Synge's satire:

The Gaels have conquered. A Pan Celtic congress is being held in Dublin. A large prize is offered for any Irishman who can be proved to know no English. A committee is sitting to try them. They bring in each man in turn, throw a light on him and say, "God save Ireland" and "To Hell with the Pope." Men are detected again and again. One is found at last who baffles all tests. In delight the congress is called in glorious robes; the victor is put up to make a speech in Irish, he begins talking on his fingers—he is deaf mute and advocates a deaf mute society as only safeguard against encroaching Anglo-Saxon vulgarity! (218)

There is a vast distance between Synge the temperate, controlled reviewer and Synge the satirist who, in the scenarios, hits at numerous targets with abandon. It is in the plays themselves that we will see Synge attempting to bridge this gap as he turns cultural conflict into comic drama.

These sketches show Synge giving full vent to his hostility toward, and contempt for, the ideas and ideals of the cultural nationalists. Indeed, Synge seems to have written a number of scenarios for plays that would surely not be staged—certainly not at the Abbey. They show Synge rather gleefully indulging in mean-spirited and crude satire; writing them must have given Synge a good deal of satisfaction after the criticism that was directed at him over the production of *The Shadow of the Glen* in October 1903. This delight in tweaking the nationalists can be seen in Synge's response to Willie Fay's request in 1904 for a play on the subject of the rebellion of 1798, "showing what the peasantry had to endure" and convincing potential audience members that the Abbey was not "irreligious and politically unsound" (cited by Saddlemyer in Synge, *Collected Works* 3:215). Fay's request certainly waved a few red flags at Synge, who responded with a decidedly irreverent sketch called *Bride and Kathleen: A Play of 98*, which featured a Catholic woman and a Protestant woman quarreling over who should have the privilege of hiding in a piece of shrubbery; another section of dialogue shows the women commiserating together before realizing that they are on opposite sides in the uprising (see *Collected Works* 3:215–17). This piece got as far as a reading with the company before it was, of course, rejected.

It is clear that Synge was capable of writing topical satire and of launching attacks on specific targets, such as Arthur Griffith and D. P. Moran. However, he chose a different strategy for his overall critique of cultural nationalism: despite his indulgence in the occasional satiric scenario, he avoided topical, overtly political dramas.[2]

Synge's acute interest in this matter is reflected in his plays, in which the central figures invariably face this same imperative that faced Ireland: to make their own histories, often from a kind of void, to the best possible ends. Synge's characters are notable for their rejection of a known present, a joyless reality, for a better—if fictional—world. In *The Shadow of the Glen*, the unhappy wife

Nora Burke faces two interpretations of her future. Her husband, who feigns his death and then throws her out of their cottage, paints a gruesome picture of the fate of his wife, whom he believes has been unfaithful and worthless:

It's lonesome roads she'll be going, and hiding herself away till the end will come, and they find her stretched like a sheep with the frost on her, or the big spiders, maybe, and they putting their webs on her, in the butt of a ditch. (*Collected Works* 3:55)

The Tramp, in turn, offers Nora an alternative ending:

Come along with me now, lady of the house, and it's not my blather you'll be hearing only, but you'll be hearing the herons crying out over the black lakes, and you'll be hearing the grouse, and the owls with them, and the larks and the big thrushes when the days are warm. . . . it's fine songs you'll be hearing when the sun goes up, and there'll be no old fellow wheezing the like of a sick sheep close to your ear. (57)

This duel of interpretations appears in virtually all of Synge's full-length plays, particularly in the love scenes (the contrast of images here, for instance, is closely echoed in the contrasting views of Christy Mahon's possible life with the Widow Quinn presented to him by the Widow and Pegeen in Act II of *The Playboy of the Western World*). The alternatives painted by the characters show the extremes of shameful lowliness and lyric heroism—the very options the cultural nationalists routinely offered to Ireland.

As Synge's works faced growing and vocal opposition from the nationalists, they increasingly showed an interest not only in the way characters could spin contrasting versions of their futures, but also in the way interpretations of the *past* could determine the course of characters' lives. In *The Well of the Saints* (1905), Synge's next drama after the controversy over *The Shadow of the Glen*, the blind couple Mary and Martin Doul are described by the locals as a "wrinkled wizened hag" and a man "with fat legs on him, and the little neck like the ram" (3:93, 97); however, they believe themselves to be youthful, noble, and enviable figures. When their eyes are opened by a miracle wrought by a passing saint, they see their history together as a lie and a sham:

MARTIN DOUL: Isn't it after yourself is playing lies on me, ten years, in the day, and in the night, but what is that to you now the Lord God has given eyes to me, the way I see you an old, wizendy hag, was never fit to rear a child to me itself.

MARY DOUL: I wouldn't rear a crumpled whelp the like of you. It's many a woman is married with finer than yourself should be praising God if she's no child, and isn't loading the earth with things that would make the heavens lonesome above, and they scaring the larks, and the crows, and the angels passing in the sky.

MARTIN DOUL: Go on now to be seeking a lonesome place where the earth can hide you away, go on now, I'm saying, and you'll be having men and women with their knees bled, and they screaming to God for a holy water would darken their sight, for there's no man but would liefer be blind a hundred years, or a thousand itself, than to be looking on your like. (99)

Eventually, these two will come to prefer their blindness, which restores to them their illusions, and refuse to have their sight restored when blindness comes on them again. Now viewing the world as a cruel, vulgar place, they decide to return to the "ignorance" of their past.

In *The Well of the Saints*, the characters are all rather unlikable sorts who are much given to argument and bitterness. The central characters move from their self-pity and dismay at their present situation to a determination to reject it, and the people they know, for a past that is full of illusions. This sort of railing at the present—at cruel facts—is itself a feature of the writings of cultural nationalists, and Mary and Martin Doul show a remarkably similar response, removing themselves from the "bad looks" and "villainy" of the world where they have no proper place and creating their own world through what Martin Doul calls "cute thinking" (129).

In his preoccupation with characters who have no "place"—who must make for themselves an alternate world—Synge evokes a central issue of Celtic nationalism, which perpetually contrasted the "spiritual" qualities of Celtic culture with the crass materialism of Anglo culture, interpreting all that was bad in modern society as a result of British influence. This view of Celtic culture as otherworldly and nonmaterialistic goes back at least to Matthew Arnold's *On the Study of Celtic Literature* (1867), and can be seen in its more modern form in A. E.'s *The Inner and Outer Ireland* (1921). The *Leader* and the *Catholic Bulletin* harped relentlessly on this theme in their attacks on contemporary society and, especially, popular culture.[3] Synge clearly preferred to attack the cultural nationalists with their own weapons. At the same time that he was turning out such devilish scenarios as *Deaf Mutes for Ireland* and *The National Drama: A Farce*, he was also working out his anger and frustration at the direction the Celtic Revival was taking by creating a more subtle lampoon of their ideas in his masterwork, *The Playboy of the Western World*. In this play, the attack on Synge's opposition is on a deeper level, making use of the most cherished notions of D. P. Moran, Arthur Griffith, and others of the "transformative" effects of a knowledge of Irish cultural history. Christy Mahon's story is a travesty of the Celtic Revivalist's views on the uplifting of the Irish people.

Christy, at the beginning of the play, is one of the sulky, downtrodden misfits, "gloomy and resentful," as described by such as Charles Gavan Duffy. The *Leader* gives us a good example of the way in which the degenerate Irish were to be raised to their proper place in the world:

The Irish revival, the arriving at the conviction of its necessity by process of thought, the effort to follow where that conviction leads, the immediate effect on the self-respect of an Irishman once he is possessed of the Irish-Ireland conviction—all this at once tends to operate on our energies, to give us real ideals, and drag us out of the ruck of general mediocrity. (24 May 1902, 8)

Christy would seem to be a prime candidate for the plan of cultural regeneration described by Duffy, Griffith, Moran, and the rest. He is described in the play as the quintessential man without a "place": he has, throughout his life, been a failure at all things. Just as Christy is about to reach his height and prove himself at the games, his father is denying that he has any good qualities at all. Christy, he insists, is a "dunce," a "poor fellow" who would "get drunk on the smell of a pint," "the laughing joke of every woman where four baronies meet" (*Collected Works* 4:123). Later, when Old Mahon sees his son win the race, he moans, "I never till this day confused that dribbling idiot with a likely man. I'm destroyed surely" (143).

Christy certainly does "fill up the blanks" of his education, as Duffy would suggest is necessary for an Irishman (47), but with results that are, from a nationalist standpoint, seriously awry. His "heroic" past does indeed transform him from a misfit into a poet, lover, and athlete (the fact that Christy's elevation includes demonstrations of physical prowess surely pokes fun at the Gaelic League's notion of sports as a conduit for the moral development of the Celts). But his heroic past is not only out of tune with reality; it is also centered on a gruesome act of familial violence. By basing Christy's rise and fall (and subsequent rise) on the crude image of a father with his skull split, Synge draws attention to all the bizarre and violent elements of Irish myth that were *not* easily incorporated into a pragmatic program of national renewal. The great hero Cuchulain, whom Declan Kiberd sees parodied in Christy, was given to spasms of bloody rage and had, in fact, slain his own son (see Kiberd 109–21).

However, here, in fact, Synge's parody has more layers. He is using the Celtic Revival's own creation, its cherished Celtic-peasant hero, to critique the very purpose of many of the revival's adherents. Far from having any beneficial social purpose, the transformative history making in Synge's plays puts his central characters on a collision course with the common people around them. They are seen as endangering the everyday workings of society, and in each case are banished or exile themselves from their surroundings. It is notable that the plays discussed here all close on scenes not of the myth-making characters themselves, but of the rejecting and, in turn, abandoned homes or societies. These characters who remain—Nora's husband and would-be husband, and the locals in *The Well of the Saints* and *The Playboy of the Western World*—are both relieved and disturbed at the departure of the trouble-making dreamers (with the exception of Pegeen, who promptly mourns the loss of her playboy). Far from being practical or socially useful, the exercises in history making in these plays are not easily controlled, and they have the result of making their central characters themselves into misfits, albeit heroic ones. Synge determinedly severs the tie between the making of one's own myth and making a prosperous and virtuous nation, and he points up an internal contradiction in the thinking of cultural nationalists who would use the otherworldly nature of Ireland's Celtic past for what were, in fact, practical and materialistic ends.

If Synge was using the creations of the Celtic Revival to critique it, the next logical step was to use the myths themselves. In *Deirdre*, Synge's ambitious attempt to handle Irish sagas, he would make a similar play upon the politics of history making by having his central characters self-consciously work out their own myth. In Synge's version of the tale, the individual is hardly at the mercy of the myth, the prophecy. While Synge's *Deirdre* is similar to Yeats's play in theme—the relation of the living to the mythic—it is radically different in concept and effect. Synge's Deirdre and Naoise prove to exert a great degree of control over "their" story.

There is every indication that this play was to be a departure for Synge, in which he could refine his ideas of the "realistic" and the "fantastic" in his drama. In a letter to Molly Allgood, his fiancée and the original "Deirdre," he would write: "I want to do something quiet and stately and restrained" (*Letters to Molly* 67); but elsewhere he expressed concern that "the 'Saga' people might loosen my grip on reality" (*Collected Letters* xxvii). The play was subject to extensive revision, and it was unfinished at the time of his death. The manuscript was prepared by Yeats and Gregory, and the play was performed at the Abbey in 1910.

Evidence from the manuscripts of the play shows that Synge consistently deleted references to the prophecy and to other supernatural elements. Both Lavarcham and Naoise were given speeches on prophecy and omens in the earlier drafts (*Collected Works* 203, 208), and Deirdre was originally intended to retain some of her visions (389). With the supernatural element thus downplayed, Synge permits his characters to create their own myth.

Coinciding with the suppression of prophecy, vision, and omen in the manuscripts is the development of a common, more earthy quality in the play. Holloway would later claim that Synge "vulgaris[ed] the beautiful legend" (Holloway 133), and his perception of Synge's interpretation of the legend, though unfavorable, is accurate. Many of the characters are given devious and unheroic moments: the sons of Uisliu threaten to break into Deirdre's house and are rude to Lavarcham, who in turn attempts to trick them; Conchobor is made to seem an imperious and pathetic old man fixated on a young girl; Owen, Conchobor's spy, makes fun of everyone; and Deirdre and Naoise are depicted as quarreling in a most undignified fashion just before their deaths. Indeed, in Deirdre's last lines to her husband she calls him a "laughing-stock" (257). The characters are at their best when they assume their mythic roles, and our measure of them derives from their willingness to choose the eternal and perfect in death.

In this play the very subjects of an Irish myth—part of the heritage that was itself seen to have a transformative value—are themselves subject to that process of change. Deirdre and Naoise are elevated into myth from a reality that is shown to be decidedly common. By rehumanizing the characters of this very well-known and beloved tale, Synge depoliticized their myth. In a deliberate inversion of the process described by Duffy, Moran, and others, Deirdre and Naoise themselves desire to flee the mutable world into the perfection of myth, to become the beautiful and inhuman pieces of a cultural legacy that Synge has carefully shown to belong outside the realm of practical politics.

NOTES

1. Ann Saddlemyer suggested that these two scenarios might have been written during the attacks on Synge by Arthur Griffith's *United Irishman* early in 1905 (Synge, *Collected Works* 3:218).

2. Synge's refusal to direct his energies into plays on political subjects can be seen in his response to a request by John Quinn that he

take some work like Sinn Fein, and trace a hero like "Shame-us" MacManus [Seumas MacManus, who wrote nationalist pieces in American newspapers] or Griffith who thinks he is a nation builder and who surrounds himself by some women and a lot of young asses who look upon him as a statesman and a nation-builder . . . and laugh at them. Show their mixture of cunning, bragging, and hypocrisy[,] . . . two of the great weaknesses of Irish character—their tendency to brag, their lack of that fine sense of honor in dealing with other people in intellectual matters, and their subservience to priests. (cited in Synge, *Collected Letters* 2:50)

Synge replied that he was "interested," but never made use of the outline (47–50).

3. For useful accounts of the categorizing of "Celtic" and "Anglo" cultures as hopelessly opposed, see O'Driscoll, and Lyons, ch. 3. A quotation from the *Catholic Bulletin* suggests how simple the connection between Celtic culture and high morals was to the nationalists:

The spruce and dapper Edwin, stepping from his mansion to woo and win some soulless Angelina, a vision of furs and laces, should be replaced by the blithe and merry working man who sings at his plough, greeting the pure-souled, cheery milkmaid as she croons on her milking stool. (cited in Garvin 105)

WORKS CITED

A. E. [Russell, George.] *The Inner and the Outer Ireland*. Dublin: National Library of Ireland, 1921.

Duffy, Charles Gavan, George Sigerson, and Douglas Hyde. *The Revival of Irish Literature: Addresses by Sir Charles Gavan Duffy, K.C.M.G., Dr. George Sigerson, and Dr. Douglas Hyde*. 1894. Reprint. New York: Lemma, 1973.

Garvin, Tom. *Nationalist Revolutionaries in Ireland, 1858–1928*. Oxford: Clarendon Press, 1987.

Gregory, Lady Augusta. *Cuchulain of Muirthemne: The Story of the Men of the Red Branch of Ulster*. London: John Murray, 1902.

Heaney, Seamus. "A Tale of Two Islands: Reflections on the Irish Literary Revival." *Irish Studies* 1 (1980): 1–20.

Holloway, Joseph. *Joseph Holloway's Abbey Theatre: A Selection from His Unpublished Journal, Impressions of a Dublin Playgoer*. Ed. by Robert Hogan and Michael J. O'Neill. Carbondale and Edwardsville: Southern Illinois University Press, 1967.

Kiberd, Declan. *Synge and the Irish Language*. Totowa, N.J.: Rowman and Littlefield, 1979.

Lyons, F. S. L. *Culture and Anarchy in Ireland, 1890–1939*. New York: Oxford University Press, 1979.

O'Driscoll, Robert. "The Aesthetic and Intellectual Foundations of the Celtic Literary Revival in Ireland." In *The Celtic Consciousness*, ed. Robert O'Driscoll. New York: George Braziller, 1982, 401–25.

Synge, John Millington. *The Collected Letters of John Millington Synge*, ed. Ann Saddlemyer. 2 vols. New York and Oxford: Clarendon Press, 1983–1985.

———. *Collected Works*, ed. Ann Saddlemyer. 4 vols. 1962–1968. Reprint. Gerrards Cross, U.K.: Colin Smythe; Washington, D.C.: Catholic University of American Press, 1982.

———. *Letters to Molly: John Millington Synge to Maire O'Neill*, ed. Ann Saddlemeyer. Cambridge: Belknap Press of Harvard University Press, 1971.

Thompson, William Irwin. *The Imagination of an Insurrection: Dublin, Easter 1916*. 1967. Reprint. New York: Harper, 1972.

Yeats, William Butler. *Explorations*. New York: Macmillan, 1962.

13

The Devil and Auld Mahoun: Exposing the Trickster Archetype in Synge's Christy Mahon by Way of Rushdie's Muhammad/Mahound

Gale Schricker Swiontkowski

What Salman Rushdie did with apparent awareness in 1989, John Millington Synge seems also to have done with less self-consciousness in 1907. Rushdie is suffering through a socially imposed purgatory as punishment for what many Muslims see as the open denigration of their religion and particularly of their prophet, Muhammad, in Rushdie's novel *Satanic Verses*. Synge, much like Rushdie, was declaimed as a devil during the first production of his drama *The Playboy of the Western World* and endured two years of significant social censure in Ireland and the United States before his death.[1] Riots and protests accompanied both the publication of Rushdie's novel and the production of Synge's play. But similarities between the two works run deeper than their receptions; the two writers offended their audiences with the same literary provocateur. Both Rushdie and Synge evoked violent response through their literary invocations of the trickster archetype as the dramatic union of their cultures' socially sanctioned divine prophets and socially condemned demonic figures. That Rushdie's compound Muhammad/Mahound inflamed Muslims in a tricksterly manner is clear. Christy Mahon's role as trickster is not so obvious. He seems in name and context to be a Christ figure: Christ, son of man. But our understanding of the contemporary controversy over Rushdie's Mahound casts a bright light back on Synge's Mahon, on both his name and role as trickster, and helps to explain more adequately than a mere reference to "shifts" can do why Christy caused such an uproar in Ireland ninety years ago.

The Oxford English Dictionary provides no more precise a definition of "trickster" than "one who practises trickery; a rogue, cheat, knave." But to psychologists and anthropologists, the trickster is a well-known and consistent character, permeating cultures throughout time, apparently endemic in the human psyche—what C. G. Jung termed an archetype. Jung describes the trickster in these terms: "He is a forerunner of the saviour, and, like him, God, man, and animal at once. He is both subhuman and superhuman, a bestial and divine being" (*Archetypes* 263). As this description suggests, the most marked feature of the trickster is his duality, to which Jung also refers as his "contradictori-ness":

Something of this contradictoriness also inheres in the medieval description of the devil as *simia dei* (the ape of God). . . . A curious combination of typical trickster motifs can be found in the alchemical figure of Mercurius; for instance, his fondness for sly jokes and malicious pranks, his powers as a shape-shifter, his dual nature, half animal, half divine, his exposure to all kinds of tortures, and—last but not least—his approximation to the figure of a saviour. These qualities make Mercurius seem like a daemonic being resurrected from primitive times. (*Archetypes* 255)

The self-contradictory duality of the trickster may be most obviously that of god/animal, but ultimately it is that of savior/demon—that is, one who might save us or destroy us, and that crucial duality is the essence of his timeless association with human culture. The trickster enacts on the social level the in-dividual's interplay between conscience and shadow, that dark side of the self we prefer to suppress rather than face (Jung, *Archetypes* 262). Because of his embodiment of both cultural aspiration and denial, the trickster's social actions often yield very dramatic results. Jung discusses this relationship between ar-chetype and society in terms of the savior/destroyer:

This image has lain buried and dormant in the unconscious since the dawn of history; it is awakened whenever the times are out of joint and a great error deflects society from the right path. For when people go astray they feel the need of a guide or teacher, and even of a physician. The seductive error is like a poison that can also act as a cure, and the shadow of a saviour can turn into a fiendish destroyer. (*Spirit* 103)

   Salman Rushdie's composition of *The Satanic Verses* seems to demonstrate the relationship of personal shadow and archetypal trickster. Indeed, Rushdie seems to have anticipated his own dilemma; at least, toward the end of the novel, his narrator records premonitions of disaster that now seem prophetic:[2]

The thumb-sucking artist with his infernal views. A book is a product of a pact with the Devil that inverts the Faustian contract. . . . Dr. Faustus sacrificed eternity in return for two dozen years of power; the writer agrees to the ruination of his life, and gains (but only if he's lucky) maybe not eternity, but posterity, at least. Either way . . . it's the Devil who wins. (459)

These are the views of the character Gibreel, who later returns to his own art form, acting, with similar results:

Gibreel had embarked on a modern-dress remake of the Ramayana story in which the heroes and heroines had become corrupt and evil instead of pure and free from sin. Here was a lecherous, drunken Rama and a flighty Sita; while Ravana, the demon-king, was depicted as an upright and honest man. "Gibreel is playing Ravanna," George explained in fascinated horror. "Looks like he's trying deliberately to set up a final confrontation with religious sectarians, knowing he can't win, that he'll be broken into bits." (539)

What was prophetic for Gibreel within the novel comes true as well for his author/creator, who flirted with heresy and has been suffering the consequences since.[3] The specific flashpoint for the Muslim world—the correlative to the word "shifts" in the mouth of Christy Mahon for the Irish nationalists earlier in the century—was the novel's transformation of the prophet Muhammad into the satanic figure Mahound. The transformation occurs as Muhammad seeks revelation from Gibreel, in his archangel role; Muhammad seems to insist, at least in one instance, on a revelation that would allow him to comply with the civil authority's request that a few pagan goddesses be assimilated into Islam. Certain rewards are promised to Muhammad in his role as a businessman; that is, Muhammad manipulates the prophetic process for personal gain. Rushdie's narrator is clear on the ethical consequences of this act; the message that Muhammad wrests from Gibreel on this occasion is the satanic verses themselves. And the prophecy that procures Muhammad/Mahound his material privileges is clearly not only received but also initiated by him; Gibreel functions to reflect back the prophet's own projections:

It happens: revelation. . . . an angel hung, scared silly, in the sky above the sufferer, held up like a kite on a golden thread? The dragging again the dragging and now the miracle starts in his my our guts, he is straining with all his might at something, forcing something, and Gibreel begins to feel that strength that force, here it is *at my own jaw* working it, opening shutting; and the power, starting within Mahound, reaching up to *my vocal cords* and the voice comes. (112)

Thus Muhammad, who seems to induce his own prophetic revelations, becomes Mahound by the nature of the revelations themselves:

His name, a dream-name, changed by the vision. . . . Here he is neither Mahomet nor MoeHammered; has adopted, instead, the demon-tag the farangis hung around his neck. To turn insults into strengths, whigs, tories, Blacks all chose to wear with pride the names they were given in scorn; likewise, our mountain-climbing, prophet-motivated solitary is to be the medieval baby-frightener, the Devil's synonym: Mahound. (93)

The process that the fictional prophet uses (consciously or not) to increase his profit as a businessman (the pun is surely not accidental) is not unlike Christy Mahon's eager acceptance of the heroic reflections the villagers provide him, thereby raising himself into that role. A key difference, however, is that Muhammad/Mahound eventually renounces the satanic verses, protesting that he was tricked by a duplicitous devil and thereby disowning responsibility, whereas Christy Mahon clings to his new self-image and struts from the stage at the end of the play "master of all fights from now" and "a likely gaffer in the end of all" (Synge, *Plays* 2:173). Both characters, however, show a detachment from or transcendence beyond the social code of accepted truths, which relates them to the archetypal trickster figure, as characterized here by anthropologist Paul Radin:

Trickster is at one and the same time creator and destroyer, giver and negator, he who dupes others and who is always duped himself. . . . He knows neither good nor evil yet he is responsible for both. He possesses no values, moral or social, is at the mercy of his passions and appetites, yet through his actions all values come into being. (xxiii)

The trickster seems to act in his own interest, but his actions affect the whole of his society because they draw on social conflicts between acknowledged and suppressed truths.

Rushdie, like Jung, traces elements of the trickster, the compound figure of good and evil, to the archetypal character developed in medieval mystery plays known by the name of Mahound or by variants of Mahound. In *Satanic Verses*, Rushdie lists several alternates: "Muhammad-Mahon-Mahound, a synonym for evil" (401). Thus, Mahound's potential relation to Christy Mahon becomes clearer. *The Oxford English Dictionary* (*OED*) confirms Rushdie's erudition, offering literary sources for a number of variant spellings of mahound, including "mahound" in Book VI of Spenser's *Fairie Queene* (VI.vii.47) and "mahon" in *Mirour Saluacioun* (c. 1450): "A grete dragon Wham alle that landes folk held god and thare mahon." Even more provocatively for scholars of Synge's play, the *OED* offers a passage from Robert Burns's "The De'il's awa" as source for "mahoun": "The De'il cam fiddling thro' the town, And danc'd awa wi' the Exciseman; And ilka wife cry'd *Auld Mahoun*, We wish you luck o' your prize, man" (emphasis added). Joseph Wright, editor of *The English Dialect Dictionary*, also cites this same passage from Burns in support of his definition of "mahoun": "A name given to the Devil; *gen.* in phr. *Auld Mahoun.* . . . OFr. *Mahon*, name of one of the principal devils, prop. a form of 'Mahomet.' " Synge read Spenser and Burns as a young man; wrote up a definition of mahometanism in an undergraduate notebook; studied medieval literature in many languages, including English, French, and Irish; spoke of the Celtic drama of Brittany as "a survival of the sincere, if sometimes grotesque, religious drama of the Middle Ages" (*Prose* 393); and further discussed the grotesque in drama in these terms: "the gaiety of life is the friction of the animal and the divine" (*Plays* 1:186), a duality that echoes the most common characterization of the trickster.[4] Did Synge, with his extensive interest in and exposure to medieval literature, know of the literary etymology of the Irish surname Mahon before giving it to the hero of *The Playboy of the Western World*? The evidence that he may have is compelling.

Not only does Christy Mahon's name contain a potential reference to the devil, but so does the word *playboy*, the term supplied to characterize Christy in the title and at various points in Synge's work. In one of the earliest critical responses to the play, Maurice Bourgeois disregards any satanic undertones to Synge's use of the term *playboy*, but also raises some provocative questions in doing so:

The word "playboy" (Irish *buachaill barra*, literally "boy of of the game," a term used in the Irish game of "hurling" . . .) is Hibernian slang. Its exact meaning (not to be found in Wright's *English Dialect Dictionary* . . . ,which gives only the older acceptations of the word . . .) is "hoaxer, humbugger, mystificator (*not* imposter), one who does sham things." (193, n. 1)

Wright's dictionary, published in 1903 and thus available to Synge when he was writing *Playboy*, provides two definitions for the term *playboy*: "the devil" and "a playful woman." In support of the first definition Wright offers a quote from a collection of tales by Seumas MacManus, entitled *The Bend of the Road*, which appeared in a second edition in 1906, a year Synge spent composing his play. In the tale "Toal, Theologian," Toal, a Donegal shoemaker, takes an opportunity to scold an impoverished Protestant minister who appears in his shop in need of new soles. The good Catholic, Toal, preaches:

Martin Luther, the first haratic, afther he dissolved himself from the wan, thrue, an' only Church o' Rome, had the divil sittin' cheek be jowl with him in his own chimbly-corner! Cheek be jowl! with his hoof on the fendher, an' his tail up lake my brannet cow's on a hot day! That, sir, is positive and proven fact—an' himself an' the Playboy *shoughed* out o' the same pipe! (107)

Wright clearly takes the Playboy in this quote to refer to the devil. It seems equally likely that Martin Luther could be the Playboy, next to the devil "himself," but the point of the cozy relationship that Toal depicts is that they are close buddies; Martin Luther is the devil's agent on earth in his act of breaking from the authority of the pope, thus a notable parricide and, in that sense, one of Christy Mahon's progenitors.

Did Synge, who was continually interested in literary representations of peasant dialect, read this edition of MacManus's popular collection of tales by fictional Donegal peasants, or its first edition in 1898, or did he perhaps also hear this vernacular usage of the term *playboy* among the peasants he lived with and studied? I have found no proof that he did, but there is enticing evidence of at least parallel thought: in Act I of *Playboy*, as the Mayo villagers are guessing at the nature of Christy's crime, Jimmy Farrell speculates, "Did you marry three wives maybe? I'm told there's a sprinkling have done that among the holy Luthers of the preaching North" (*Plays* 2:71).[5] In addition, Arthur Nethercot cites the etymological judgment of two Celtic scholars who disagree with Bourgeois's definition of *playboy* in a way that supports the possibility that Synge knew of connotations of trickster in the term:

It is clear that the Irish term most nearly equivalent to English "playboy" is *buachaill baire* (not *barre*). Tomas de Bhaldraithe cites [it] in his study of Connemara Irish . . . and translates it "fly-boy." He also gives *cailin baire*, "girl trickster." . . . The dialect he reports on in this book is the same Synge would have heard in Connemara and the Aran Islands. (116)

Moreover, both MacManus's story and Wright's dictionary were available to Synge during the period he was writing *Playboy*, but the source that Bourgeois prefers for his nondemonic definition of "playboy" was not. To contradict Wright's "older acceptations" of the term, Bourgeois refers to an article entitled "The Irish Dialect of English" by Mary Hayden and Marcus Hartog, published in three parts in *The Fortnightly Review* in 1909, two years after the first production of Synge's play. In fact, Hayden and Hartog do mention the devil, even if only in a derivative way, in their discussion of the Irish use of the term *playboy*: "The clown, or buffoon, of a class, whether at school or college, is an 'artist,' and a wild dare-devil is termed a 'play-boy.' " Unfortunately for Bourgeois's defense of this more innocent sense of the term as that which Synge intended, Hayden and Hartog footnote the source of their definition thus: "As in Synge's well-known comedy" (779). Hayden and Hartog cannot supply the denotation of the term *playboy* as Synge inherited it if they also use Synge as their source.

The drafts of Synge's play show that he arrived at the term *playboy* in his title rather late in the evolution of the drama. Previous titles include *Murder Will Out* and *The Fool of the Family* and, most interestingly, *Christy Mahon*, before Synge settled on *The Playboy of the Western World* (Synge, *Plays* 2:51, n. 1). And Christy's name evolved over quite a long period of composition as well; various typescripts and notebook entries reveal that while Synge seems to have used the given name of Christy from very early in his development of the plot, he contemplated quite a few surnames for his hero before settling on "Mahon" (Synge, *Plays* 2:76, n. 4, 362, n. H). Interestingly, one early name that Synge used consistently for Christy and his father was "O'Flaherty," which Synge finally retained as the surname of Pegeen and Michael James, in the form of "Flaherty." Ann Saddlemyer, in her appendix to the play, reproduces passages from one of Synge's notebooks showing that Christy's father is called both "Old O'Flaherty" and "Old Man" in one early draft (Synge, *Plays* 2: 298). It is tempting to speculate that the name "Flaherty" held Synge's interest right into the final version (as other surnames did not) because it is a near-homonym of "flattery." At least four stage directions in the final version of the play specify that Christy is flattered or that others are flattering him (63, 69, 101, 103). If Synge were consciously working with such a descriptive name, it likewise would be a small step from "Old Man" in the early versions to the homonymic and punning "Old Mahon" of the final version. It seems clear from the evolution of the play that Old Mahon earns his surname first and Christy's follows as a matter of course, so the significance of the surname may relate more to the symbolic standing of the father than the son. Christy is the son of Mahon, but what is the allegorical essence of this Old Mahon—is he God, mankind, or the devil? Synge read Burns and apparently admired his work, for he classified Burns in a 1908 notebook with Shakespeare as a poet of real life (*Prose* 347). But did Synge consciously develop his Old Mahon with Burns's Auld Mahoun in mind?

In the final analysis, speculations about Synge's intent cannot be confirmed, and the play must speak for itself. The possibility that the name "Christy Mahon" carries associations of both savior and infidel in tandem demands a significant rereading of the play, for most critics have discussed only the divine connotations of the given name "Christy" and have developed, thus, his potentially redeeming nature.[6] Zack Bowen has most recently summarized the play's Christian allegory as it clearly centers on Christy (72). Bowen is not, however, content to present only the straight Christian allegory; he also refers to the play as a "degradation of Irish Roman Catholicism in this biblical father-son parody" (72) and to the appearance in it of "our Jungian shadow side" (74). Similarly, Robin Skelton has augmented Synge's own comparison of Christy to Don Quixote by emphasizing the duality inherent in each character: "at once saviour and fool, hero and clown, visionary and madman" (117).[7] As clearly present as the Christ analogy is, just as clearly some darker element functions in the play as well. As Anthony Roche has put it, "Even in a relatively straight reading of the Christ/Christy parallel, it is impossible to suppress completely the disturbing ironic disruptions that refuse to conform and complete the parallel" (130).

Stanley Sultan (52) has pointed to Christy's first speech of the play, "God save all here!" (*Plays* 2:67), as introducing the Christian allegory, and indeed Christy refers to God numerous times in the play. But there are also a good many references to Satan or the devil. In Act I, Christy initially associates the devil with his own anticipated punishment, describing himself as "a poor orphaned traveller, has a prison behind him, and hanging before, and hell's gap gaping below" (71). But the villagers respond to Christy's revelation of his crime with awe at his courage: "Bravery's a treasure in a lonesome place, and a lad would kill his father, I'm thinking, would face a foxy divil with a pitchpike on the flags of hell" (75). Almost immediately, the villagers' veneration turns Christy's fear of punishment into bravery, as the devil image in their dialogue turns from punisher of Christy to potential victim of his own prey. Significantly, Christy gives his surname only after this reputation as father killer and devil threatener is established; he then sprinkles several bragging references to the devil into his conversation with Pegeen (81, 83); and by the end of Act I, Christy has learned that a devilish rebellion against authority can bring the rewards of independence and a new life.

In Act II, references to the devil are associated more specifically with what

Christy has stood up to and escaped from in his past, his father in particular. In his monologue at the beginning of the act while looking in a mirror, Christy reveals his memories of a hellish past homelife in contrast to the heavenly life he expects in his new home with Pegeen:

Didn't I know rightly I was handsome, though it was the divil's own mirror we had beyond, would twist a squint across an angel's brow, and I'll be growing fine from this day, the way I'll have a soft lovely skin on me and won't be the like of the clumsy young fellows do be ploughing all times in the earth and dung. (95)

A bit later, as he develops his flare for figurative language, Christy recreates the scene that drove him to strike his father with the loy, including this exchange with his father: " 'Go on,' says he, 'or I'll have the divil making garters of your limbs tonight.' 'You will not if I can help it,' says I" (103). But when Old Mahon appears in Act II, it is clear that Christy fears him and, in fact, associates him with the devil; he cries to Widow Quin, "Where'll I hide my poor body from that ghost of hell?" (119). It is equally clear that Old Mahon disdains his son for lacking the gumption of a more sinister character, using the term "divil" here to mean, ironically, the absence of devilish spunk: "It was my own son hit me, and he the divil a robber or anything else but a dirty, stuttering lout" (121). In Act II, Old Mahon calls on the devil as ritually as Christy calls on God in Act I.

In an earlier version of the play, where Christy calls his father a "black walker of hell" (356), the conflict in Christy's mind between himself as a God-fearing man and his demonic father (still Old Flaherty here) is developed much more openly and thoroughly:

OLD F. [*shaking his stick*]. Now the day of quitment has been sent from God. Now you'll get your wages for your demon doings in the north and south.

CHRISTY [*slinking round behind* SALLY]. May God help and pity me this dreadful day.

OLD F. Let you not be tormenting the Lord God. Would you have him sending down droughts and big winds, and the blight on the spuds and typhus and typhoid, and the "ould hin," and the Cholera Morbus?

CHRISTY. What'll I do at all from this day if I can't say my prayers out itself without bringing torment on me head?

OLD F. Come along I'm saying till I work the evil from your heart.

CHRISTY. Oh, Sally Quin for the love of God protect [me] from his hands. What did I ever do that I should have him badgering, and badgering round as if I was an evil person or a son of hell.

OLD F. Doesn't the whole world know you're a poor good for nothing and isn't it by the likes of you that the sins of the whole world are committed. Didn't the divil himself lay his mark on you the day you were born the way yourself or me would put a black mark on the thighs of a lamb?

CHRISTY. Oh, Sally Quin for the love of Heaven won't you step out between the two of us now?

SALLY QUIN. What would you have me do for you at all?

CHRISTY. Let you not have me sent out this day to be a lonesome poor tramper on the face of the world, walking from Union to Union with the ground white and hard to my feet, and the old lad pacing behind me the way the lost spirits do be following and following the saints of God.

SALLY. How would I stop him? . . .

CHRISTY. . . . Oh, let you wed me Widow Quin for the love and kindness of the holy Christy. (332–33)

Synge must later have deemed this dialogue too heavy-handed, for the final version of the play preserves parts of this scene in Act III without such obvious imagery; "for the love and kindness of the holy Christy," for instance, becomes the more muted "for the love of Christ" (131). But this early version casts into relief the great achievement of Christy's strong exit at the end of the final version—"like a gallant captain with his heathen slave" (173), and it also highlights Synge's concern not only with Christy's Christ-like nature, but also with his satanic father. In this draft, Christy seems clearly to be the son of Auld Mahoun (or "son of hell," as he says) and thus a man of devilish as well as saintly qualities—a trickster by constitution.

Indeed, in his indignation at his mistreatment by the villagers at the end of the play, Christy's language turns markedly toward the devilish terminology of his father, and his references to the devil seem to record his achievement of independence and self-respect, as if he has incorporated the strength of his father into his own, more timid identity, and thus stands on his own rather than running from his father or any other authority: he has become his own authority, and the frightened villagers have become the ignorant oppressors. In incorporating the demonic inheritance from his father and the self-assertion that accompanies it, Christy grows out of an initial timidity not unlike Shawn's and into an assurance at the end of the play that carries him away from his audience and into a state of gleeful independence:

SHAWN [shrieking]. My leg's bit on me! He's the like of a mad dog, I'm thinking, the way that I will surely die.

CHRISTY [delighted with himself]. You will, then, the way you can shake out hell's flags of welcome for my coming in two weeks or three, for I'm thinking Satan hasn't many have killed their da in Kerry and in Mayo too. (Plays 2:171)

It is at this point that Old Mahon reappears, but the fact that Christy has twice failed to kill his father does not undercut his new confidence; he bosses his father out the door and taunts the villagers with his freedom. Even Old Mahon's happy craziness at Christy's more assertive behavior at the end may affirm Christy's new acceptance of his father's own demonism, for Old Mahon has previously confided to Widow Quin that his madness has been associated with devils (143).

Pegeen's ending lament, "Oh my grief, I've lost him surely. I've lost the only playboy of the western world" (173), assumes a different tone in light of the demonic element that seems to give Christy the power to walk away exulting. Pegeen, who has been pining for a young man plucky to the point of sinfulness or heresy (59, 151), realizes at the end of the play that she has just spurned the one man likely to meet her desires and deliver her from her subjection. Numerous critics have noted the play's theme of rebellion against father/ authority and its implications for the young nationalist movement at the time the play was first produced. Augustine Martin has perhaps best developed the theme of rebellion in terms of Christy's growth as an individual. Martin celebrates *Playboy* as a "Dionysiac comedy," in that "it celebrates the victory of the aggressive individual will over the immoveable forces of society" (64). And he shows that this victory is achieved not just through parricide but through the mastery of the father that follows rebellion:

When Norman Podhoretz suggests that the play's underlying myth is "rebellion against the father" he gives us, I believe, precisely half the story. The other half is the recognition and acceptance of the father. . . . [Old Mahon] is not ready yet for the real recognition— that Christy is truly his son, an even greater "playboy" than himself. This insight can only be reached when Christy recognizes Mahon as his real father, thereby rejecting the men of Mayo and their law-fearing timidity and transcending his infatuation for Pegeen. (65, 68–69)

Martin's analysis of the Dionysiac character of Christy and the positive aspect of the disorder he brings to the villagers is remarkably close to anthropologist Karl Kerenyi's analysis of the Winnebago trickster, whose "Dionysian ecstasy" (188) has the virtue of abolishing boundaries:

Disorder belongs to the totality of life, and the spirit of this disorder is the trickster. His function in an archaic society . . . is to add disorder to order and so make a whole, to render possible, within the fixed boundaries of what is permitted, an experience of what is not permitted. (185)

Irving Suss has reached further into the implications of rebellion in *Playboy*, into the challenge it presented to the contemporary audience and to the society of the time, and in this analysis he touches also on the work of the trickster:

In the political context of the time, there was . . . a touchiness among the Irish that is characteristic of any subjugated group fighting against the inferior status to which it is condemned. . . . In this social context [of power of priest/peeler/parent] the self-liberation of the Playboy by violence—especially by violence—was a picture of the hidden dream of the Irishman brought into the light of day. There was no intervening censor, no concealing dream-work to distort the wish and make it acceptable to the consciousness.

Freud's reality principle operated in the mass, and there was a violent effort to suppress the feeling that the play generated and made recognisable. (40, 42)

Several contemporary editorial comments on the first production of *Playboy* affirm this insight—that the audience was moved to reject the play because its truth was too painful to admit into consciousness. The *Freeman's Journal* of 28 January 1907 reminded its readers: "It has ever been the custom of traducers of the Irish people to charge them with sympathy with all forms of crime. Over and over again this same lie has been made the justification of Coercion" (quoted in Kilroy 19). While this statement was intended to brand Synge and his supporters as traitors to the nationalist cause in depicting the virtuous Irish peasant as sympathetic to a parricide, it also speaks clearly to the motivations of the rioting audiences: how could the theatergoers accept a negative depiction of the Irish peasantry that echoed England's excuse for subjugating them? More to the point, why would Synge wish to present his audience with such a dilemma? The *Irish Times*, on 30 January 1907, attempted an answer:

He has led our vision through the Abbey street stage into the heart of Connaught, and revealed to us there truly terrible truths, of our own making, which we dare not face for the present. The merciless accuracy of his revelation is more than we can bear.... "Shaneen" accepts terror as the regular condition of his existence, and so there is no need for him to emigrate with the strong and clever ones who insist on freedom for their lives.... Such are Synge's insights into life and character in Connaught. Can the Western peasantry have a truer friend than the one who exhibits to criticism and to condemnation the forces afflicting their lives? (quoted in Kilroy 37–39)

The villagers' initial admiration for a parricide and their subsequent degradation in the wake of Christy's apotheosis as a hero demonstrates the psychological truth that it is only by accepting one's own shadow and not projecting it onto others that one achieves self-possession and freedom. Synge would likely have agreed with the *Freeman*'s insight that the Irish could not accept such a critical picture of their countrymen because it would seem to confirm England's negative view of them and thus to reinforce the supposed justice of England's oppression of Ireland. Especially at that time of renewed national interests, it seemed crucial to present the Irish people as pure and moral—the antithesis of England's condemnatory stereotype. Synge would likely also have agreed with a comment by Townsend Walsh, former drama critic of the *New York World*, in a letter to John Quinn in March of 1907: "If Synge had made Christy murder a peeler instead of his father, the Nationalists would have crowned him a genius" (cited in Synge, *Letters* 2:49, n. 7). However, it is when Christy accepts his father, sins and all, that he is set free.

Christy's assumption of control over his father and his incorporation of the villagers' new view of him as a demonic character are strongly reminiscent of Rushdie's Muhammad becoming Mahound, accepting the derogatory label of the enemy and thus disabling it. Rushdie has elsewhere described this as an act of triumph and self-empowerment:

What "Islam" now means in the West is an idea that is not merely medieval, barbarous, repressive and hostile to Western civilization, but also united, unified, homogeneous, and therefore dangerous. . . . We are back in the demonizing process which transformed the Prophet Muhammad, all those years ago, into the frightful and fiendish "Mahound." . . . Central to the purposes of *The Satanic Verses* is the process of reclaiming language from one's opponents. . . . Something of the same spirit lay behind my use of the name "Mahound." (*Imaginary Homelands* 382, 402)

Many of Rushdie's readers have shown their inability to appreciate that freedom follows a refusal to project the shadow and a willingness to incorporate it into the self. Synge likewise challenged his audience to accept the shadow side of their own national character along with its more consciously ideal manifestations (a unity of opposites symbolized when Christy and Old Mahon stride off together) in order to possess their own sins and weaknesses and thus be free of England's exploitation of them. Jung has said:

If only people could realize what an enrichment it is to find one's own guilt, what a sense of honour and spiritual dignity! . . . When we are conscious of our guilt we are in a more favourable position—we can at least hope to change and improve ourselves. . . . Without guilt, unfortunately, there can be no psychic maturation and no widening of the spiritual horizon. . . . Such an experience brings about an inner transformation, and this is infinitely more important than political and social reforms which are all valueless in the hands of people who are not at one with themselves. (*Civilization* 202, 215–16)

This is probably why Thomas Whitaker has spoken of the *Playboy* as "a 'score' for a participatory event" (11) and focused on the duality of Christy's character as the catalyst of that event: "Not for nothing is Christy Mahon a potato-digging poet, ostensible father-murderer, seeming savior, lord of misrule, and consequent scapegoat. He is a richly symbolic man" (2). Christy embodies the opportunity of freedom for himself and the villagers, but at the end of the play the villagers deny their own guilt and project it onto Christy, as they earlier projected their fantasies of rebellion onto him. Christy, to the contrary, assumes his own guilt and seems truly to be transformed at the end of the play.

Interestingly, if Christy's role is, ideally, to offer freedom to the villagers and, by extension, the audience of the play, by demonstrating how to accept the shadow and cease projecting it onto others, this role accords quite closely with what anthropologist Paul Radin has said about the origin of the trickster figure in the mythology of the Winnebago Indians, that he was created as an adversary or antidote to other spirits that caused harm to humans (60). Alternatively, in reference to a variant trickster figure, Radin notes, "His task is to grow up and to see that human beings grow up with him" (166). The Winnebago trickster performs these two functions in a very indirect way—by acting the fool, acting out all the potential weaknesses of mankind, thereby incorporating them into humanity and removing them from the projected realm of evil spirits. The society that can accept his behavior, which includes breaking all social taboos, like the villagers of *Playboy* in their initial admiration of Christy's story of parricide, will benefit from participating in this ritual tale:

What we really have here is something equivalent to certain semi-religious mediaeval performances where the participants feel that no harm can come to them and where they can pretend to themselves that they cannot be accused of sacrilege or of ridiculing the traditionally accepted order. (Radin 152)

Of course, the villagers do benefit from a playful participation in Christy's tale of parricide, testing their own desires and strengths, until Synge has Christy do within the play what the more traditional, mythological tricksters do not—bring the breaking of taboos out of the realm of fantasy and into the realm of reality. Then the villagers prove unable to step out of the confines of their restrictive social order and walk in self-assumed responsibility into a freer but unknown and undefined future. Christy does, as do so many of the more interesting characters in Synge's dramas: the tinkers who bag the priest in *The Tinker's Wedding*, Nora and the Tramp of *The Shadow of the Glen*, Martin and Mary Doul in *The Well of the Saints*. Synge seems to admire these daring characters, but he does not follow them into the future to record whether anyone can, as Christy promises to do, "go romancing through a romping lifetime from this hour to the dawning of the judgment day" (*Plays* 2:173).

While Synge at times complained of frights during childhood from his mother's warnings of Hell, he also appreciated as an adult the benefits of a healthy awareness of the demonic or at least the rebellious, especially in the arts.[8] In a draft of a letter to Stephen MacKenna in 1904, Synge wrote of the need in literature for the trickster archetype, without using that terminology:

I think squeamishness is a disease, and that Ireland will gain if Irish writers deal manfully, directly and *decently* with the entire reality of life. I think the Law-Maker and the Law-Breaker are both needful in society—as the lively and volcanic forces are needed to make earth's crust habitable—and I think the Law-Maker is tending to reduce Ireland or parts of Ireland to a dismal morbid hypocracy [*sic*] that is not a blessed unripeness. (*Letters* 1:76)

So William Blake observes in his *Marriage of Heaven and Hell* that the devil brings energy to the world.[9] And so Christy Mahon is, in at least this sense, more Mahound than Christ, a liberating character who challenges the stultifying order of society and awakens energy and desire in the Mayo villagers—or perhaps he is like Christ, but not the Christ bringing laws from the Father so much as the Christ challenging the corrupted social order of his time, introducing concepts of spiritual transcendence to a society that initially thought them evil.

It is clear from his letters during the composition and after the first production of *Playboy* that Christy Mahon was a liberating and then challenging Law-Breaker, not only for the Mayo villagers in the play and the play's audience, but also for the playwright himself. During the composition of *Playboy*, Synge complained at times of the infrequency of his meetings with his fiancee, Molly Allgood, in terms such as these, from a letter dating from the last months of his work on the play: "I believe it is that wretched Playboy who has been making all the mischief, it is unnatural that we should be so near each other, and still not be able to see each other oftener" (*Letters* 1:233). Such a comment demonstrates an instinctive, if not conscious, comprehension of the puckish quality of the trickster figure—his insistence on having his own way, especially at the inconvenience of others. But in later letters Synge suggests not a subordinate association with his own trickster character, but more of an identification with him. Again to Molly Allgood, he writes at the end of the *Playboy*'s first week on stage: "Cheer up, my little heart, the P.B. will soon be getting his rest I hope, and then, we'll be able to see a lot of each other. . . . The mountains looked lovely today. I cannot tell you how much I longed to be away among them with Pegeen Mike" (Molly's role in the play) (*Letters* 1:287–88). *Playboy* was not destined to produce rest for anyone in the near future, but Synge seemed to accept that controversy was its proper role. After opening night he wrote to Molly, "It is better any day to have the row we had last night, than to have your play fizzling out in half-hearted applause. Now we'll be talked about. We're an event in the history of the Irish stage" (285). And several months later, after a good review and a request to translate the play, Synge was confident enough to exult, "So you see Christy is making his way" (335).

The Playboy of the Western World is unquestionably Synge's masterpiece, a drama that seemed to work its way through Synge's life and talent before his early death. After its production, the playwright was most closely identified with that play. More than six years after the first production of the play and four years after Synge's death, in June 1913, Padraic Pearse remembered Synge as a symbol of sacrifice, a Christ figure who tried to assist his fellow countrymen by introducing them to the liberating potential of rebelling against a restrictive authority—a living Christy Mahon:

When a man like Synge, in whose sad heart there glowed a true love of Ireland, one of the two or three men who have in our time made Ireland considerable in the eyes of the world, uses strange symbols which we do not understand, we cry out that he has blasphemed and we proceed to crucify him. (quoted in Greene and Stephens 272)

Pearse here confronts his own initial condemnation of *Playboy*; it was he who called Synge "a sort of Evil Spirit" in response to the play (quoted in Greene and Stephens 272). But this passage also clearly shows that Pearse has learned much from Synge and his *Playboy*—in less than three years after writing these approving words on Synge, Pearse would choose Easter as the symbolic moment to begin the rebellion he and a few others orchestrated in defiance of the English authority in Ireland, sacrificing their lives, Christ-like, for the liberation of their fellow countrymen.

It took six years for one of the prominent nationalists in Ireland to recognize that Synge and his apparently insulting play were potential agents of redemption. Just as long after the initial publication of *Satanic Verses*, Salman Rushdie pursues his life in hiding from the Muslim extremists who have branded him a traitor and his novel treason to their fundamentalist cause and have cast a death sentence on him. Only time will tell if Muslim culture will come to appreciate the opportunity for liberation that may be lurking in Muhammad/Mahound of *Satanic Verses*.[10] But both cases of Synge's and Rushdie's literary provocation of social censure through the manifestation of the trickster archetype demonstrate two dominant characteristics of the trickster—its flexibility and durability:

Every generation occupies itself with interpreting Trickster anew. No generation understands him fully but no generation can do without him. . . . for he represents not only the undifferentiated and distant past, but likewise the undifferentiated present within every individual. This constitutes his universal and persistent attraction. . . . If we laugh at him, he grins at us. What happens to him happens to us. (Radin 168–69)

The trickster is an agent of redemption or ruin, depending on our abilities to comprehend and confront him. As Pegeen learns, he merely mirrors our own desires and capacities.

NOTES

1. Joseph Holloway wrote in his diary during the furor over the first production of Synge's *Playboy*, "Synge is the evil genius of the Abbey and Yeats his able lieutenant" (81); Padraic Pearse wrote in *An Claidheamh Soluis* of "the generation of a sort of Evil Spirit in the shape of Mr. J. M. Synge" and of his "gospel of animalism" (quoted in Greene and Stephens 272).

2. While Rushdie has more recently "embraced Islam," he also makes it clear that this action has not freed him of the social censure that threatens his life. (See "Why I Have Embraced Islam" in *Imaginary Homelands* 430–32.) Rushdie disputes that he "knew exactly what [he] was doing" when he wrote *The Satanic Verses* but also admits, "It's true that some passages in *The Satanic Verses* have now acquired a prophetic quality that alarms even me" (*Imaginary Homelands* 407).

3. Rushdie has claimed that he cannot have intended heresy since he never embraced Islam (before writing *Satanic Verses*): "To put it as simply as possible: *I am not a Muslim*. It feels bizarre, and wholly inappropriate, to be described as some sort of heretic after having lived my life as a secular, pluralist, eclectic man" (*Imaginary Homelands* 405). But in this statement Rushdie begs the question of the relation of religion and culture—can he really claim not to be a Muslim when he acknowledges being raised in a Muslim family within a Muslim cultural group? Rushdie may possess the flexibility to make the distinction between individual belief and cultural heritage (see *Imaginary Homelands* 376–77), but this would not be true for many of his readers.

4. The most thorough account of Synge's knowledge of medieval literature is Toni O'Brien Johnson's *Synge: The Medieval and the Grotesque*. Evidence of Synge's readings is provided in his notebooks (especially MS 4373) and in MS 5205, a list of Synge's readings up to 1888, both in Trinity College Library, Dublin. The entry for mahometanism, in which Synge does not use the term "mahound," is on leaf 31 of MS 4373. My thanks to the librarians who helped me to examine the Synge manuscripts at Trinity College Library, Dublin, and at the National Library of Ireland.

5. Whether Synge knew of this particular collection of tales, he did know of its author, MacManus. The Irish National Theatre Society produced his play *The Townland of Tamney* in 1903, when Synge was associated with that group, and Synge comments in a strongly negative way on an article by MacManus on Sinn Fein in a letter to John Quinn in September 1907. (See Greene and Stephens 167, 298–99, and *Letters* 2:46.)

6. Mitsuhiko Ito recently published an essay on the Gaelic derivations of the names in *Playboy* that accepts Christy as Christ but traces the surname Mahon to "the Irish word *mathghamhain* [meaning] 'bear' in English, which implies strength" (96).

7. Synge compared his *Playboy* to *Don Quixote* in an interview published in the Dublin *Evening Mail* on 29 January 1907. (See Kilroy 24.)

8. Synge lamented "the well-meant but extraordinary cruelty of thrusting/throwing the idea of Hell into the imagination of a nervous child" and observes approvingly, "In Irish and non-Christian texts no hell" (quoted in Roche 110–11). But the Hell of which Synge speaks here seems to be that used by the "Law-Makers" of society (to use the term Synge himself uses in his letter to MacKenna) and thus a stultifying force, a reinforcement of the life-restricting rules that the "Law-Breaker" will challenge.

9. Interestingly, Rushdie cites William Blake's *Marriage of Heaven and Hell* as one of the "two books that were most influential on the shape *[Satanic Verses]* took" (*Imaginary Homelands* 403).

10. Ghassan Maleh has written appreciatively of the example Synge and Yeats have set for the Arabic world, in terms of a "literary and dramatic movement [being] an offshoot of their political struggle for freedom and independence" (246).

WORKS CITED

Bourgeois, Maurice. *John Millington Synge and the Irish Theatre*. 1913. Reprint. New York: Blom, 1968.

Bowen, Zack R. "Synge: *The Playboy of the Western World*." In *A J. M. Synge Literary Companion*, ed. Edward A. Kopper, Jr. Westport, Conn.: Greenwood Press, 1988, 69–86.

Greene, David H., and Edward M. Stephens. *J. M. Synge, 1871–1909*. 1959. Rev. ed. New York: New York University Press, 1989.

Hayden, Mary, and Marcus Hartog. "The Irish Dialect of English, I: Its Origins and Vocabulary." *Fortnightly Review* 85 (April 1909): 775–85.

Holloway, Joseph. *Joseph Holloway's Abbey Theatre: A Selection from His Unpublished Journal. Impressions of a Dublin Playgoer*. Ed. by Robert Hogan and Michael J. O'Neill. Carbondale: Southern Illinois University Press, 1967.

Ito, Mitsuhiko. "Naming the Characters of Synge's *Playboy of the Western World*." *Eire-Ireland* 27(2) (1992):93–101.

Johnson, Toni O'Brien. *Synge: The Medieval and the Grotesque*. Irish Literary Studies

11. Gerrards Cross, U.K.: Colin Smythe; Totowa, N.J.: Barnes and Noble, 1982.

Jung, C. G. *The Archetypes and the Collective Unconscious.* Vol. 9, part 1, of *The Collected Works of C. G. Jung.* Trans. by R. F. C. Hull. Bollingen Series 20. Princeton, N.J.: Princeton University Press, 1959.

———. *Civilization in Transition.* Vol. 10 of *The Collected Works of C. G. Jung.* 2d ed. Trans. by R. F. C. Hull. Bollingen Series 20. Princeton, N.J.: Princeton University Press, 1970.

———. *The Spirit in Man, Art, and Literature.* Vol. 15 of *The Collected Works of C. G. Jung.* Trans. R. F. C. Hull. Bollingen Series 20. Princeton, N.J.: Princeton University Press, 1966.

Kerenyi, Karl. "The Trickster in Relation to Greek Mythology." In *The Trickster: A Study in American Indian Mythology,* ed. Paul Radin. 1956. Reprint. New York: Schocken, 1972, 173–94.

Kilroy, James. *The "Playboy" Riots.* Irish Theatre Series 4. Dublin: Dolmen Press, 1971.

MacManus, Seumas. *The Bend of the Road.* 2d. ed. Dublin: Gill/Duffy, 1906.

Maleh, Ghassan. "Synge in the Arab World." In *A Centenary Tribute to John Millington Synge, 1871–1909: Sunshine and the Moon's Delight,* ed. S. B. Bushrui. New York: Barnes and Noble, 1972, 245–52.

Martin, Augustine. "Christy Mahon and the Apotheosis of Loneliness." In *A Centenary Tribute to John Millington Synge, 1871–1909: Sunshine and the Moon's Delight,* ed. S. B. Bushrui. New York: Barnes and Noble, 1972, 61–73.

Nethercot, Arthur H. "The *Playboy* of the *Western World.*" *Eire-Ireland* 13(1) (1978): 114–20.

Oxford English Dictionary: Compact Edition. New York: Oxford University Press, 1971.

Radin, Paul, ed. *The Trickster: A Study in American Indian Mythology.* 1956. Reprint. New York: Schocken, 1972.

Roche, Anthony. "J. M. Synge: Christianity versus Paganism." In *A J. M. Synge Literary Companion,* ed. Edward A. Kopper, Jr. Westport, Conn.: Greenwood Press, 1988, 107–34.

Rushdie, Salman. *Imaginary Homelands.* New York: Viking Penguin, 1991.

———. *The Satanic Verses.* New York: Viking Penguin, 1989.

Skelton, Robin. *The Writings of J. M. Synge.* Indianapolis, Ind., and New York: Bobbs-Merrill; London: Thames and Hudson, 1971.

Sultan, Stanley. "A Joycean Look at *The Playboy of the Western World.*" In *The Celtic Master,* ed. Maurice Harmon. Dublin: Dolmen Press, 1969, 45–55.

Suss, Irving. "The 'Playboy' Riots." *Irish Writing* 18 (1952): 39–42.

Synge, John Millington. *Collected Letters.* Vol. 1: *1871–1907,* ed. Ann Saddlemyer. Oxford: Clarendon Press, 1983.

———. *Collected Letters.* Vol. 2: *1907–1909,* ed. Ann Saddlemyer. Oxford: Clarendon Press, 1984.

———. *Plays, Book I.* Vol. 3 of *J. M. Synge: Collected Works,* ed. Ann Saddlemyer. London: Oxford University Press, 1968.

———. *Plays, Book II.* Vol. 4 of *J. M. Synge: Collected Works,* ed. Ann Saddlemyer. London: Oxford University Press, 1968.

———. *Prose.* Vol. 2 of *J. M. Synge: Collected Works,* ed. Alan Price. London: Oxford University Press, 1966.

Whitaker, Thomas R. "Introduction: On Playing with *The Playboy*." In *Twentieth-Century Interpretations of the Playboy of the Western World: A Collection of Critical Essays*, ed. Thomas R. Whitaker. Englewood Cliffs, N.J.: Prentice-Hall, 1969, 1–20.

Wright, Joseph, ed. *The English Dialect Dictionary: Being the Complete Vocabulary of All Dialect Words Still in Use, or Known to Have Been in Use during the Last Two Hundred Years*. London: Henry Frowde, 1903.

14

J. M. Synge's Vagrant Aesthetic

William Atkinson

Ireland's particular historical situation as one of the last European nations to achieve self-government contributes to the confusion and the energy of its early-twentieth-century literature. While Yeats was not alone in pointing to the fragmentary nature of modern life, he and his fellow writers, as Irish men and women, were unusually placed in that the political goal of Irish independence presented a concrete correlative to the more abstract goal of spiritual reintegration. The dramatists of the Irish literary revival wrote for a national theater that was expected to play its part in the regeneration of Ireland, and the inseparability of the political and the poetic is made plain by the riots at the first performances of John Millington Synge's *The Playboy of the Western World* in January and February 1907.

This chapter seeks to establish Synge's aesthetic and locate it in the political context of the time. In order to do so I first show that in the late nineteenth century Irish writers were encouraged to create rather than simply reflect their national spirit; but the separation of spirit and materiality that such a project entailed was perilous. In the preface to *The Playboy*, Synge contrasts the rich aestheticism of Stéphane Mallarmé and Joris-Karl Huysmans with the pallid realism of Henrik Ibsen and Émile Zola. Nonetheless, Synge rejected aestheticism because it severed art from reality, creating autonomous artworks that valued the artificial over the natural. A number of recent scholars have pointed out that Synge's female characters represent a critique of the patriarchal family system dominant in nineteenth-century Ireland, and Synge's plays understand that system to be culturally determined rather than a function of "natural" Irishness.[1] If his drama is to be more than a critique, he must represent an alternative, so he set about elaborating a communal creation that appreciated the life of the spirit without severing itself from material reality. But Synge most valued those people who are peripheral to society—tramps and artists—and their vision is consistently represented as antithetical to the everyday world. The result is usually the same: the protagonist leaves the stage in search of an enhanced reality, described but seldom represented, which can exist only at or beyond society's boundaries, arguably in a realm of pure art. The protagonists of *The Well of the Saints* must leave the text to pursue imagination. Time itself wears down the reality that Deirdre and Naisi generate in *Deirdre of the Sorrows*. The Mayoites' moment of carnival in *The Playboy of the Western World* comes to grief in the twin gaps "between a gallous story and a dirty deed" and between the first-nighters' expectations and their perceptions of the play. For these reasons I differ from a number of recent readers of Synge in that I do not, like Simon Williams, regard Synge's drama as ultimately "optimistic" in effect (96), nor can I agree with Joan Templeton in seeing most of his heroines as "able to refuse what society would have them be" (155); moreover, I find Christy and his father's return to the road at the end of *The Playboy of the Western World* more problematic than does George Bretherton (333).

The role of literature in Irish history was much discussed toward the end of the nineteenth century. Richard Fallis writes that John O'Leary regarded great literature as a prerequisite for the formation of a national identity (5). However, since O'Leary also saw nationality as a precondition for great literature, we seem to be left with a chicken-and-egg problem. Standish James O'Grady— generally acknowledged to have been a seminal influence on the Irish Renaissance—wrote, in his "Introduction to the Bardic History of Ireland," of national gestation and the delicate relationship between art and history. His essay helps me to establish some of the parameters for my discussion of Synge's aesthetic.

The first five pages of O'Grady's essay are spent looking about for some solid fact in the "empurpled mist" of Irish legendary history—a fact as solid as that which Descartes sought once he had established his "adamantine" *cogito* (O'Grady 25). The Cartesian *cogito* is effectively the establishment of individual subjectivity, whereas O'Grady is referring to a moment of collective identity when the nation as a whole is able to claim existence. In contemporary terms, O'Grady might be said to be alluding to the moment when the discourse of Ireland became aware of itself as other than English or continental. The place to look for a fact would be in history, but history is "the vulgarity of actual things" (27); circumstantial and unthinking, there is no mind behind it, no sense of the ideal. O'Grady contrasts history with legends, which represent

the imagination of the country; they are that kind of history which a nation desires to possess. They betray [*sic*] the ambition and ideals of the people, and in this respect, have a value far beyond the tales of actual events and duly recorded deeds, which are no more history than a skeleton is a man. (27)

Because Irish history since the twelfth century had been a narrative of oppression from the neighboring island, "actual things" would indeed seem vulgar to an

Irishman hoping for independence. A history that mirrors the reality of Ireland will show its readers an oppressed people, so legend takes precedence over history; it is the soul to history's skeleton, projecting ideals and ambitions, manifesting independent life and will. Legendary history is the nation thinking itself into being—its *cogito*—and is the proof of its identity. O'Grady maintains that "romance, epic, drama, and artistic representation are at all times the points to which history continually aspires—there only its final development and efflorescence. Archaeology culminates in history, history culminates in art" (42). Possibly he envisions art as the spirit of history, expressing the spirit in form as history does in action. But the final clause—"history culminates in art"— clearly establishes art at a developmental peak. It strives to move beyond the restraints of history: "To express the whole nature of the race or nation, the artist needs that absolute escape from positive history and unyielding despotic fact" (42–43). Whereas O'Grady's concept of legend suggested some sort of communal generation or plural subjectivity, he has now posited "the artist," the individual subjectivity striving to break free of the restraints of his or her own time and to express the soul of the nation.

Herbert Marcuse, in "The Affirmative Character of Culture," argues that nineteenth-century capitalism, with its valorization of the marketplace and material gain, implies a space for values other than the pragmatic. This space is filled by art, which affirms values that bourgeois society acclaims but ignores.[2] Art can be said to be protesting against a reality that affords no practical value to its truths, but the world of these truths now only exists in memory or imagination—fiction (95–122). Aestheticism is the culmination of such a process, the point at which artists come to feel so alienated from a reality that ignores their values that they deny any relationship between "the unyielding despotic" facts of everyday reality and of art. "All art," wrote Oscar Wilde, "is quite useless" (7). He was claiming that it has no "use value," as Karl Marx would have said, because it cannot be used in the world. Art is completely separate from the world of bourgeois exchange, where everything has its cash value. Extreme aestheticism even denies moral value to its production, valuing only the surface:

There is no such thing as a moral or an immoral book. Books are well written or badly written. That is all. . . . All art is at once surface and symbol. Those who go beneath the surface do so at their peril. (Wilde 5–6)

Art that does not opt out, as does aestheticism, is the tool of bourgeois culture, which is happy to exile commercially inappropriate values to the realm of imagination, to be visited only during leisure hours. The Irish artist who ignores everyday reality cannot possibly be taken seriously by men and women of affairs, and therefore will have no significant voice in the creation of the new Ireland.

Synge's position on these matters can be seen in his article, "The Vagrants of Wicklow,'' in which he establishes the vagrant as the type of the artist. Purporting to write factual reportage, Synge maintains that ''the tramp in Ireland is little troubled by the laws, and lives in out-of-doors conditions that keep him in good humour and fine bodily health'' (2:202). Since the oppression of the law would be known to someone like Synge—of the landlord class, he had seen the ill-health of those who live in substandard housing in the Dublin slums or the Congested Districts of the West of Ireland—he can hardly be accused of making this implausible claim from mere ignorance.[3] The reason is that Synge wishes to distance the vagrant/artist from any accusation of decadence, while placing him or her outside the central core of society, with its compromised bourgeois values.

Synge writes that while some vagrants have been ''on the road for generations,'' many have drifted from the villages and retain much in common with their original class (2:202); thus, they are a good statistical sample of the Irish peasantry. But he wants to claim that these people of the road are more talented than their stay-at-home brothers and sisters: ''In the middle classes the gifted son of a family is always the poorest—usually a writer or artist with no sense for speculation—and in a family of peasants, where the average comfort is just over penury, the gifted son sinks also, and is soon a tramp on the roadside'' (2: 202). It is clear that Synge's idea of ''gifted'' is nearer the general notion of cursed. Whichever it may be, the son is set apart, and moves away to the periphery of society as if unclean. Although marginal to society, the vagrants are free of many of its most contingent oppressions. Synge does not see the tramp as unfit, but rather as a vigorous sport. The vagrant is the peasant analogue of the middle-class artist, so the men and women of the road in Synge's plays can be read at one level as artists. He continues his comparison:

In all the circumstances of this tramp life there is a certain wildness that gives it romance and a peculiar value for those who look at life in Ireland with an eye that is aware of the arts also. In all the healthy movements of art, variations from the ordinary types of manhood are made interesting for the ordinary man, and in this way only the higher arts are universal. (2:208)

It is essential that the ordinary not be disvalorized, for it is the ground against which the wildness of the vagrant or the artist stands out. Synge's idea of art is ''founded on the variations which are a condition and effect of all vigorous life'' (2:208). This is contrasted with the freakish growth that is too far from the ordinary. ''To be quite plain,'' Synge writes, ''the tramp in real life, like Hamlet and Faust in the arts, are variations; but the maniac in real life, and Des Esseintes and all his ugly crew in the arts, are freaks only'' (2:208). Thus, the tramp has been raised to the highest station of Western literature, on a dais with Shakespeare and Goethe. In *Against Nature*, Huysmans's character Des Esseintes considered ''that the imagination could provide a more than adequate substitute for the vulgar reality of actual experience'' (35). When he essays a trip to London, a meal in an English restaurant in Paris is quite enough for him (132–43). Synge dumps the decadent aestheticism that privileges the artificial over the natural in the same category as the maniac, a word covering those whose conception of personal history is too far from the accepted facts—persons clearly not fit to contribute to the making of a new nation. The tramp and the healthy artist move around on the margins of society, marking the boundaries; the maniac and the decadent are unnatural and beyond the pale. Bonnie Kime Scott has insisted on the importance for Synge of nature, a realm that he saw as essentially feminine. He "entertained feminine models of creativity," and she quotes him in *Vita Vecchia* comparing women, flowers, and artists. Unlike precious gems which are beautiful, but feel nothing, they "fulfil [*sic*] their swift task of propagation and pass in a day" (185). It is surely no coincidence that Des Esseintes is particularly fond of gemstones. The question will be, however, whether Synge's protagonists use the imagination as a means to enhance reality or to replace it.

The Well of the Saints, Synge's first full-length play, concerns Martin and Mary Doul. Aging and ugly, both are also blind, a condition that is to their advantage since they believe each other to be fine and sightly (a fiction that the villagers encourage). But Molly Byrne, the local beauty, is reluctant to continue this play reality. Although Martin is becoming a little skeptical about his wife's beauty, Mary always has an answer, and they are in no position to verify either point of view until a saint cures their blindness. Their relationship is thereby shattered. "Go on now," says Martin to Mary, "to be seeking a lonesome place where the earth can hide you away" (3:99). Visual reality, unyielding and despotic, has overpowered verbally generated imagination, and the couple must now share the same world as everyone else.

The oppressiveness of reality is made plain in Act II when Martin, now sighted, must work; he finds Timmy the smith a hard taskmaster. He attempts to romance the beautiful Molly Byrne with his vision of the south, "Where you won't set down the width of your two feet and not be crushing fine flowers. . . . Come along now, let you come on the little path through the trees" (3:117). This path is surely first cousin to Kipling's "Way through the Woods" or Eliot's "passage which we did not take/ Towards the door we never opened/ Into the rose-garden" (13).

Molly's response, "It's the like of that talk you'd hear from a man would be losing his mind" (3:117), suggests Patch Darcy of *The Shadow of the Glen*, who fell in love with Nora Burke, went mad, and died. At the end of that play, ordered out by her husband, Nora goes with the tramp—"'I'm thinking it's myself will be wheezing that time with lying down under the Heavens when the night is cold, but you've a fine bit of talk, stranger, and it's with yourself I'll go" (3:57). Similarly, the conclusion of *The Well of the Saints* suggests that Martin and Mary, now blind again, will be drowned on their way south, crossing the flood rivers. It would seem that the realm of imagination can be dangerous. However, reality can be sterile and loveless, and, ten years on, Molly Byrne, as bored and lonely as Nora Burke, may well remember Martin Doul's fine bit of talk.

Molly, whom Martin took for Mary when he first recovered his sight, is his vision of the ideal made flesh. However, she had been the one who told the truth about Mary's ugliness, while Timmy had been one of the leaders in the deception practiced upon the blind couple, and is himself middle-aged and un-prepossessing, locked into a world of physical toil. Molly, whose beauty is self-sustaining since she sees it every morning in the glass, has no conception of the need to generate perceptions. Both Timmy and Martin do understand that, as both are fabricators in one way or another.

The second act is a struggle between the appeal of Timmy, the maker of things, and Martin, the fabricator of stories. Objects are in the realm of facts. Their text is one of presence, of immediate, indicative verification. Martin's text is subjunctive: "Let you come on now" (3:107), referring to a world whose extension is in possible time, but whose enjoyment is in the moment of speech. Its principal appeal lies in the fact that it ignores time, but for the young, like Molly, time is not yet problematic. Deirdre, on the other hand (from Synge's last play), becomes aware that Naisi will not always look at her with the same desire and that her looking glass will not always reflect the same beauty that she now projects. A text with no concrete referent is not faced with the problem of verification: there is nothing against which to measure it, so it is like O'Grady's factless history. That is its strength, but also its weakness, so Molly chooses Timmy's strong arm and solid house in preference to Martin's way through the trees, the imaginative space he could open up amid the solid facts of the everyday.

The Well of the Saints sets reality against imagination, but the dichotomy is either the relatively simple one of visible ugliness against verbalized beauty or of everyday reality against an unverified projected narrative of vagrancy in the south. Only when Mary Doul perceives that she can idealize herself by pro-jecting forward to the time when her hair will be white—"an I seen it that I'd a face would be a great wonder" (3:129)—does the possibility of escape from the ugly present emerge. Martin consoles himself with the thought of a long white beard. Their imaginations thus provide them with the possibility of change and movement away from an unacceptable present. The indicative eye throws back what is, not what might be: for that, imagination is needed.

The play chronicles the failure to establish an alternative communal reality. The Douls' other reality is in the south, off-stage, and the general view of the villagers is that Martin and Mary will lose their lives in getting there. In short, the path through the trees leads to a world beyond the periphery: it is either death or a realm of art outside communally accepted reality. The play ends with the saint marrying Timmy the smith and Molly Byrne, whose relationship is to be given ecclesiastical and public validity.

Molly Byrne is not a very fully developed character, but in *The Playboy of the Western World*, Synge moves the potential bride to the foreground. Randolph

Parker points out that until the very last draft Synge had Pegeen Mike set off after Christy Mahon and his father in their "romping lifetime" (83). As it is, rather than following the lead of Nora Burke, she is left to her famous lament, "I've lost the only playboy of the western world" (173). On the first night of *The Playboy*, the piece was prefaced by a performance of Synge's earlier play, *Riders to the Sea*, which presents the response of three women to the deaths of the last two men in their family. Drowned at sea, the men have passed quite beyond the material world, and the play closes with the women keening for the loss of their men. Had the first night's audience allowed *The Playboy* to reach its end, they would have seen Pegeen Mike cover her head and keen for the lost Christy, acknowledging that he has passed out of her world. But the performance broke up because, as David Cairns and Shaun Richards demonstrate, the play contradicted the nationalist construction of "peasant man as nature's nobleman and of peasant woman as pious, virtuous and submissive" ("Reading a Riot" 232). Synge's reality was too far from the nationalists' idea of the natural.

Indeed, the play's premise—a confessed parricide is made into a hero—seems "a freakish growth" rather than a variation from the ordinary, and, in fact, some reviewers attacked the play from what was, ironically, Synge's own ground. The *Evening Mail* thought that the premise was "absurd and un-Irish, and smacks of the decadent ideas of the literary flaneurs of Paris rather than of simple Connaught" (cited in Kilroy 13). Nevertheless, the reviewer was unperturbed as he considered the story "entirely unconvincing," and declared that he saw no reason to work himself into a state of "pallid indignation" (13). The *Freeman's Journal*, on the other hand, took the parricide theme at face value and read the play as a "hideous caricature [that] would be slanderous of a Kaffir Kraal" (Kilroy 9).

This was why nationalists took note of the Abbey Theater. If it was to represent itself as a national theater, it would be appropriating the voice and ambitions of the Irish people, objectifying them on the stage for general scrutiny. Abstracted Irishness would be made public in a way not seen since the days of Parnell at Westminster. Many nationalists, particularly the new "Davisites"— or the *Nation* school—and the members of the Gaelic League, were critical of the Abbey (Cairns and Richards, "Reading a Riot" 223). Arthur Griffith had attacked *The Shadow of the Glen* for its slander on "the women of Ireland," Nora Burke being "a foul echo from degenerate Greece" (cited in Greene and Stephens 176). In the same issue of the *United Irishman* that contained his first attack on Synge, Griffith printed articles by James Connolly and Maud Gonne, both critical of the National Theatre for allowing "foreign ideas" to distort its presentation of Irish men and women (149). We are dealing with competing myths, and the nationalists were clearly allying themselves with the legend of pure Irish womanhood. Lorna Reynolds has commented on how much without foundation was any such myth. The women of heroic Irish legend are forceful and sexually independent—not unlike Maud Gonne herself. But the nationalists apparently had no interest in seeing such values transferred to contemporary stage women. An Irish Nora Helmer might raise too many hard questions.[4] It is very clear from Yeats's response to the Irish Free State that as far as he was concerned independence brought little or no moral renewal for Ireland. The same bourgeois values prevailed in the revived Land of Saints as in England. The kind of propagandist drama that the nationalists wanted should not open up debate about the nature of the new Ireland. They wanted to be sure that their values were projected as those of all Ireland.

Synge, on the other hand, wanted to use his drama to stretch the boundaries of the national consciousness. *The Well of the Saints* had outlined the theme of a community playing with the self-conscious fiction of the Douls' beauty. In *The Playboy of the Western World*, Synge analyzes the communal construction of reality much more closely. As Randolph Parker and George Bretherton have shown, the theory of carnivalization helps us understand how he deals with competing realities in *The Playboy of the Western World*.[5]

During carnival the laws and rules that normally govern the order of life are suspended. The carnivalesque is suggested at the beginning of *The Playboy* by Michael James and his friend, who are planning to set out for Kate Cassidy's wake. There are to be sports, indicating some kind of fair or festival, and the arrival of Christy Mahon offers the opportunity for the crowning of a carnival king.

Christy does not arrive at Michael James's *shebeen* as a hero; he has to be made into one. This begins when the people in the pub try to find out why he is afraid of the police. Their questions quickly become a riddle-game in which Christy does little more than deny each of their guesses. The key moment comes when he declares, "But I'm not calling to mind any person, gentle, simple, judge or jury, did the like of me. [*They all draw nearer with delighted curiosity*]" (4:71). He is declaring himself to be an anomaly and in a category of one. He is thus to some extent holy—his name is surely no coincidence. An anomaly is just what is needed for the game of reversed values, of life out of the rut. Christy must remain anomalous and thus be like nothing known to them, thereby outside their "history." Shawn Keogh, friend of the priest and representative of standard morality, is shocked, and sees Christy for what he claims to be, "A bloody-handed murderer the like of . . .". But Pegeen silences him: "We'll take no fooling from your like at all" (4:77). When the condemnation of parricide is regarded as fooling, then things are surely upside down.

Bakhtin relates carnivalized literature to Menippean satire, which he traces back to Socratic dialogue. The Socratic technique

is counterposed to the official monologism which claims *to possess the ready-made truth.* . . . The truth is not born and does not reside in the head of an individual person; it is born of the dialogical intercourse *between people* in the collective search for truth. (90; emphases in original)

Christy's story or truth is first presented in a dialogic manner. He does not enter the *shebeen* and monologically recount what he has done. Everything has to be dragged out of him. The story is built up little by little, with the interlocutor's responses made plain at every point. Indeed, the parricide itself has to be forced out by Pegeen threatening Christy with a broom. It is only when all crimes and all ways of committing Christy's particular crime have been voiced and responded to that he can begin to embellish the tale. Only when its credentials as heroic have been established by the other people in the play, and when all events and circumstances are known, can Christy begin to encrust his base tale with the linguistic gems of heroism. In short, Christy is only a hero because he has been told to be, and this heroism is a far more social and dialogic affair than a simple matter of an individual artist/monologist imposing his will upon the group. A new social reality is created, but it is a purely carnivalesque reality. The *Freeman's Journal* had missed this point entirely; the other papers caught it somewhat bewilderedly, although their criticism of the language showed a fundamental unhappiness with a key element of the carnivalesque.

The heroic status of Christy's deed having been clearly established, the text moves on to mark his marital desirability with the contest between Pegeen and the Widow Quin. Again, we find a reversal of the expected in that rather than two men fighting for the heroine, here are two women fighting for the hero. Heroines are cultural constructs of female desirability and customarily passive. Christy's passivity shows the notion of the heroine in a new light as a value and behavior neither inevitable nor other than culturally determined. The experience of being desirable later permits Christy to open his romantic floodgates and live the role he has been ascribed.

In the second act, the four girls bring their gifts of food for the carnival hero, and the Widow Quin has him take part in the sports so that he may win play-glory. The girls and the Widow Quin are an even more eager audience than Christy had the night before, and again the narrative is built up and elaborated upon communally. Questions and comments punctuate it so that the structure and value of the tale is kept in public control. The narrative ends with a toast drunk by Christy and the Widow Quin. Pegeen's entry brings everything back to the normality of buying and selling. Indeed, she seems to imply that the carnival is really over when she sets Christy to work like the pot-boy that nominally he is.

Pegeen's teasing about hanging brings Christy to talk about the loneliness of the roads and allows him to begin generating another persona—the artist/vagrant: "It's well you know it's a lonesome thing to be passing small towns with the lights shining sideways when the night is down" (4:109). This is the gravitational pull from the center that the vagrant experiences, and it parallels that which Pegeen feels toward the moving margin.[6] It is a fine thing to be outside looking in, but also a fine thing to be inside looking out.

The "coaxing" quality that Pegeen perceives in Christy comes from the fact that she has given him permission to expand. She is unique to him even as he is to her. She has never known a parricide nor a man who made vagrancy so alluring, and he has never known a young woman who did not laugh at him. The facts of his history have been washed away and he is as legendary a creation as O'Grady's Ireland. Christy can be sustained as a heroic subject because he is based on the absence of fact and on the reversal of normal values. Martin and Mary Doul's romancing will not quite work because the portrait and its original are constantly before our eyes. *The Playboy* establishes a topsy-turvy world to accommodate the upside-down values, and it also keeps the narrative and its deed well apart. But the appearance of Old Mahon brings an alternative and unheroic narrative to set against that which the Mayoites have created.

The sports are finished, and Michael James has returned from Kate Cassidy's wake. The time of carnival is drawing to a close, and Christy's heroic stature is undone by the presence of he who should be absent, beyond the periphery. Having, as he believes, finally killed his father and remade history so as to match the legend, Christy assumes that Pegeen will take him back—but no: "I'll say, a strange man is a marvel with his mighty talk; but what's a squabble in your back yard, and the blow of a loy, have taught me there's a great gap between a gallous story and a dirty deed" (4:169). Pegeen gives too much credit to Christy's monologic power—even their "love duet" in Act III (4:147–51) is fully dialogic, and Pegeen has quite as much to say as Christy. The playboy phenomenon is a product of Michael James's *shebeen* and of Christy, but what is present and visible—at the center—has less glamor than what is absent—at the periphery. After all, the Widow Quin's "sneaky" murder of her husband "did win small glory with the boys itself" (4:89). There is a great gap between a fine story and despotic fact, and Pegeen's faith collapses at the first sign of a fact. She can find no way to integrate imagination within the everyday world, and her lament at the loss of the Playboy is a lament for her own wiping away of the glamor.

Christy and his father leave Mayo. Their exit from the set is their return to the realm of narrative and carnival. The indicative mood of Christy's second attempt at murder gives way to the subjunctive of "romancing through a romping lifetime" (4:173). Bakhtin writes: "Carnival celebrates change itself, the very process of replaceability, rather than that which is replaced" (103). It concentrates on those moments when the imagination disburdens itself of its chains and runs free for a while. These moments of freedom and the glimpses of alternative worlds and orders can bring society to an awareness that its present set of "chains" is not the only one available. But above all, it valorizes dialogue. Those who shouted down *The Playboy of the Western World* were denying the theater's right to establish, if only temporarily, its own social reality, and, by implication, denying the possibility of any alternative reality.

Thus *The Playboy* celebrates the power of the imagination to allow renewal, hold off reification, and fly in the face of history. However, such a state could not be maintained indefinitely, for a full-time carnival would, by definition, not be carnival. What is the world to which Christy and his father have committed themselves? It seems perilously close to the aesthetes' self-generated world of art. Pegeen stays on stage, within *our* consciousness, while the Mahons leave the set and pass beyond the border of the text. They have found, perhaps, "that absolute freedom" that O'Grady saw as a precondition for expression of "the whole nature of the race" (42–43), but in their escape from "unyielding despotic fact" have they not moved beyond the pale, beyond the nation's consciousness? If the community rejects the artist, there is nothing else for him or her to do, and we might see the Mahons as forced into the roles of grotesque aesthetes, turning their back on Mayo to devote themselves to "a romping lifetime."

Pegeen is the mirror image of Nora Burke from *The Shadow of the Glen*. Nora leaves with the tramp for an uncertain life; Pegeen stays, and that is her tragedy. In *Deirdre of the Sorrows*, Synge allows his female protagonist to sample life on the periphery. In the first act he shows Deirdre herself as a lover of the fields and the open sky, and it is she who tempts Naisi to the road. However, after seven years, when the world of the center calls to them, Deirdre admits:

It's lonesome this place, having happiness like ours, till I'm asking each day will this day match yesterday, and will tomorrow take a good place beside the same day in the year that's gone, and wondering all times is it a game worth playing, living on until you're dried and old, and our joy is gone forever. (4:219)

The word "game" suggests she realizes that her years with Naisi have been only a provisional reality. The world of Conchubor and the determining prophecy that she will be the ruin of the sons of Usna is stronger. More telling, however, is her fear that the love between Naisi and herself can only weaken before the onslaught of age. She is thus refusing to acknowledge any alternative realm that can compete with the central reality, not even love.

Arthur Griffith was right about *The Shadow of the Glen*: it did present a radical challenge to the familial system. However, Synge's last two plays suggest that "the yahoos have won," and the only option is coming to terms with the world as the nationalists said it was: Pegeen will do as her father and Father Reilly want and marry Shawn Keogh; Deirdre must do as the old men said and marry Conchubor, the man who raised her to be his wife. But she kills herself rather than do so. It had been his father's insistence that he marry the woman who nursed him that provoked Christy to "parricide," and there was no happy ending for him within the text. Synge's last play brings the vagrants back to center, as if acknowledging their freakishness. He gestures toward the valorization of a world of ideals or of art, but turns back to a reality that his audiences would recognize as their own, while leaving the memory of the taste of what might be.

NOTES

1. On the family system of the time, see Bonnie Kime Scott, Gail Finney, and David Cairns and Shaun Richards (*Writing Ireland*, chs. 3, 4).

2. Religion also fills these spaces, and plays a similar role to art. In many cases, art is the secondary substitute, after a loss of faith in God.

3. Synge's mother held property in Galway that provided £400 a year (Greene and Stephens 5), and his brother was a land agent.

In 1885 Synge's brother Edward was busily evicting tenants in Cavan, Mayo and Wicklow. When Synge argued with his mother over the rights of the tenants and the injustice of evicting them, her answer was, 'What would become of us if our tenants in Galway stopped paying their rents?' To this he could find no answer and was forced to hold his tongue. In the summer of 1887 Edward's activities came much nearer home when he evicted a tenant from his aunt's estate at Glanmore. The cruelty and efficiency with which he went about his duties made it an event Synge never forgot. (11)

4. Joan Templeton has pointed out that there is no shortage of such figures, however. Writers of the Irish Renaissance value their heroines "precisely because they refuse society's established norms" (151).

5. Although he uses the term, Parker prefers Victor Turner's concept of liminality, "the potentially transformative experience of being on the threshold between two recognized cultural loci or in a break in the continuity of life" (Parker 65). He is most interested in the "gap" between real life and the world of the imagination: "Synge seems committed to exploring central gaps in human experience and demonstrating the importance of what happens to people in those gaps" (68).

6. Gail Finney observes that Pegeen "as a girl 'was tempted often to go sailing the seas' (151.III)" (89).

WORKS CITED

Bakhtin, Mikhail. *Problems of Dostoevsky's Poetics*, trans. R. W. Totsel. N.p.: Ardis, 1973.

Bretherton, George. "A Carnival Christy and a Playboy for All Ages." *Twentieth Century Literature* 37 (1991): 322–34.

Cairns, David, and Shaun Richards. "Reading a Riot: The 'Reading Formation' of Synge's Abbey Audience." *Literature and History* 13 (1987): 219–37.

———. *Writing Ireland: Colonialism, Nationalism and Culture*. Manchester, U.K.: Manchester University Press, 1988.

Eliot, T. S. *Four Quartets*. New York: Harvest, 1977.

Fallis, Richard. *The Irish Renaissance*. Syracuse, N.Y.: Syracuse University Press, 1977.

Finney, Gail. "The 'Playgirl' of the Western World: Feminism, Comedy, and Synge's Pegeen Mike." In *Women in Theatre*, ed. James Redmond. Themes in Drama 2. Cambridge: Cambridge University Press, 1989.

Greene, David H., and Edward M. Stephens. *J. M. Synge, 1871–1909*. New York: Macmillan, 1959.

Huysmans, J. K.. *Against Nature*, trans. Robert Baldick. Harmondsworth, U.K.: Penguin, 1973.

Kilroy, James. *The "Playboy" Riots*. Dublin: Dolmen Press, 1971.

Marcuse, Herbert. "On the Affirmative Character of Culture." In *Negations, Essays in Critical Theory*, trans. Jeremy J. Shapiro. London: Free Association, 1988, 88–133.

O'Grady, Standish. *Selected Essays and Passages*. Dublin: Talbot Press, n.d.

Parker, Randolph. "Gaming in the Gap: Language and Liminality in *Playboy of the Western World.*" *Theatre Journal* 37(1) (1985): 65–85.

Reynolds, Lorna. "Irish Women in Legend, Literature and Life." In *Women in Irish Legend, Life and Literature*, ed. S. F. Gallagher. Gerrards Cross, U.K.: Colin Smythe, 1983.

Scott, Bonnie Kime. "Synge's Language of Women." In *A J. M. Synge Companion*, ed. Edward A. Kopper, Jr. Westport, Conn.: Greenwood Press, 1988.

Synge, John Millington. *Collected Works.* Gen. ed., Robin Skelton. 4 vols. 1962–1968. Gerrards Cross, U.K.: Colin Smythe, 1982.

Templeton, Joan. "The Bed and the Hearth: Synge's Redeemed Ireland." In *Themes in Drama: Drama, Sex and Politics*, ed. James Redmond. Cambridge: Cambridge University Press, 1985.

Wilde, Oscar. *The Picture of Dorian Gray.* Vol. 4 of *The Complete Works of Oscar Wilde.* 12 vols. Garden City, N.Y.: Doubleday, 1923.

Williams, Simon. "John Millington Synge: Transforming Myths of Ireland." In *Facets of European Modernism: Essays in Honour of James McFarlane. Presented to Him on His 65th Birthday, 12 December 1985*, ed. Janet Garton. Norwich, U.K.: University of East Anglia Press, 1985.

Selected Bibliography

Agostini, Rene. "J. M. Synge's *Deirdre of the Sorrows*: Some Aspects of Its Relation to the Myth and to Synge's Other Plays." *Etudes Irlandaises* 13 (1988): 95–114.

———. "Patterns of Poetry and Ironic Meaning in John Millington Synge's *The Well of the Saints*." *Cahiers Victoriens et Edouardiens* 3 (1976): 79–96.

———. "A Reading of John Millington Synge's *The Playboy of the Western World*: The Problem of Identity." *Cahiers Victoriens et Edouardiens* 9–10 (1979): 253–71.

Akin, Warren, IV. " 'I Just Riz the Loy': The Oedipal Dimensions of *The Playboy of the Western World*." *South Atlantic Bulletin* 45(4) (1980): 55–65.

Benson, Eugene. *J. M. Synge*. New York: Grove Press, 1983.

Bigley, Bruce M. "*The Playboy of the Western World* as Antidrama." *Modern Drama* 20(2) (1977): 157–67.

Bloom, Harold, ed. *John Millington Synge's "The Playboy of the Western World."* Modern Critical Interpretations. New York: Chelsea House, 1988.

Boyd, E. A. *The Contemporary Drama of Ireland*. Dublin: Talbot, 1918.

Bushrui, S. B., ed. *A Centenary Tribute to John Millington Synge, 1871–1909: Sunshine and the Moon's Delight*. New York: Barnes and Noble, 1972.

Cairns, David, and Shaun Richards. " 'WOMAN' in the Discourse of Celticism: A Reading of *The Shadow of the Glen*." *Canadian Journal of Irish Studies* 13(1) (June 1987): 43–60.

Cardullo, Bert. "*Riders to the Sea*: A New View." *Canadian Journal of Irish Studies* 10(1) (1984): 95–112.

Carpenter, Andrew. "Synge and Women." *Etudes Irlandaises* 4(1) (1979): 89–106.

Clark, David R., ed. *John Millington Synge: Riders to the Sea*. Merrill Literary Casebook Series. Columbus, Ohio: Charles E. Merrill, 1970.

Collins, Michael J. "Christy's Binary Vision in *The Playboy of the Western World*." *Canadian Journal of Irish Studies* 7(2) (1981): 76–82.

Corkery, Daniel. *Synge and Anglo-Irish Literature*. 1931. Reprint. Cork: Mercier Press, 1966.

Cronin, Anthony. *Heritage Now: Irish Literature in the English Language*. Dingle, Ireland: Brandon, 1982.

Dasenbrock, Reed Way. "Synge's Irish Renaissance Petrarchism." *Modern Philology* 83(1) (1985): 33–44.

Deane, Seamus. *Celtic Revivals: Essays in Modern Irish Literature, 1880–1980*. London and Boston: Faber and Faber, 1985. Reprint. Winston-Salem, N.C.: Wake Forest University Press, 1987.

———. *A Short History of Irish Literature*. London: Hutchinson; Notre Dame, Ind.: University of Notre Dame Press, 1986.

Donoghue, Denis. *We Irish: Essays on Irish Literature and Society*. New York: Knopf, 1986.

Driver, Tom. *Romantic Quest and Modern Query: History of the Modern Theatre*. New York: Delacorte, 1970.

Dumbleton, William A. *Ireland: Life and Land in Literature*. Albany: State University of New York Press, 1984.

Ellis-Fermor, Una. *The Irish Dramatic Movement*. London: Methuen, 1939. Reprint. New York: Barnes and Noble, 1967.

Fallis, Richard. *The Irish Renaissance*. Syracuse, N.Y.: Syracuse University Press, 1977.

Faulk, C. S. "John Millington Synge and the Rebirth of Comedy." *Southern Humanities Review* 8(4) (1974): 431–48.

Fay, Gerard. *The Abbey Theatre, Cradle of Genius*. London: Hollis and Carter, 1958.

Fitz-Simon, Christopher. *The Irish Theater*. London: Thames and Hudson, 1983.

Flannery, James W. *W. B. Yeats and the Idea of a Theatre: The Early Abbey Theatre in Theory and Practice*. New Haven, Conn., and London: Yale University Press, 1976.

Fleischmann, Ruth. "Fathers Vanquished and Victorious—A Historical Reading of Synge's *Playboy*." In *Critical Approaches to Anglo-Irish Literature*, ed. Michael Allen and Angela Wilcox. Irish Literary Studies Series 29. Gerrards Cross, U.K.: Colin Smythe, 1989, 63–74.

Foster, Leslie D. "Maurya: Tragic Error and Limited Transcendence in *Riders to the Sea*." *Eire-Ireland* 16(3) (1981): 98–117.

Free, William J. "Structural Dynamics in *Riders to the Sea*." *Colby Library Quarterly* 11(3) (1975): 162–68.

Genet, Jacqueline, and Richard Allen Cave, eds. *Perspectives of Irish Drama and Theatre*. Gerrards Cross, U.K.: Colin Smythe, 1991.

Gerstenberger, Donna. *John Millington Synge*. Twayne's English Authors Series 12. New York: Twayne, 1964. Rev. ed. Boston: G. K. Hall, 1990.

Gibbs, A. M. "J. M. Synge's Forms of Romance." *Modern Drama* 31(4) (1988): 479–94.

Gonzalez, Alexander G. "A Pair of Notes on Synge's *The Tinker's Wedding*." *Notes on Modern Irish Literature* 2 (1990): 10–11.

Greene, David H., and Edward M. Stephens. *J. M. Synge, 1871–1909*. New York: Macmillan, 1959. Rev. ed. New York: New York University Press, 1989.

Harmon, Maurice, ed. *J. M. Synge: Centenary Papers 1971*. Dublin: Dolmen Press, 1972.

Hart, William E. "Synge's Ideas on Life and Art: Design and Theory in *The Playboy of the Western World*." *Yeats Studies* 2 (1972): 35–51.

Henn, T. R., ed. *The Plays and Poems of J. M. Synge*. London: Methuen, 1963. Reprint. London and New York: Methuen, 1981.

Hirsch, Edward. "The Gallous Story and the Dirty Deed: The Two *Playboys.*" *Modern Drama* 26(1) (1983): 85–102.

Hogan, Robert. *Laying the Foundations, 1902–1904.* Atlantic Highlands, N.J.: Humanities, 1976.

Hogan, Robert, and James Kilroy. *The Abbey Theatre: The Years of Synge, 1905–1909.* Dublin: Dolmen; Atlantic Highlands, N.J.: Humanities, 1978.

Holder, Heidi J. "Between Fiction and Reality: Synge's *Playboy* and Its Audience." *Journal of Modern Literature* 14(4) (1988): 527–42.

Jain, Praveen C. "Synge's Playboy and the Idea of Heroic Life." *Indiana Journal of English Studies* 22 (1982–83): 77–85.

Jeffares, A. Norman. *Anglo-Irish Literature.* New York: Schocken, 1982.

Johnson, Kenneth E. "J. M. Synge's *When the Moon Has Set.*" *Canadian Journal of Irish Studies* 9(2) (1983): 35–42.

Johnston, Denis. *John Millington Synge.* New York and London: Columbia University Press, 1965.

Kavanagh, Peter. *The Story of the Abbey Theatre.* New York: Devin-Adair, 1950.

Kenner, Hugh. *A Colder Eye: The Modern Irish Writers.* New York: Knopf, 1983.

Kiberd, Declan. *Synge and the Irish Language.* Totowa, N.J.: Rowman and Littlefield, 1979.

King, Mary C. *The Drama of J. M. Synge.* Syracuse, N.Y.: Syracuse University Press, 1985.

Kopper, Edward A., Jr. "J. M. Synge." In *Modern Irish Writers,* ed. Alexander G. Gonzalez. Westport, Conn.: Greenwood Press, 1997.

———. *John Millington Synge: A Reference Guide.* Boston: G. K. Hall, 1979.

———. *Synge: A Review of the Criticism.* Modern Irish Literature Monograph Series 1. Lyndora, Pa.: Kopper, 1990.

———, ed. *A J. M. Synge Literary Companion.* Westport, Conn.: Greenwood Press, 1988.

Krause, David. *The Profane Book of Irish Comedy.* Ithaca, N.Y.: Cornell University Press, 1982.

Levitt, Paul M. "The Two-Act Structure of *The Playboy of the Western World.*" *Colby Library Quarterly* 11(4) (1975): 230–34.

MacPhail, Ian, and M. Pollard, comps. *John Millington Synge, 1871–1909: A Catalogue of an Exhibition Held at Trinity College Dublin Library on the Occasion of the Fiftieth Anniversary of His Death.* Dublin: Dolmen Press, 1959.

Malone, Andrew E. *The Irish Drama.* 1929. Reprint. New York and London: Blom, 1965.

Maxwell, D. E. S. *A Critical History of Modern Irish Drama, 1891–1980.* Cambridge and New York: Cambridge University Press, 1984.

McHugh, Roger, and Maurice Harmon. *A Short History of Anglo-Irish Literature.* Totowa, N.J.: Barnes and Noble, 1982.

McMahon, Sean. " 'Leave Troubling the Lord God': A Note on Synge and Religion." *Eire-Ireland* 11(1) (1976): 132–41.

Mikhail, E. H. *J. M. Synge: Interviews and Recollections.* New York: Barnes and Noble; London: Macmillan, 1977.

Morrisey, Thomas J. "The Good Shepherd and the Anti-Christ in Synge's *The Shadow of the Glen.*" *Irish Renaissance Annual* 1 (1980): 157–67.

————. "Synge's Doorways: Portals and Portents." *Eire-Ireland* 17(3) (1982): 40–51.

Murphy, Brenda. "Stoicism, Asceticism, and Ecstasy: Synge's *Deirdre of the Sorrows.*"
    Modern Drama 17(2) (1974): 155–63.

Neff, D. S. "Bartley's Fall: Pyrolatreia and *Riders to the Sea.*" *Notes on Modern Irish
    Literature* 1 (1989): 26–31.

————. "Synge's Hecuba." *Eire-Ireland* 19(1) (1984): 74–86.

O'Casey, Sean. "John Millington Synge (1946)." In *Blasts and Benedictions: Articles
    and Stories by Sean O'Casey*, ed. Ronald Ayling. London: Macmillan; New York:
    St. Martin's, 1967, 35–41.

O'Driscoll, Robert, ed. *Theatre and Nationalism in Twentieth-Century Ireland.* Toronto:
    University of Toronto Press, 1971.

O'hAodha, Michael. *Theatre in Ireland.* Oxford: Blackwell, 1974.

Orel, Harold. "Synge's Concept of the Tramp." *Eire-Ireland* 7(2) (1972): 55–61.

Parker, Randolph. "Gaming in the Gap: Language and Liminality in *Playboy of the
    Western World.*" *Theatre Journal* 37(1) (1985): 65–85.

Partridge, A. C. *Language and Society in Anglo-Irish Literature.* Dublin: Gill and Mac-
    millan; Totowa, N.J.: Barnes and Noble, 1984.

Pearce, Howard D. "Synge's Playboy as Mock-Christ." *Modern Drama* 8(3) (1965):
    303–10.

Pierce, James C. "Synge's Widow Quin: Touchstone to the *Playboy's* Irony." *Eire-
    Ireland* 16(2) (1981): 122–33.

Popkin, Henry, ed. *John Millington Synge, The Playboy of the Western World and Riders
    to the Sea.* New York: Avon Books, 1967.

Price, Alan. *Synge and Anglo-Irish Drama.* London: Methuen, 1961.

Rafroidi, Patrick, Ramonde Popot, and William Parker, eds. *Aspects of the Irish Theatre.*
    Lille, France: Publications de l'Université de Lille, 1972.

Robinson, Lennox. *Ireland's Abbey Theatre.* London: Sidgwick and Jackson, 1951.

————, ed. *The Irish Theatre.* 1939. Reprint. New York: Haskell House, 1971.

Robinson, Paul N. "The Peasant Play as Allegory: J. M. Synge's *The Shadow of the
    Glen.*" *CEA Critic* 36(4) (1974): 36–38.

Roche, Anthony. "The Two Worlds of Synge's *The Well of the Saints.*" *Genre* 12
    (1979): 439–50. Reprint. In *The Genres of the Irish Literary Revival*, ed. Ronald
    Schleifer. Norman, Okla.: Pilgrim; Dublin: Wolfhound, 1980, 27–38.

Saddlemyer, Ann. *J. M. Synge and Modern Comedy.* Dublin: Dolmen Press, 1967.

————. "Synge and the Nature of Woman." In *Woman in Irish Legend, Life and Lit-
    erature*, ed. S. F. Gallagher. Irish Literary Studies 14. Gerrards Cross, U.K.: Colin
    Smythe; Totowa, N.J.: Barnes and Noble, 1983, 58–73.

————, ed. *The Collected Letters of John Millington Synge.* 2 vols. Oxford: Clarendon
    Press; New York: Oxford University Press, 1983–1984.

————, ed. *Letters to Molly: John Millington Synge to Maire O'Neill, 1906–1909.* Cam-
    bridge, Mass.: Belknap Press of Harvard University Press, 1971.

————, ed. *Some Letters of John M. Synge to Lady Gregory and W. B. Yeats.* Dublin:
    Cuala, 1971.

————, ed. *Theatre Business: The Correspondence of the First Abbey Theatre Directors:
    William Butler Yeats, Lady Gregory and J. M. Synge.* Gerrards Cross, U.K.: Colin
    Smythe; University Park and London: Pennsylvania State University Press, 1982.

Sekine, Masaru, ed. *Irish Writers and the Theater.* Gerrards Cross, U.K.: Colin Smythe,
    1986.

Setterquist, Jan. *Ibsen and the Beginnings of Anglo-Irish Drama.* 1951. Reprint. New
    York: Gordian, 1974.

Skelton, Robin. *J. M. Synge*. Lewisburg, Pa.: Bucknell University Press, 1972.

————. *J. M. Synge and His World*. New York: Viking, 1971.

————. "The Politics of J. M. Synge." *Massachusetts Review* 18(1) (1977): 7–22.

————. *The Writings of J. M. Synge*. Indianapolis, Ind., and New York: Bobbs-Merrill; London: Thames and Hudson, 1971.

Spangler, Ellen B. "Synge's *Deirdre of the Sorrows* as Feminine Tragedy." *Eire-Ireland* 12(4) (1977): 97–108.

Stephens, Lilo, ed. *J. M. Synge: My Wallet of Photographs*. Dublin: Dolmen Press, 1971.

Strong, L. A. G. *John Millington Synge*. London: Allen and Unwin, 1941.

Sultan, Stanley. *J. M. Synge: The Playboy of the Western World*. Barre, Mass.: Imprint Society, 1970.

Synge, J. M. *J. M. Synge: Collected Works*. Gen. ed., Robin Skelton. 4 vols. London: Oxford University Press, 1962–1968. Reprint. Gerrards Cross, U.K.: Colin Smythe; Washington, D.C.: Catholic University of America Press, 1982.

Taaffe, Maura. "Legend of an Irish Outlaw in Synge's *Playboy of the Western World*." *Papers in Comparative Studies* 2 (1982–83): 207–16.

Templeton, Joan. "Synge's Redeemed Ireland: Woman as Rebel." *Caliban* 17 (1980): 91–97. Revised and reprinted as "The Bed and the Hearth: Synge's Redeemed Ireland." In *Drama, Sex and Politics*, ed. James Redmond. Themes in Drama 7. Cambridge: Cambridge University Press, 1985, 151–57.

Thornton, Weldon. "J. M. Synge." In *Anglo-Irish Literature: A Review of Research*, ed. Richard J. Finneran. New York: Modern Language Association of America, 1976, 315–65.

————. "J. M. Synge." In *Recent Research on Anglo-Irish Writers: A Supplement to "Anglo-Irish Literature: A Review of Research,"* ed. Richard J. Finneran. Modern Language Association of America Reviews of Research. New York: Modern Language Association of America, 1983, 154–80.

————. *J. M. Synge and the Western Mind*. Irish Literary Studies 4. New York: Barnes and Noble; Gerrards Cross, U.K.: Colin Smythe, 1979.

Waters, Maureen. *The Comic Irishman*. Albany: State University of New York Press, 1984.

Watson, G. J. *Irish Identity and the Literary Revival: Synge, Yeats, Joyce, O'Casey*. New York: Barnes and Noble; London: Croom Helm, 1979.

Whelan, F. A. E., and Keith N. Hull. " 'There's Talking for a Cute Woman'! Synge's Heroines." *Eire-Ireland* 15(3) (1980): 36–46.

Whitaker, Thomas R., ed. *Twentieth-Century Interpretations of The Playboy of the Western World: A Collection of Critical Essays*. Englewood Cliffs, N.J.: Prentice-Hall, 1969.

Williams, Raymond. *Drama from Ibsen to Eliot*. London: Chatto and Windus, 1961. Reprint. New York: Oxford University Press, 1967.

Williams, Simon. "John Millington Synge: Transforming Myths of Ireland." In *Facets of European Modernism: Essays in Honour of James McFarlane. Presented to Him on His 65th Birthday, 12 December 1985*, ed. Janet Garton. Norwich, U.K.: University of East Anglia Press, 1985, 79–98.

Worth, Katharine. *The Irish Drama of Europe from Yeats to Beckett*. Atlantic Highlands, N.J.: Humanities, 1978.

————. "O'Casey, Synge and Yeats." *Irish University Review* 10(1) (1980): 103–17.

Index

About the Editor and Contributors

ALEXANDER G. GONZALEZ, Professor of English, is the Irish-literature specialist at Cortland College of the State University of New York. Educated at Queens College and at the University of Oregon, where he received his doctorate, he has also taught at both these institutions, as well as at The University of California at Santa Barbara, at The Ohio State University, and at The Pennsylvania State University as a Distinguished Scholar in Residence (Summer 1991). He has authored two books: *Darrell Figgis: A Study of His Novels* (1992) and *Peadar O'Donnell: A Reader's Guide* (forthcoming, 1997), and edited two more: *Short Stories from the Irish Renaissance: An Anthology* (1993) and *Modern Irish Writers: A Bio-Critical Sourcebook* (forthcoming, 1997). In addition he has published over thirty articles in journals such as *Studies in Short Fiction, Irish University Review, Eire-Ireland, Colby Library Quarterly, The Journal of Irish Literature, Notes on Modern Irish Literature*, and many others. He is currently writing a monograph on Daniel Corkery.

WILLIAM ATKINSON is an assistant professor at Appalachian State University. He was educated in England and then pursued his graduate studies in the United States. He has published mostly on twentieth-century British literature.

DAN CASEY is President of Burlington College in Vermont. He has founded and directed Irish Studies programs at the State University of New York and at other colleges and universities in the United States, Ireland, and elsewhere in Europe. He has more than a hundred publications—books, monographs, articles, and reviews—on Irish and Irish-American subjects. His *Critical Essays on John Millington Synge* was published in 1994. Dan Casey is also a writer of fiction, nonfiction, and poetry.

DANIEL DAVY is an assistant professor in the Theater Division of the Department of Speech Communication, Theater, and Dance at Kansas State University. He holds a Ph.D. in Dramatic Art from the University of California at Santa Barbara and also taught there, as well as at Ohio University. Davy has written about Grotowski's "poor theater" for *Essays in Theater* (May 1989) and on *The Cenci* for the *Journal of Dramatic Theory and Criticism* (Fall 1990). "Tragic Self-Referral in *Riders to the Sea*" originally appeared in slightly different form in *Eire-Ireland* (Summer 1994).

EILEEN J. DOLL, Associate Professor of Spanish at Loyola University, New Orleans, has published several articles on early twentieth-century Spanish drama and prose, often with a comparative approach. She is the author of "Don Juan y Cristo en las *Comedias Bárbaras* y *The Playboy of the Western World*," which appeared in *Suma Valleinclaniana* (Barcelona, Spain, 1992). She is currently at work on a book analyzing the parallel use of symbols by John M. Synge and Spanish playwright Ramón del Valle-Inclán.

JANE DUKE ELKINS graduated with a Ph.D. in English Literature from The University of North Carolina at Chapel Hill in 1994.

MARY FITZGERALD-HOYT is Professor of English at Siena College, where she teaches a variety of courses in Irish literature. She has published articles on such contemporary Irish writers as Brian Friel, William Trevor, Julia O'Faolain, and Ciaran Carson, and is currently working on a book, *"An Imperial Affliction": The Impact of Colonization in William Trevor's Irish Fiction.*

JOHN P. HARRINGTON is Associate Professor and Dean of Humanities and Social Sciences at The Cooper Union in New York City. The author of many essays on Irish literature, his books include *The Irish Beckett, The English Traveller in Ireland*, and the *Modern Irish Drama* volume in the Norton Critical Editions series.

HEIDI J. HOLDER received her Ph.D. from the University of Massachusetts at Amherst and is a Lecturer in English at Smith College. She has published essays on J. M. Synge, Harley Granville Barker, and imperialism and the British stage. She is currently at work on a book about realism, genre, and censorship in the Victorian and Edwardian theaters.

CAROLYN L. MATHEWS is a Visiting Instructor in the Department of English at Wake Forest University, where she teaches writing and American literature. Her research interests include clothing as material culture in American realist novels, turn-of-the-century British and American popular fiction, and Irish literature.

CÓILÍN D. OWENS, Associate Professor of English at George Mason University, has edited *Family Chronicles: Maria Edgeworth's Castle Rackrent*, co-edited *Irish Drama: 1900–1980*, and written numerous articles on Irish drama, language, and literature.

ROBERT E. RHODES is Emeritus Professor of Anglo-Irish Literature at Cortland College of the State University of New York, where he taught literature for over thirty years. He has coedited, with Daniel J. Casey, *Views of the Irish Peasantry, 1800–1916* (1977), *Irish American Fiction: Essays in Criticism* (1979), and *Modern Irish-American Fiction: A Reader* (1989), and has published scores of articles and reviews. Past President of the American Conference for Irish Studies, he is also a SUNY Faculty Exchange Scholar.

ELLEN POWERS STENGEL is Instructor of Writing in the Writing Program at the University of Central Arkansas in Conway, Arkansas. Holding a B.A. from Smith College and an M.A. and a Ph.D. in English from Duke University, she has presented papers and published articles and book chapters on a variety of medieval and modern British and American authors and on learning theory and writing anxiety. Currently, she is completing a book about the ghost stories of Edith Wharton.

GINGER STRAND is currently a Visiting Scholar and Adjunct Assistant Professor at Columbia University. Her published work includes articles on early American drama, Percy Shelley's *The Cenci*, and Sophie Treadwell's *Machinal*, and a film column for the New York newspaper, *Downtown*. She is completing a book about American news-based dramas.

GALE SCHRICKER SWIONTKOWSKI is Associate Professor of English at Fordham University, where she teaches modern poetry and modern Anglo-Irish literature. She is the author of *A New Species of Man: The Poetic Persona of W.B. Yeats*, and numerous articles, including studies of the work of Samuel Beckett, Seamus Heaney, and Micheal O'Siadhail. She has recently concluded research on the Irish poet Joseph Campbell.

ISBN 0-313-29714-2

90000>

EAN

9 780313 297144

HARDCOVER BAR CODE